JOHN L. SHOVER is associate professor of history at San Francisco State College. He received his bachelor's degree from Ohio Wesleyan University and his master's and doctorate degrees from The Ohio State University.

FIRST MAJORITY—LAST MINORITY

The Transforming of Rural Life in America

Minorities in American History

FIRST MAJORITY
–LAST MINORITY

The Transforming of Rural Life in America

John L. Shover

Northern Illinois University Press
DE KALB

John L. Shover is professor of History at University of Pennsylvania, Philadelphia, Pennsylvania

The illustrations used in this book were obtained through the courtesy of the U.S. Department of Agriculture, the Smithsonian Institution, Mrs. Fay Bouic, William Clark, and Mrs. Paul Reese.

We wish to thank the following publishers for permission to quote from their publications:

Holt, Rinehart and Winston, Inc., for material from Frederick Jackson Turner's *The United States, 1830–1850.*

Houghton Mifflin Co., for an excerpt from page 529 of Harold Dean Cater's *Henry Adams and His Friends: A Collection of His Unpublished Letters.*

Charles Scribner's Sons, for an excerpt from page 56 of Curtis Stadtfeld's *From the Land and Back.*

We also wish to thank Prentice-Hall, Inc., for permission to quote from Charles Josiah Galpin, *Rural Life,* © 1918, page 71. Reprinted by permission of Prentice-Hall, Inc., Englewood Cliffs, New Jersey.

Library of Congress Cataloging in Publication Data

Shover, John L 1927-
First majority, last minority.

(Minorities in American history)
Bibliography: p.
Includes index.
1. Agriculture—Economic aspects—United States—History.   2. United States—Rural conditions.   I. Title.   II. Series.
HD1761.S556   301.35'0973   75-26473
ISBN 0-87580-056-4
ISBN 0-87580-522-1 pbk.

In Memory
Walter S. Shover
of Ostrander, Scioto Township, Ohio

Contents

Foreword

Minority History, once a euphemism disguising unpleasant or intractable social realities, has come in our time to be viewed as a source of American vitality and self-illumination. In an era when American society has been undergoing a vast realignment of its human resources, institutions, and habits of mind, Americans are more prone than ever to see that the experiences of ethnic, regional, social, economic, occupational, political, religious, intellectual, and other well-defined groups have spotlighted and personalized strategic problems in the American past.

The Minorities in American History series will encompass a whole range of such group experiences. Each is intended to illuminate brightly a critical event, movement, tradition, or dilemma. By so doing, these books will individualize the problems of a complex society, giving them both broad pertinence and sharp definition. In addition, the special insights afforded by the increasingly sophisticated methodology of the "new history" will be reflected in an expanding list of ethnohistory studies where sociological theory and quantitative analysis will further inform, document, and shape the dramatic narrative.

No characteristic of the American past has been more wedded to the nation's sense of itself than has its rural image. Jefferson's farmer is still seen as central presence, exemplar of the good life, and bulwark of democracy. Even in post-agricultural and post-industrial America, the rural vision has been dimmed only slightly. It comes as a shock to learn that the country town is near death and that in the 1970s only one out of twenty-five Americans is a member of a farm family. But, as John Shover makes clear, the first majority has become a minority on the verge of extinction just as its function, ironically, as the world's greatest food exporter has become ever more critical to the maintenance of human life on this earth.

A singularly versatile historian of twentieth-century America, John Shover is by birth, education, and intellectual resources uniquely equipped to portray in this authoritative study the transformation of the yeoman farmer republic into the agro-industrial empire. His academic career, which has taken him from his native Ohio to Indiana, California, and finally Pennsylvania, has included wide travel and lectureships in American history in India, Pakistan, and the Soviet Union. A specialist in agricultural and political history, Shover is well-versed in the sophisticated grammar of the social sciences and is also a recognized historian of the urban scene. To his probing analysis of American agricultural developments, broad-sweeping personal exposure to the American scene, and critical world perspective, he brings a command of contemporary history that leaves no doubts about the merits of the discipline. By juxtaposing the older farm patterns with the modes of the agro-industrial revolution of the last three decades, he makes vivid the abrupt eclipse of a whole dimension of American life at whatever the cost to all those affected by such unprecedented change. In the book's closing chapters, Shover explores the unparalleled effects in 1973–1974 of international problems on the American economy, most especially upon its agricultural sector. Without becoming apocalyptic, he spells out the implications of food scarcity for the world's hunger belt and lays out the dilemma that faces this nation of agricultural plenty. Shover's unique combination of talents lends unusual cogency, range, and humanity to his perceptions in this historical inquiry into the strategic role that the first majority, now the last minority, has played and will continue to play in shaping the nation's and the world's future.

Moses Rischin, Series Editor
San Francisco State University

Introduction

Suppose there was a revolution and no one knew it. Incredible? Impossible? With a few concessions to rhetoric, this is precisely the proposition this book asserts. This revolution has been a major one, too. It is equal in scope to the great scientific revolutions that have periodically reshaped human knowledge, and its impact is as far-reaching as some of the historic social revolutions that have convulsed political systems around the world.

What is this revolution? At its core it is a vast technological upheaval that has swept across the farmlands of America in the years since World War II. In its thrust, it has overwhelmed traditional family farming and the village life that existed symbiotically with it. In its wake, the traditional yeoman farmer, celebrated in popular folklore as the apotheosis of virtue, individualism, and independence, has become a part of history. It has transformed the little team-haul communities beyond recognition. The functions these places perform now are a world apart from those of a brief thirty years ago. It has carried rural dwellers into crowded cities and faceless suburbs. With few persons noticing, the technological changes since 1945 have brought about the consolidation of many old family farms into large, mechanized food-producing factories. Farming, one of the last vestiges of the individual entrepreneur, has been absorbed into the complex infrastructure of a vertically and horizontally integrated mass production industry.

The changes are more than technological. Rural folklore and agrarian values have deep and cherished roots in the American culture. Years ago Frederick Jackson Turner postulated that the frontier had disappeared and that this marked a great watershed in the nation's experience. Factually, Turner was in error. At best his concept of a frontier was romanticized and sentimental. In the brief time since 1945, the fundamental transmutation of rural life, as it had existed for more than a century, is most certainly a historical watershed of greater importance than the mythological passing of a frontier in the 1890s. Accordingly, I have designated this historical turning point the "Great Disjuncture."

As far-reaching and significant as the rural transformation has been, more amazing is the fact that it has been so little noted or discussed. Even those who shape agricultural policy and act as spokesmen for agrarian interests evoke in mythological terms a way of life that existed in the past. How many informed persons realize, for example, that emigration from country to city in the years since the Great Depression has been greater in numbers than the entire immigration from foreign shores to the United States in the 100 years between 1820 and 1920? How many have pondered the fact that less than 5 percent of Americans remained farmers in 1970, or that in California, where agriculture is the state's greatest single business enterprise, only 1 percent of the population was engaged in farming?

The consequences of radical change reverberate through most facets of contemporary American life. The urban crisis is an outgrowth of the migratory tides that have swept cityward from the countryside. The concentration of more and more of the American population in less and less of the nation's land space manifests this same phenomenon of change. And the ramifications have not ceased. As these words are being written, the process of rapid change in agriculture continues. Some of the most vexing of the social paradoxes of our time follow its wake. Thus, even as technological and scientific innovations have shattered all production records of the past, population pressures throughout the world mount so recklessly that with each passing year the fateful question of the capacity of the finite earth to feed its human inhabitants looms more and more portentous. Thus, while we take pride in the scientific miracles that make American agriculture the most productive in the world, there remains the ominous question of what the price of this progress has been in terms of possibly irreparable damage to the fragile and tenuous ecological system that sustains us all.

The purpose of this book, then, is to attempt to capture and synthesize the scope, the importance, and the effects of what I consider one of the most significant and extensive social transformations of our day. Issues so vast and so interwoven can be treated only by a painful process of selection and synthesis. Accordingly, I believe that the best way to attempt to convey and understand the change that has taken place is through a series of case studies. I harbor the somewhat heretical notion that history involves more than the activities of the great, the ambitious, and the cultural elite; it involves, also, the impact of change upon the lives of ordinary people who leave little behind in the way of memorabilia or written records.

In the chapters that follow, the first, "The Ways of Change," will attempt a macroview of the transformations that have swept across the countryside these last three decades, and will attempt to place them in a theoretical perspective. Chapter 2 will give to the same theme a more concrete reference point by compartmentalizing changes in terms of geographic areas and demographic groupings. Then in chapters 3 and 4 the focus will be upon some very specific places and people whose simple lives and experiences, I think, mirror part of the process by which rural Americans passed euphemistically from the "first majority" to the "last minority." Thus we will examine, in broad time-perspective, patterns of social change in Scioto Township, Delaware County, Ohio, and Bedford County, Pennsylvania, and we will attempt to recreate traditional family farm life by looking carefully at just two among the many thousands in the Middle West: Tarpleywick, in late nineteenth-century Iowa, and a farm in Mecosta County, Michigan, in the 1930s. In terms of time perimeters, chapters 2 through 4 deal with a period of evolutionary change and, rather than following a strict chronology, sweep generously and selectively over the decades from the Civil War until 1945. To trace longitudinal development on several occasions, we will even return to the pioneer period.

Then, as the process of change unfolds and grows more involved, the "Great Disjuncture" takes place. Change becomes so sharp and decisive after 1945 that the very ideas, words, and constructs that describe rural life in the years before are no longer adequate. The final four chapters, after we have crossed the dividing line of World War II, will focus with greater time specificity on the more drastic and temporally compressed revolutionary transformations of the past three decades. Once we move beyond the forties, the localistic and personalistic frame of reference, which describes farming and country life effectively all the way through the depression years, disappears. Although I retain the case-study approach throughout, the case studies of the last four chapters are broader in scope and weave through a maze of economic and political complexities. They are unabashedly presentist. Chapter 5 will address specifically the patterns of technological change. Discussion of contemporary agriculture and rural life outside of the context of the infrastructure of the vast food-processing and food-retailing industry becomes impossible. There is no better case study of this industry than to focus upon the monolithic agribusiness enterprise that reaches from factories in the fields, through marketing and retailing, all the way into the intricacies of international commerce. The best case study in the modern economics of agriculture and food production, it seems to me, is to attempt to explain the rapid price inflation of the years since 1973. These are the themes of chapter 6. Chapter 7 will examine some of the forces and considerations that shaped and influenced federal agricultural policy during the period when the "Great Disjuncture" was taking place. Finally, in chapter 8, we will ask: How have the people of this earth arrived at a time in history when the seemingly insatiable demands of a perilously expanding population press upon the finite resources of the environment and, although the output of the American farms that remain is more bountiful than ever before, millions of people are threatened with starvation?

I bring some value judgments to the exposition that follows which had better be voiced than inferred. I share a feeling of sadness and loss for the disintegration of that simpler world of the traditional farm and village. While I certainly make no case for parochialism, I am, regretfully, convinced that the sense of community (however one chooses to interpret that elusive word) is rapidly being lost in modern America. I have been privileged to find it only in a few places—one place was in the crowded center of a great city where a sense of ethnic identity and belonging persisted; the other places have been in small rural communities, and in a rural commune in the redwoods of northern California, where I believe the last and best of the flower children of a decade past tenuously persist. I have a profound respect for the ingenuity and patience of those traditional farmers and ranchers who remain. And although I do not choose to follow them, I deeply sympathize with those émigrés who are going back to the land. I am a supporter of the most determined efforts to rescue the environment from technological degradation and to expose the all too frequent frauds and dishonesties of the omnipresent food processing and retailing oligopolies. Yet I am aware that nostalgia for a world that is lost is a fruitless indulgence—to use a horrifying term, there is no turning back from the "deterministic" forces that have destroyed that more personable, more secure world. No doubt such a contradiction is fertile breeding ground for a cynicism that borders on contempt for many of the vaunted material benefices, life-styles, and cultural achievements of contemporary life. This cynicism will, I believe, become obvious to the patient reader who chooses to continue beyond these prefatory remarks.

During the preparation and writing of this book I incurred a number of obligations. First of all, I am obliged to those scholars of agricultural history, economics, and sociology, who are far too cautious to have embarked upon a project so bold in scope and inchoate in form, but whose patient studies have provided much of the data and theory upon which my discussion rests. Although I cite his work infrequently, and suspect he might dissent from many of my interpretations, I acknowledge my debt to one of the unrecognized giants of the historical profession, James C. Malin. The implicit theoretical assumptions that support the organization of this book have been influenced by the fertile ideas and writings of Samuel P. Hays. Any student of agriculture is privileged to have readily available the comprehensive statistical data gathered by the Economic Research Service of the United States Department of Agriculture.

I am indebted to my colleague Michael Zuckerman who applied his keen mind and profound insight into American social history to a ruthless critique of this manuscript and made it a better work as a result. Thomas C. Cochran read the chapters dealing with recent economic developments and reminded me that many of the trends and tendencies I discussed were not confined to the agricultural sector alone. Jack Reece critiqued the chapter on family farming, not from his professional perspective as a distinguished young scholar of modern Europe, but as a Michigan farm boy, which he was for eighteen years of his life. In the process he rescued me from several embarrassing errors. In addition, Moses Rischin and Paul Kleppner made helpful comments. Two talented students at University of Pennsylvania, William Clark and Bruce Baker, served both as research assistants and astute critics. However ardently I might wish to place all responsibility for the shortcomings of this volume on these kind friends and helpmates, and reserve all potential plaudits for myself, I must nonetheless accept full personal responsibility for both.

Finally, my apologies to a close young friend whom I believe would have liked more hours with her stepfather than the preparation of this book allowed. Perhaps one day she will read it and understand.

John L. Shover

Philadelphia, Pennsylvania

PART 1

TRADITION AND TRANSITION
Before 1945

CHAPTER ONE

The Ways of Change

Ill fares the land, to hastening ills a prey
Where wealth accumulates, and men decay:
Princes and lords may flourish, or may fade,
A breath can make them, as a breath has made.
But a bold peasantry, their country's pride,
When once destroyed, can never be supplied.

—Oliver Goldsmith

How are you going to keep them down on the farm
after they've seen—the farm?

—Groucho Marx

In the beginning they were many. When the first federal census was enumerated in 1790, of the four million inhabitants of the United States, nineteen of every twenty were rural dwellers and only twenty-four population centers qualified for the minimal definition of "urban territory," that is, an inhabited place of more than twenty-five hundred residents. In the 1820 census 93 percent of the population was designated "rural" and 73 percent of workers were engaged in agriculture. The soldiers in blue and grey who fought in the Civil War came overwhelmingly from the villages, plantations, and piney woods tracts of the South and from the farms and tiny commercial centers of the

North. In 1870, 79 percent of the American population still lived on the land or in rural villages, and 53 percent of the nation's workers made their living from agriculture. The first census that revealed more than half the United States' population to be living in places of more than twenty-five hundred inhabitants was that of 1920.[1]

Despite the early preponderance of rural dwellers, their proportion to urban inhabitants declined with every census beginning in 1820. The trend slowed in the depression decade of the 1930s, but with the coming of World War II, what had been a gradual erosion became a mass exodus.

Between 1929 and 1965 more than 30 million people moved away from American farmlands. During the 1940s, 8.6 million migrated, nearly a third of the rural population at the decade's beginning; the rate spiralled to a million annually in the 1950s and averaged 750,000 each year in the sixties—and this from a far smaller base.[2] Spanning just three and a half decades, this mass outpouring represents one of the great migrations in history, greater in scope and numbers than the great exodus of European and Asians to the United States in the 140 years from 1820 to 1960. An estimated 47 million migrated to the United States during these years, and 22 million returned, leaving a net increment from foreign immigration of about 25 million.[3]

The 1970 census classified just 26.5 percent of the total population of the United States of 203,211,926 as rural, but even this figure must be explicated. First, rural dweller does not mean farmer. Only one of five of the rural population lives in farm operator or farm worker families. The remaining 80 percent reside in villages under 2,500 in population; others are service people such as shopkeepers, repairmen, schoolteachers, and an increasing portion are industrial workers who commute to urban centers from countryside or village homes.[4] Second, the nature of the farming enterprise itself needs to be examined. Reliable estimates tell us that in 1973 only 4.5 percent of the nation's working population was engaged in agriculture—quite a contrast to the 27 percent in 1920 or the 14 percent at the end of World War II. Just what does "engaged in agriculture" mean? In 1959, 24 percent of all farm operators worked away from their farms for more than 200 days yearly; a recent survey in Wisconsin found that 40 percent of farm operators or members of their families moonlighted away from their farms for more than 100 days.[5] Earnings off the farm are critically important items in the budgets of farm families. In 1950, nearly one-third of per capita personal earnings of the farm population came from nonfarm income; from 1967 to 1972 nonfarm income of the farm population exceeded that from farming. The smallest of farm operators, those with less than $2,500 in sales, averaged $9,628 in off-farm income in 1972—nine times the amount they realized from farming. Even on the largest of farms where net sales averaged over $100,000, an average of more than $8,500 in off-farm income was realized in 1972. In 1971–1972, 73 percent of all hired farm laborers lived in nonfarm residences.[6]

Stated in antiseptic statistical language, changes of scope so sweeping are difficult to conceptualize. To note that the United States is overwhelmingly an urban nation is trite and self-evident. It is not so trite to observe that in 1974, 70 percent of the population lived in just about 1½ percent of the nation's land area. The Bureau of the Census estimates that by 1985 half the population will reside in three integrated "strip cities," one stretching from Boston to Washington, D.C., another on an east-west axis from Buffalo to Chicago, and a third along the Pacific Coast from San Francisco to Los Angeles.[7]

Why the outpouring of people away from farming? The most direct response is to answer simply: they aren't needed. In 1820 one farm worker was required to supply subsistence for four people; in 1945 the ratio was 1 for 14.6; in 1969 the estimate was 1 for 45.3. In 1948 about 140 manhours of labor produced one bale of cotton; in 1969 about 25 man-hours did the job.[8] A technological takeoff, apparent most dramatically since 1945, has turned traditional farming upside down. Concentration, specialization, a declining

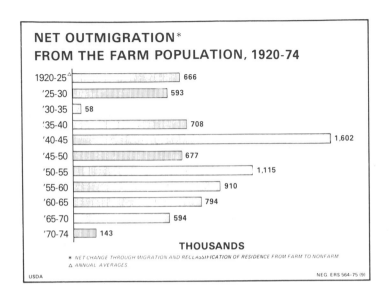

NET OUTMIGRATION*
FROM THE FARM POPULATION, 1920-74

Period	Thousands
1920-25△	666
'25-30	593
'30-35	58
'35-40	708
'40-45	1,602
'45-50	677
'50-55	1,115
'55-60	910
'60-65	794
'65-70	594
'70-74	143

THOUSANDS

* *NET CHANGE THROUGH MIGRATION AND RECLASSIFICATION OF RESIDENCE FROM FARM TO NONFARM*
△ *ANNUAL AVERAGES*

USDA   NEG ERS 564-75 (9)

number of productive units, rational planning with considerable government assistance, scientific expertise, skilled management, large capital investments, technical rather than physical skills—these are the hallmarks of the agricultural enterprise as it is being carried out in the seventies.

Despite the removal of much of its human component, the total production of foodstuffs on the farms of America has remained constant and even increased.[9] The reason is farm consolidation. Nine-hundred thousand fewer farms operated in 1970 than in 1960, but virtually all the land except that diverted by government policy, remained in production.[10] While the total number of farms was decreasing between 1960 and 1968, larger farms with value of sales of $20,000 or more increased by 50 percent. In 1960, these units made up 8.6 percent of all farms; in 1972, 24.4 percent. Gross production differentials among farms are nothing new, for many of the smaller units with less than $10,000 annual sales are semi-farms or part-time operations. In 1948 the largest 10 percent of farms were responsible for 24 percent of total farm output; this increased to 48 percent in 1964. Meanwhile the smallest 20 percent of farms produced 3 percent of output in 1949, 1959, and 1964.[11] Farms with sales of more than $20,000 received more than 34 percent of net farm income in 1960, 70 percent in 1972. Stated another way, 24 percent of farms took in 70 percent of net farm income. This ranged from an average of $52,815 for the 2.4 percent of farms with value of sales above $100,000 to $977 for the 35 percent with sales less than $2,500. The overall average for the approximately three million operating farms in 1972 was $6,856.[12]

Complex technologies and high production costs that follow arc making of traditional diversified farming an obsolete business. Estimated production expenses for all farms ($25 billion in 1970) have increased fourfold since 1930. An Illinois farmer raising corn on 400 acres would require an investment of more than $250,000 in land and equipment, and his yearly costs would likely be in excess of $25,000.[13] The farmer, William Jennings Bryan exclaimed in his "Cross of Gold" speech, is a businessman, and of course that has always been true, but it is difficult to consider a profitable modern farm a small business. This does not mean that corporation farming is taking the place of individual proprietary operations. About 80 percent of all farms are still owned by individuals or partners, but these family farms of the seventies are something far different from those Bryan described with pastoral rhapsodies in 1896.[14]

Technological disemployment isn't the only factor that has eliminated small farms and pushed rural people into the cities and suburbs. Throughout history most voluntary mass movements of population have been prompted by the quest for better economic opportunities. Migrants out of America's countryside have had a fair chance of finding them. Consistently, per capita income from farming has been less than in nonfarm occupations, and, contrary to popular belief, a greater percentage of country people live in poverty than do residents of the crowded centers of our largest cities. In 1960 the per capita income of a farm resident was $1,100, 54.5 percent of the $2,017 earned by a non-farm resident. Higher farm prices and the flight of marginal earners narrowed the gap by 1972, but farm income was still 82.7 percent of nonfarm.[15] Poverty figures are even more striking. A 1965 study estimated that 18 percent of central city residents and 9.6 percent of those in metropolitan suburbs lived in poverty, but in nonmetropolitan areas, 22 percent of nonfarm residents and 29 percent of those living on farms were poor. In 1972, 9.3 percent of all families in the United States fell below the low-income level; inside central cities the percentage was 11.3, among nonmetropolitan nonfarm families, 12.0, but on farms, 14.3.[16] As Groucho Marx said it, "How are you going to keep them down on the farm after they've seen—the farm?"

Poverty in America has never been measurable in economic terms alone; poverty is a cultural phenomenon, and that is especially true in rural areas. In the countryside, as in the cities, a disproportionate number of the poor are black people, Mexican-Americans, or American Indians; the only nonethnic group appreciably represented are the poor whites dispossessed from the deteriorating coal mining areas of Appalachia. These four groups made up 20 percent of the rural population of 1950, but their movements constituted 50 percent of the net migration in the 1950–1960 decade. The most dramatic residential and occupational transformation has been that of the black population. In 1890, 60 percent of all employed blacks were farmers; in 1910, 83 percent lived in the former states of the Confederacy. By 1960, 42 percent of blacks lived in the South and only 8 percent were farmers. Outside the South, about 80 percent of black people lived in standard metropolitan areas like Chicago, New York City, or Philadelphia, and of the blacks who remained below the Mason-Dixon line, two of every three lived in some standard metropolitan area like Atlanta, Nashville, or Washington, D.C. Depressing as it may seem, the blacks who flocked to city ghettos lived better, at least statistically, than they had before, or better than those who stayed behind. In the South, in 1966, 19 percent of metropolitan blacks lived in substandard housing (50 percent of those on the urban fringes) as contrasted to 75 percent of those who resided in small towns or rural areas.[17] Outside the South, 15 percent of the housing occupied by urban blacks was substandard, but in villages and rural areas the figure was 32 percent. In 1972, 29 percent of blacks had incomes below the low income standard, but among the more than one million who lived outside metropolitan areas, the figure was 40.5 percent, and of the ninety-nine thousand who lived on farms, it was 46.5 percent.[18]

In addition to technological and economic factors, simple demographic differentials influence migration rates. A recent study of the small Minnesota town of Benson concluded that the community's major export was its young people,[19] a generalization that applies to virtually every village and rural area in the nation. One reason for this is the important matter of birthrates. Two-thirds of the population growth from the last generation of American women who have recently completed childbearing came from the 27 percent of all women who resided in rural areas.[20] Not only have rural areas fewer economic opportunities, they have proportionately more young people to export.

Finally, the place one lives has something to do with the decision to migrate. The South consistently has the highest rate of emigration. One who lives close to a large city is more likely to move than one who resides in the remoter hinterlands. In addition, the process of population erosion in any particular community is self-reinforcing. The smaller the community, the more rapid the rate of decline and the more confidently it can be predicted that the rate of decrease will be maintained. Those small towns and rural townships where population has increased are usually located within a magic fifty mile radius of a metropolitan center and thus benefit from the decentralization that pushes people and functions to the urban and suburban fringes of standard metropolitan areas.[21]

The implications of a population transformation so comprehensive as the one described here, and one that still continues, force a reconceptualization of some of the ways the American experience has been categorized. In the light of the upheaval since 1945 alone, the alleged disappearance of the American frontier in the 1890s does not appear as a major historical turning point. When restrictions ended mass foreign immigration into the United States in 1924, the process of gross population transfers didn't end; on the contrary, it was just beginning![22] The absorption and assimilation of displaced persons into new social, cultural, political, and economic milieus is not a social issue appropriately relegated to reflective analysis in history books. The problems of adjustment of the rural migrant to a metropolitan center in the 1960s or 1970s are strikingly similar to those that confronted the Italian or Jewish newcomer to New York or Boston in the early twentieth century. In some important ways, the earlier migrants had it better: substantial numbers of them came from urban centers in Europe, bringing skills readily transferable to jobs in the new country; fewer of them suffered the social handicaps of having a black skin. Census data gives no help at all in trying to understand what has happened to the modern day uprooted people in American cities, and rural sociologists and economists have only recently begun to give the matter careful attention. Calvin L. Beale, the leader of the Population Studies Group of the Economic Research Service, United States Department of Agriculture, remarked in 1968: "I think it is only partly an exaggeration to say that many economists largely overlooked the rural-urban migration until 2 or 3 years ago."[23]

Nevertheless, a sampling of several of the narrow studies undertaken give some fleeting impressions. Forty-two percent of rural migrants to one northern city took up blue-collar jobs (slightly higher than the national average); a third of the newcomers were in the city of their employment for the first time, and half of them knew nothing about the city before they moved there to find work.[24] An investigation of one migrant group (221 Appalachian white families who came to Cincinnati, Ohio) found that in comparison to other families in the neighborhoods of settlement, more of the newcomers were lower class (judged by occupation of family head, schooling, and quality of housing), and generally persons in this lower class category had greater problems in adjusting than did migrants classified in two higher status groups. Taking into account these class differences and the length of time they had resided in Cincinnati, people of southern Appalachian origin were less well integrated into the community, judging from their markedly lower participation in lodges, labor unions, neighborhood clubs, and community center activities.[25]

A nation with a situation where less than 5 percent of its popultion is employed in farming and three-quarters of its migrant farm laborers are living in towns and villages, and where migrants have poured away from the countryside at rates often more than one million yearly, is in stark contrast to the images of rural life that still prevail in our culture.

Traditions die hard, particularly those so deeply imbedded as those of the agrarian society that for the major span of United States' history underwrote economic development and shaped political institutions. Agrarian attitudes and values have survived, even though they are more consonant with a rural life that existed, if ever, sixty years ago.

Economically, the United States was nurtured and grew to maturity as an agricultural nation. During the critical period of its economic development, 1840–1890, cheap exports from American plantations and farms built up the balances on the international market that allowed for needed imports of technology and raw materials. Investments in land and the purchasing power of the people who inhabited it sustained the growth of a nationwide market for the products of American industry. Even today, the United States is the world's largest exporter of agricultural products, and it accounts for nearly one-fifth of total international commerce in agricultural commodities.

The nation's political structure reflects its rural heritage. Only in the last two decades has the Supreme Court moved to rectify the long-standing policy of representing trees and acres, not people, in the apportioning of seats in state legis-latures.[26] In urban states such as New York and California, rural counties were grossly over-represented at the cost of burgeoning metropolitan centers. In Kansas, constitutional mandate required reapportionment every five years, but the state legislature had neglected to do so for half a century. The result of such policies was that, prior to the intervention of the Supreme Court, in twenty-four states less than 30 percent of the voters could elect a majority in the upper house of the legislature, and in fourteen states they could elect a majority in both houses.[27] Even in the face of the rapidly depleting rural population, diehards in the United States Senate made an abortive attempt to push through a constitutional amendment to nullify the court's decision. The Senate, where Nevada and Alaska have equal voting power with California and New York, has through much of its history been the bulwark of agrarian interests. The House of Representatives, except where the seniority system afforded long-tenured rural representatives access to sensitive positions of influence, has been less a bastion for agriculture. By 1969 only 60 of the 435 members of the House represented districts with a farm population greater than 15 percent.[28]

The agrarian past lingers with peculiar tenacity in popular thought and culture. In a 1953 public opinion poll, 73 percent of a nationwide sample felt that the farmer was better off than the city dweller.[29] More recent Gallup polls (1966 and 1970) reveal that most people would prefer to live outside of cities.[30] Real farmers are not quite so enthusiastic. A Wisconsin survey in 1966 found that only 44 percent of those participating said they would choose farming if they could do it over again.[31]

When a Texas farm woman declared at a 1969 listening conference called by the secretary of agriculture, "I only want to remind you that when the farmer falls, the nation falls," she was, perhaps unknowingly, giving voice to sentiments that have permeated American culture since the nation's beginnings. The words could have been those of

Thomas Jefferson: "Those who labor in the earth are the chosen people of God, if ever He had a chosen people, whose breasts He made His peculiar deposit for substantial and genuine virtue." Vivid and colorful expressions of such ideas are an occupational hazard associated with the office of secretary of agriculture. One, a few decades ago remarked:

> We have always had a feeling that there is something basically sound about having a good portion of our people on the land. Country living produces better people. The country is a good place to rear a family. It is a good place to teach the basic virtues that have helped to build this nation. Young people on the farm learn how to work, how to be thrifty and how to do things with their hands. It has given millions of us the finest preparation for life.[32]

Thanks in part to the pervasive influence of Frederick Jackson Turner, a rural metaphor, transposed as the frontier thesis, has conditioned Americans' interpretation of their own history. In his most celebrated but not most significant essay, Turner lamented that after 1890 the census bureau no longer saw fit to demarcate a frontier line, beyond which (westward!) the ratio of settlers to acreage was less than two per square mile. (Why the ratio of two persons per square mile should define a frontier is not logically clear.) Since it was America's experience with the frontier of unsettled land that had fortified two of the most important ingredients of the national character, nationalism and individualism, the exhaustion of such free land had obvious and not too happy implications for the nation's future. Avid and not particularly discriminating successors to Turner extrapolated his central premise, "The existence of an area of free land, its continuous recession, and the advance of American settlement westward explain American development," into an overarching economic and geographic determinist position that left scant allowance for cultural or technological variables and gave short shrift to the urban ingredients in American development.[33]

Social change, whether conceptualized as progress or as degradation, is at the core of all social sciences, including history. Change, however, is too inclusive and pervasive to be abstracted in and of itself; it must be constricted, and if it is to be analyzed, applied to specific defined areas of human activity.[34] The kind of social change that has transformed an agrarian society to an urban-industrial one is not unique to the United States, and it is not unique to the last three decades—far from it.

The uprooting of agrarian, peasant societies, a process crystallized by the inclusive term "modernization," is a phenomenon that touches every continent and nearly every nation. The process is swifter in industrial societies like the United States; it is more urgent and more threatening in those vast areas of the world where the race of food supply with population growth is a losing one. Judging from the statistics in the *Demographic Yearbook*,[35] more than two-thirds of the 3.5 billion people who inhabit the planet derive their livelihood from some form of agriculture or stock raising.[36] Depopulation of the countryside cuts across most of the social variables that separate nations. If advanced technology drives farmers out of rural America, grinding poverty forces more and more peasants into the teeming slums of Calcutta, Delhi, and Bombay. Migration from the country takes place in those Latin American nations where the birthrate is the highest in the world; it occurs in the Soviet Union irrespective of the millions who perished in World War II.

The basic fact is that agriculture is losing people in unprecedented numbers in practically all parts of the world; and in the countries where the flow is just now beginning in a massive way, its major sociocultural consequences are yet to be felt. India, China, Latin America, Africa, and all other areas stand on the verge of a rural to urban migration that will make previous movements in these places seem modest by comparison. Concomitantly, it is certain to produce problems that are now also minor by comparison.[37]

While migration from country to urban area is accelerating, the process has been going on for centuries. Contemporaries are not the first to have voiced concern for its social consequences. Nostalgic bards and formulators of classic social theories alike have contemplated the effects of changes of social structure as extensive in proportion and intensive in impact as any history records. These words, penned in 1770, have been traditional perorations for more than one orator of rural fundamentalist persuasion:

Ill fares the land, to hastening ills a prey
Where wealth accumulates, and men decay:
Princes and lords may flourish, or may fade;
A breath can make them, as a breath has made.
But a bold peasantry, their country's pride,
When once destroyed, can never be supplied.

The author, Oliver Goldsmith, remarking that some critics questioned the empirical foundations for his prognosis, noted in the dedication: "... I sincerely believe what I have written. ... I have taken all possible pains, in my country excursions, for these four or five years past, to be certain of what I have alleged."[38]

On a level more profound, the classic social theorists, whose concepts underlie most of modern social science, were acutely cognizant of the rural to urban migration that was already a worldwide phenomenon in the nineteenth century. Most of them—Marx, Weber, Tönnies, Durkheim —addressed it directly; for several it was at the core of their theories. Insofar as these masters of the past have informed and enlightened modern social theory, any study such as this one which claims to have an implicit and explicit theoretical grounding is in their debt.

Central to Karl Marx's powerful formulation was the process of transition in Europe, particularly in England, which undermined the traditional manor system, swelling the industrial proletariat with refugees from the countryside. These provided the surplus of labor which held wage costs down and helped propel the capitalist or bourgeois revolution. By sharpening class differences, the availability of cheap labor lay the groundwork, once the oppressed could become conscious of their class status, for the final stage in

Marx's cyclical theory of change, the proletarian revolution, and the creation of a classless society. Marx, however, had scant sympathy for or interest in peasant society; only when the "idiocies of rural life" could be surmounted, rural isolation overcome, and peasants made into wage workers, could the social interactions that might lead to class consciousness occur. Marx's exclusive focus on the industrial proletariat and his relegation of peasants to the "lumpenproletariat" category proved no small obstacle for those of his followers who sought to transform Marxist theory into political action.[39]

Ferdinand Tönnies distinguished social structures that integrated individuals in a network of personal and subjective relationships (*gemeinschaft*), which by implication were more manifest in traditional and rural societies, from the impersonal, isolated, and objective patterns of personal association (*gesellschaft*) that linked the individual with work and political authority in industrial society.

Max Weber spoke less directly to the question of rural-urban transition, but in an early study of agrarian enterprise in nineteenth-century Germany he noted the difference in social context of bonded workers, whose obligation to their Junker landlords consisted of an enmeshed set of rights and obligations, and the status of wage workers, whose only link to their job and employer was economic. Since the latter's interest was confined to a higher wage, the commercialization of German agriculture accentuated economic conflict between workers and employers. Despite the "organic solidarity" in which bonded workers were encompassed, Weber found a definite inclination among them to desire escape from the bonds of dependence and, in a quest for personal freedom, exchange their position of security—and dependence—for the more uncertain position of the wage worker.[40] Even this capsule summary suggests Weber's extension of the analysis of change beyond the sphere of economic relationships into the realm of the deep-seated values held by members of society.

The transformation of American agriculture from traditional farm to modern complex enterprise, the scope and

(Courtesy USDA)

Deserted farm, Bowling Green, Virginia.

extent of which we have been able only to suggest here, is one of the profound, if little noted, social changes of our time. To gauge it in its full complexity would require examination of the crisis of our cities, their populations swollen by the refugees from abandoned farms and deserted villages. It would require consideration of the centralizing and organizational tendencies that have spatially and culturally subsumed local and regional differences and increasingly integrated American society. It would require examination of the ways in which technological innovation occurs and the economic and social consequences that follow from creating a vast centralized and integrated food processing industry. The role of conscious political decision-making in promoting and accelerating the change process would have to enter the analysis. Finally, when this formidable task was completed, one would need to stand back and ask, "What has been wrought?"

As I have indicated in the introduction, getting a handle

on a topic so vast and inchoate requires some painful selecting and synthesizing, and I believe this can best be opera-
tionalized through a series of case studies. In the process,
I am aware that depth has often been sacrificed in favor of
breadth; topics that require microscopic investigation have
been swept up in macrocosmic generalizations or appear
only as suggestive hypotheses within the rubric of some
specific case analysis. Nonetheless, the consistent direction
in the book is from simplicity to complexity, from community to society. Thus, in broad perspective we move from
the simpler agrarian world of the nineteenth and early
twentieth century into the complex, intricate, coordinated
agricultural enterprises of the present. Likewise, within
each individual chapter an attempt has been made to repli-
cate this same thematic structure—development from simplicity to complexity.

In order to get on with the task, the natural environment
is the arena, and its inhabitants are the actors in the drama
where the processes of social change are played out. These,
of necessity, are the base points for an attempt to understand the metamorphosis that has overtaken American rural life.

Notes

1. General demographic data, unless otherwise indicated, is from U.S., Bureau of the Census, *Historical Statistics of the United States, Colonial Times to 1957* (Washington, D.C.: Government Printing Office, 1960) and U.S., Department of Agriculture [hereinafter abbreviated USDA], Statistical Reporting Service, *A Century of Agriculture in Charts and Tables,* Agriculture Handbook no. 318 (July 1966). Statistics on rural and urban populations are elusive because the definition of an urban area has been periodically changed by the Bureau of the Census, vacillating between 1,000 and 8,000 before settling upon the 2,500 figure which has been standard since 1900.
2. Statistics on the extent of the migration vary slightly. My computation is based upon those contained in USDA, *Handbook of Agricultural Charts, 1973* (Washington, D.C., 1973), p. 55. See also U.S., Congress, Senate, Committee on Government Operations, Subcommittee on Governmental Research, *National Manpower Conference, Oklahoma State University, May 17–18, 1968,* 90th Cong., 2d Sess., pp. 7, 77. [Hereinafter cited *National Manpower Conference, 1968.*]
3. *National Manpower Conference, 1968,* p. 67; Francis Fox Piven and Richard A. Cloward, *Regulating the Poor: The Function of Public Welfare* (New York: Random House, 1971), p. 214.
4. Warren R. Bailey, "Rural and Urban, The Interfaces," in USDA, *The Yearbook of Agriculture, 1970: Contours of Change,* p. 137. [Hereinafter cited, *USDA Yearbook, 1970.*]
5. Wayne C. Rohrer and Louis H. Douglas, *The Agrarian Transition in America: Dualism and Change* (Indianapolis: Bobbs-

Merrill Co., 1969), p. 52; *National Manpower Conference*, 1968, p. 105.

6. Kyle Randall and Mardy Myers, "Are They Making a Living Down on the Farm?" USDA Yearbook, 1970, p. 25; USDA, Economic Research Service, *Farm Income Situation, July, 1974* (FIS–224), pp. 49, 50, 71.

7. Paul J. Jehlik and Sheldon R. Lowry, "The Team Haul Community in a Jet Age," *USDA Yearbook, 1970,* p. 149.

8. Rex F. Colwick and Vernon P. Moore, "King Cotton Blasts Off," *USDA Yearbook, 1970,* p. 39; James L. Butler, "Winning the Race to Get the Hay In," *USDA Yearbook, 1970,* p. 53.

9. Randall and Myers, "Are They Making a Living," p. 19.

10. Donald R. Durost and Warren Bailey, "What's Happened to Farming," *USDA Yearbook, 1970,* p. 8.

11. *National Manpower Conference*, 1968, p. 65.

12. USDA, *Farm Income Situation, July, 1974,* p. 70.

13. Warren R. Bailey and John E. Lee, Jr., "The New Frontier of Finance," *USDA Yearbook, 1970,* pp. 10–11; Randall and Myers, *USDA Yearbook, 1970,* p. 24–25.

14. USDA, *Handbook of Agricultural Charts*, 1973, p. 28.

15. Ibid., pp. 5, 58. Surveys of migrants indicate that the pull of nonfarm jobs is greater than the push of low incomes. Kenneth L. Robinson, "Commodity Policies and Programs, *USDA Yearbook, 1970,* p. 122.

16. *National Manpower Conference, 1968,* p. 78. Defining poverty has troubled social scientists and government administrators. The usual measure, that of the Social Security Administration (1965), defined it as an income below $3,000 yearly for a family, $1,500 for an unrelated individual. Mollie Orshansky's more versatile index adds such variables as differences in family size and composition as well as differences in living conditions. Figures here are based on the Orshansky index.

17. *National Manpower Conference, 1968,* p. 14.

18. U.S., Bureau of the Census. *Characteristics of the Low Income Population* (Ser. p–60, #91, December 1973), p. 81.

19. Don Martindale and R. Galen Hansen, *Small Town and the Nation* (Westport, Conn.: Greenwood Publishing Co., 1969).

20. Alan R. Bird, "Population Distribution Issues," *USDA Yearbook, 1971,* p. 17.

21. See chapter 3 and Glenn V. Fuguitt, "The Places Left Behind: Population Trends and Policy for Rural America," *Rural Sociology* 36 (December 1971): 449–69.

22. To rural-urban migration, the substantial Puerto Rican influx and continuing foreign immigration must be added, plus an incredible urban to urban movement that involves nearly 25 percent of the American population annually.

23. *National Manpower Conference, 1968,* p. 13. See Varden Fuller, *Rural Worker Adjustment to Urban Life: An Assessment of the Research* (University of Michigan-Wayne State University, Insitute of Labor and Industrial Relations, 1970). A recent survey of the literature and an indication of its general poverty is Jan H. Reeger and J. Allan Beegle, "The Integration of Rural Migrants in New Settings," *Rural Sociology* 39 (Spring 1974): 42–55.

24. *National Manpower Conference, 1968,* pp. 9–10.

25. Roscoe Griffin, "Appalachian Newcomers in Cincinnati," in Thomas R. Ford, ed., *The Southern Appalachian Region: A Survey* (Lexington: University of Kentucky Press, 1967), pp. 79–84.

26. Reynolds v. Sims, 377 U.S. 533 (1964); Baker v. Carr, 369 U.S. 186 (1962).

27. Rohrer and Douglas, *Agrarian Transition in America,* pp. 91, 93.

28. Robert G. Sherrill, "Reaping the Subsidies," *Nation* 209 (24 November 1969): 561.

29. Howard W. Beers, "Rural-Urban Differences: Some Evidence from Public Opinion Polls," *Rural Sociology* 18 (March 1953): 1–11.

30. Bird, *USDA Yearbook, 1971,* p. 18.

31. Wayne D. Rasmussen and Gladys Baker, "The Farmer Speaks for a Way of Life," *USDA Yearbook, 1970,* p. 28.

32. Ezra Taft Benson, *Freedom to Farm* (Garden City, N.Y.: Doubleday & Co., 1960), p. 109.

33. See Lee Benson, "The Historian as Mythmaker: Turner and the Closed Frontier," in David M. Ellis, ed., *The Frontier in American Development: Essays in Honor of Paul Wallace Gates* (Ithaca, N.Y.: Cornell University Press, 1969), pp. 3–9, and James C. Malin, *On the Nature of History* (Copyright James C. Malin, Lawrence, Kansas, 1954), pp. 99–111.

34. See Robert C. Bealer and Frederick C. Fliegel, "A Reconsideration of Social Change in Rural Sociology," in James H. Copp, ed., *Our Changing Rural Society: Perspectives and Trends* (Ames, Iowa: Iowa State University Press, 1964), pp. 288–306.

35. While probably the most complete source of world demographic data, the Yearbook, for example, has no data from the People's Republic of China available to it for inclusion.

36. T. Lynn Smith and Paul E. Zopf, Jr., *Principles of Inductive Rural Sociology* (Philadelphia: F. A. Davis Co., 1970), pp. 44–45.

37. Ibid., pp. 77.

38. *The Poems and Plays of Oliver Goldsmith* (London: J. M. Dent and Sons, 1910), pp. 21, 24.

39. David Mitrany, *Marx Against the Peasant* (New York: Collier Books, 1961), pp. 31–65.

40. Anthony Giddens, *Capitalism and Modern Social Theory: An Analysis of the Writings of Marx, Durkheim and Max Weber* (Cambridge: At the University Press, 1971), pp. 122–23.

CHAPTER TWO

Of Lands and Peoples

> *Inevitable in such a changing country were sectional interests, sectional antagonisms, and sectional combinations. Each great area was evolving in its own way. Each had its own type of people, its own geographic and economic basis, its own particular economic and social interests. This fact is often lost sight of in the division of attention between the history of national legislation and national parties, on one side, and state history, on the other.*
>
> —Frederick Jackson Turner, *The United States, 1830–1850*

Of the 1.4 billion acres of non-federal rural land—the land available for agriculture in the United States—438 million acres are cropland, 482 million pasture and rangeland, 462 forest, with the remaining 56.2 devoted to miscellaneous uses. This vast area is divided by the Department of Agriculture into ten farm production regions which roughly approximate the continent's physical contours[1] (see map). To delineate geographical and regional differences and to trace the dynamics of regional settlement patterns is not to fall back upon a singular kind of physical determinism, often attributed to Frederick Jackson Turner. Unfortunately most students of history know Turner only through his 1892 essay, more widely publicized by recent generations of academic anthologists than it ever was when it was presented. Anyone who has studied his far more compelling last work, *The United States, 1830–1850,*[2] can detect that Turner was there attempting to piece together a more complex model that stressed geographical variables but added ethnic factors, political composition, and even attempts at value-analysis. Yet Turner tended to romanticize sectionalism as he earlier romanticized the frontier. Turner—and even more so his followers—seem to have found difficulty is confronting the difficult fact that the passage of time and the dynamics of change were muting regional differences. To the extent that discrete sections are our starting point, this analysis builds upon Turner's model but adds those forces of change that are increasingly snuffing out local distinctions, transcending sectionalism, and working to homogenize the rural society and even the rural landscape.

The Northeast

The rocky hills and river valleys of New England were never well suited for agriculture. New England presaged by a century the change and deterioration that would finally overtake most of traditional American farm life. The rural population grew rapidly when early settlements were being established, but by the mid-nineteenth century abandoned farms could be counted in the orchard lands of Connecticut and the Green Mountains of Vermont, their inhabitants having moved on to the more fertile lands that lay west or taken up employment in the small industrial towns that grew up along the region's swift flowing water courses. As the wheat and cattle of the agricultural West poured into New England over the transportation routes northeastern capital and enterprise had done much to inspire, the pioneer New England farmer's struggle for profit from the thin, rocky soil became increasingly futile. New England left an imprint on American farm life, but that imprint had little to do with the products of its soil. By the late nine-

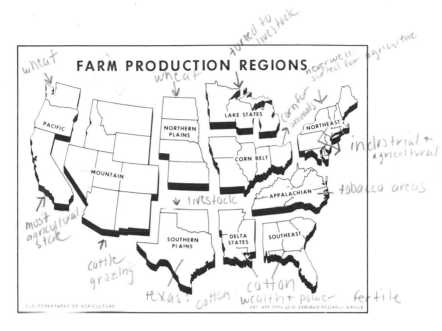

FARM PRODUCTION REGIONS

Handwritten annotations on map:
- wheat
- wheat
- turned to livestock
- never well suited for agriculture
- agriculture
- corn for animals
- industrial + agricultural
- most agricultural state
- livestock
- tobacco areas
- cattle grazing
- texas: cotton
- cotton
- cotton wealth + power
- fertile

Map region labels:
PACIFIC, NORTHERN PLAINS, LAKE STATES, NORTHEAST, MOUNTAIN, CORN BELT, APPALACHIAN, SOUTHERN PLAINS, DELTA STATES, SOUTHEAST

U.S. DEPARTMENT OF AGRICULTURE — ECONOMIC RESEARCH SERVICE

teenth century, the nascent industrial development was sputtering; in Maine, Vermont, western Massachusetts, and New Hampshire population stabilized and in some places declined.

New England's population has increased at a rate near the national norm only in the last two decades. The opening of the new federal highway system and related road projects has stimulated the growth of vast recreation areas, made isolated villages and valleys available as second homes for metropolitan professional people or for retirement centers, and opened up the floodgates for spillover from the Boston area. National corporations, decentralizing their operations into small towns in New Hampshire and Vermont, and several rapidly expanding college towns, have spurred further the most important population increase New England has experienced in more than a century.[3]

If any region reflected the economic diversity of mid-nineteenth century America, it was the Mid-Atlantic states: New York, New Jersey, and Pennsylvania. The area led in manufacturing output, contained the nation's major industrial urban centers, and supported a varied and intensive agriculture. The Mohawk Valley across northern New York opened into productive agricultural lands in the western part of the state and extended on into the Great Lakes basin. The Genesee country and adjacent areas in western Pennsylvania and northeast Ohio were major wheat and sheep raising areas. Avenues of commerce such as the Erie Canal and the narrow Hudson River valley carried the products of the region to the great natural harbor at New York City and helped propel that city to its national commercial dominance. The Great Valley of the Susquehanna through Pennsylvania widened into a rich wheat-growing flatland in the Lancaster plains and helped feed the urban growth of Philadelphia and Baltimore. New York and Pennsylvania were the nation's leading cattle raising states in 1850, and New York's dairy production was double that of any other single state.[4]

Small-scale manufacturing often intermingled with agriculture, drawing upon natural resources such as the anthracite coal of northeast Pennsylvania or the bituminous deposits of the southeast. Many Mid-Atlantic towns were less agricultural marketing centers than small manufacturing clusters—Ithaca, New York, is an example. Economic diversity, mixed-crop farming, both agricultural and industrial development: patterns that would be replicated across the northern half of the United States had their genesis in the Mid-Atlantic states.

It would be a misnomer to draw sharp distinctions between rural and urban in the metropolitania that makes up the Mid-Atlantic states at the twentieth century's three-quarter point. New Jersey is the nation's most densely populated state, claiming only 8,000 farmers; yet the state ranks third in fruit and vegetable production, behind California and Florida. In New York and Pennsylvania more and more farm areas and small towns serve as bedroom communities for commuters who drive to jobs in the branch plants and light industries that have mushroomed in the middle-sized cities that dot the area. The most successful of farmers are mechanized milk producers who serve the ever expanding milksheds of New York, Philadelphia, and Pittsburgh. Land values have escalated in many formerly remote Pennsylvania counties. Eager urban developers, taking advantage of inadequate zoning laws, purchase farmland to be converted either into tract housing or vacation homes for affluent suburbanites who can drive a few hours over federal highways to areas so primitive that one may even hear the whippoorwills call on warm summer nights—if the sound isn't drowned out by the television set.

The Not So Solid South

As homogeneous as it was in its politics during most of the late nineteenth and twentieth centuries, the label "Solid South" is inappropriate to the region's physical contours or its agriculture. The Appalachians intersect the region on a north-south axis: in the seaboard areas of the east rose the tobacco centers of Virginia and North Carolina; the mountain areas, encompassing the border states and extending all the way southward into Georgia, had closer economic ties with the commercial centers of the North than with the areas to the east and west of them. The Cotton Kingdom of the Southeast and Delta states, a misnomer when applied to the whole South, was nevertheless the center of the region's wealth and power. It consisted of a narrow fertile belt (at its widest 200 miles) that reached 1,000 miles from South Carolina to central Texas. Here were the great plantations and the vast majority of enslaved blacks. Other areas of rich productive land were interspersed in the southern landscape: the fertile bluegrass country of central Kentucky, well adapted to tobacco and hemp production; the Nashville basin, a limestone strip surrounded by the Highland Rim in central Tennessee; rich river valleys like the alluvial delta lands along the Mississippi and Yazoo, seats of the plantation aristocracy of Mississippi. This was, as Turner described it, a "complex section, full of different physical regions": mountainous east Tennessee contrasted with the rich cotton areas of the middle region of the state; the sandy pineywoods areas of southern Alabama and Georgia and upcountry Mississippi juxtaposed to the rich lands of the Black Belt.[5]

Keeping in mind the region's diversity, several important features of southern agriculture need be noted. The highest quality lands were monopolized by a few privileged owners to an extent greater than in any other region. In 1850, three to four thousand families lived on the best lands and received three-quarters of the returns from annual exports. Two-thirds of the white people of the South were never connected to the slavery system. The pattern of soil depletion and rural decline noted in New England was also manifest in the seaboard areas of the South. By the time of the Civil War, the westward moving cotton frontier had advanced to the Mississippi; today Texas is the nation's leader in cotton production. No physical variables obstructed the production of crops, other than cotton or tobacco: the South could and did grow corn and raise livestock. Eugene Genovese[6] argues that "the concentration of wealth in the hands of an aristocratic ruling class" retarded the rise of a prosperous yeomanry, got in the way of profitable investment of capital and the evolution of a home market for locally manufactured goods. Thus the South was locked into commercial subservience to the manufacturing centers of the northern states. The inefficiency of slave labor and the social accoutrements that accompanied elite economic control combined to block crop diversity, insure livestock of poor quality, and prevent efficient use of fertilizers to restore overworked soils.[7]

In the twenty years between 1944 and 1964 cotton acreage in the southeastern states declined 31 percent; yet production of cotton not only remained stable but a substantial carry-over remained each year even after about 25 percent of the crop was exported abroad. The decline was greatest in the piedmont regions of Georgia, Alabama, and the Carolinas, those areas where the mountains drain down toward the seaboard. It was here that small-scale growing had been the norm. To the west, in the large-scale production areas of the southern Plains and the Delta, both acreage and output were increasing. One careful study argues that the reason for the demise of cotton in the Piedmont was not geography but the organization of production. Producers and processors there were hesitant to break with established traditions of land tenure and experiment with innovations such as multiple tenancies; they were unwilling to invest capital in the technical innovations that would keep their products competitive. Thus with the return of cattle grazing to the Piedmont for the first time since colonial days, and with commercial poultry production a major enterprise, agricultural diversity at this late date may at last have reached the Southeast.[8]

So brief a synopsis leaves out an important dimension of southern agriculture. In no region of the United States has the agrarian tradition lingered with the same tenacity and determination. From John C. Calhoun to the intellectuals of the 1930s who attached their names to the agrarian manifesto *I'll Take My Stand,* both romanticized agrarian ideology and genuine resistance to modernism's encroachments have had their most ardent spokesmen in the former states of the Confederacy. Nevertheless, the South has not been singled out for especial attention in this book and none of the particularistic case studies are drawn from the region. The reason is a simple one, amply justified, I think, by the references to the South that will be made: the processes of homogenization that have overtaken American agriculture have transcended regional confines. The trends we detect in central Ohio, Iowa, or western Pennsylvania would apply with equal validity to most any rural enclave in the American South.

The Corn Belt and the Lake States

Prehistoric glaciers which extended across the upper reaches of the area loosely classified as Middle West left the land divided into two distinct geographical areas: to the north, limestone areas well adapted to diversified farming and heavily forested at their lake-studded northern borders with conifers and hardwoods; to the south, in a belt extending diagonally across southern Ohio, Indiana, and Illinois, a hilly area of nonglaciated volcanic rocks, ridges, and deep canyons carved out by rivers that ceased to flow millenia ago. The glaciated areas could in turn be separated into forest and prairie. Much of northeast Ohio, Michigan, Wisconsin, and Minnesota were covered by thick forest. Generally the northern prairies fanned out in a southwest direction from northern Indiana, extending to the Grand Prairie of Illinois, widening across the Mississippi into Iowa and Missouri. The rich prairie soils of the glaciated areas were ideal for diversified farming. Wheat was the crop best suited to the prairies and was usually the first one cultivated at the western fringe of settlement.

Wheat rapidly depleted the soil and was difficult to transport. Hence, when growing it ceased to be profitable, farmers in the Lake states turned to livestock. They could not produce good enough grains to fatten hogs and beef cattle, but they had abundant roughage, well suited to the sustenance of dairy cattle. To the south, farmers in the Ohio Valley and westward began to raise corn on a traditional three-crop rotation system they inherited, probably unknowingly, from medieval agricultural practices. The soil was black and fertile. The midwestern summers were hot and sticky, often broken by sudden and ferocious thundershowers; spring was damp and cloudy, the winters hyperborean. The climate, in short, was ideal for growing corn if not for human habitation.[9] The crop was fed to hogs and cattle which, once sufficiently fattened, were in the early days driven overland to markets like the thriving "porkopolis" at Cincinnati, and later transported by rail to the stockyards and meat packing centers at Chicago or St. Paul. In 1850 Ohio was the nation's leading corn producing state.

The land beyond the Mississippi was the most valuable asset the federal government owned. This was the domain of the legendary homesteader, whose 160-acre tract was made available to him only at the cost of his making a home there. Alas, the legend evaporates. Several decades of comprehensive research by Cornell University's Professor Paul W. Gates, the most distinguished scholar of American land policy, and his students have revealed a complex interplay of policy options. Commitment to democratic values meant making land freely and easily available; demands of economic development required populating these unused acres to supply food for consumption and for export, and also to provide buyers for the manufactured products issuing forth from eastern factories. In the long struggle over priorities, the small farmer lost out; by the time he arrived, prize lands had already been gobbled up by railroads, land grant colleges, and land speculators. Moreover, it is by no means clear that the railroads or the speculators were the villains of the piece—both probably hastened the process of settlement, and they certainly stimulated economic development. Neither is the distinction between a farmer and a speculator always clear. Many farmers, whose records have been examined by students of land policies, seemed as much interested in making profits from buying and selling land as from raising and harvesting crops.

The Northern and Southern Plains

Settlement paused temporarily at the borders of the Plains, and the first tentative thrusts into the new lands, first across the Mississippi, then across the Missouri, followed the natural contours of the timber-lined riverbanks. By the late nineteenth century, the farming frontier had crept all the way into the dry areas that follow a rough north-south line through western Nebraska and extend from the Canadian border south into Texas. The low rainfall areas would support only wheat, the region's prime export; at the western border of agricultural settlement an arc-shaped wheat crescent curved from the spring wheat areas of the Dakotas through western Nebraska to the winter-wheat producing regions of Kansas. Beyond that, as the snowcapped Rockies appeared on the horizon, only livestock grazing was feasible. Included in the northern and southern Plains are some of the most productive farmlands on the continent as well as areas that never should have been cultivated, although it took sad experience to learn this. Glaciation had its impact here, too. Thus the glaciated Missouri River plateau in northern Montana and the Dakotas is one of the most heavily cropped areas in the Plains, cash sales of wheat being the major enterprise. Just to the south, however, the unglaciated Missouri plateau will support only ranching, and a 6,000-square-mile geologic area, the Black Hills, rises 4,000 feet above the encircling plains. The Sand Hills of Nebraska represent the eastern fringe of the western range and the west boundary of the prairie grassland. This is almost exclusively a cattle raising area, although in recent years the extensive water resources have stimulated major irrigation projects, and a vigorous sugar beet industry thrives in Scotts Bluff County, Nebraska. The Central Plains incorporates the flat wheat-growing lands of western Kansas, central Nebraska, the Oklahoma Panhandle, and northern Texas.

In the southern High Plains of the Texas Panhandle and south, the Edwards Plateau has always been grazing country. Here all three livestock classes—cattle, sheep, and goats—may be raised on the same ranch. Three billion gallons of water daily are pumped into the Staked Plains to the immediate south to irrigate the productive fields of cotton, grain sorghum, alfalfa, and truck crops. Central Texas, culturally the most southern part of the Great Plains, sustains mixed crop and livestock farming, but has the highest percentage of blacks, low income families, and part-time farmers in the Plains.[10]

From the days of Andy Adams's cattle drives to the modern interstate highway, transportation facilities have always been crucial to the Plains. Unlike the versatile climate of the Midwest, that of the Plains will not sustain general subsistence farming. Today Interstate 80, following the Platte River valley, parallels part of the Oregon Trail and the Union Pacific right-of-way through an intensively irrigated strip that is one of the most heavily cultivated sections of the Plains. Transit routes, it will be noted, flow east to west, for, as the lack of any great metropolitan centers shows, the Plains were an area to pass through, not to stay. All major cities that service the area—St. Paul, Minneapolis, Denver, Omaha, Kansas City, Dallas—are located on its fringes.

Parts of the Great Plains, particularly the wheat growing central areas, absorbed population faster than any agricultural area of the United States in the years following the Civil War. Between 1860 and 1880, the population of Kansas increased ninefold, Nebraska's fifteenfold. Farms of gigantic acreage are not innovations of the last quarter century here. Thousands of prairie acres of the Dakotas were early occupied by hugh bonanza wheat farms; one Nebraska ranch grazed 23,000 cattle on a million acre tract in 1881. In 1945, two Sand Hills ranches encompassed more than 80,000 acres each.

Nowhere has modernization and mechanization proceeded at so rapid a pace. An agricultural service man with a $350,000 investment in his big combines may harvest wheat all the way from the Staked Plains to the Canadian border. One hundred or more feedlots, most of them located in the Plains or in the Southwest, fatten cattle with scientifically prescribed diets, and have in recent years supplied 16 percent of the nation's beef supply.[11]

The Mountain States

In the shadow of the Rockies to the west of the Plains, the Colorado Piedmont, drained in its northern reaches by the South Platte River, is extensively irrigated and contains the major urban center of the Mountain states, Denver.

The Colorado plateau extends over most of the four states of Colorado, New Mexico, Arizona, and Utah. In the high altitudes, winters are cold, the growing season short. Rainfall in sparse; much of the usable moisture is derived from melting winter snows, and even these are carried off in streambeds so deeply entrenched in stony mountain cliffs as to make access well-nigh impossible. Even though the

Desert Land Act (1877) amended the Homestead Act to permit holdings as large as 640 acres in this region, more of the land than in any other area (having never been claimed) remains federally owned. The grazing of cattle, mainly on these federal lands, is the major agricultural enterprise. The Mountain states have a long history; they were long the habitat of the nomadic Navaho, the more stable Hopis, and the mysterious Anasazi (ancient ones). They were explored early by Spanish gold and fur seekers. Yet the forbidding terrain and hostile Indians made them the last frontier of American settlement.

If glaciation was critical to the quality of agriculture in the Lake states and Corn Belt, beyond the Great Divide the success of any type of farming hinges on a single variable: rainfall. The location of the mountains is determinative. Hence, parts of northern California and Oregon are inundated with surplus water as heavy laden clouds pile up against the Sierras, while across these mountains to the east, in the great expanse until the Rockies are reached, lie barren, fallow desert lands.

Mormon Utah is an oasis. Parts of it are brilliantly-hued rocky wasteland and barren salt lake, while other irrigated areas are lush with greenery, making diversified farming and a thriving sheep-raising industry possible.

On the other hand, the only thing lush and green in adjacent Nevada is likely to be found in the coffers of the gambling lords of Reno and Las Vegas.

The propinquity of the burgeoning southern California region and the sun-belt retirement centers of Arizona, coupled with an untapped reservoir of natural resources, make the Mountain states the center of the most heated conservation battles of our time. The ecology issue has had a salience in Colorado elections in 1972 and 1974 unparalleled in any other state. Eager strip miners of coal—for example, in the Black Mesa area of Navaho territory—have discovered mineral wealth of greater potential than all the legendary gold the Spanish explorers hoped to find. Uranium and oil also are present. The urban communities in southern California and Arizona, insatiable in their needs for water and power, encourage more Hoover Dams to capture the valuable Colorado River water, and coal-burning power plants threaten to belch out even more dusty clouds of smoke over the mountains, deserts, and canyons.[12]

The Pacific States

Approaching the West Coast across the northern Plains, the land pattern of the East is reversed. The first crop to appear is wheat; in July vast areas of western Washington turn as yellow with grain as the fields of North and South Dakota. Where valleys widen between the mountain ranges, rich orchard lands appear: the Okanagan Valley across the border in British Columbia, the area around Yakima, Washington, and the fertile Willamette Valley of central Oregon. As in the East, there are sizeable milksheds at the outer reaches of Seattle, Spokane, and Portland. The forested mountain sides of Oregon and northern California support a sizeable timber industry.

California agriculture epitomizes variety and paradox. The nation's most populous state is also its most prosperous agricultural state, turning out each year farm products worth more than four billion dollars. This makes farming the largest single business enterprise in the state. California has some of the best farmland on the continent, but along its eastern mountain spurs, stretching from north to south, are barren areas where even mesquite struggles to survive; there are cold, high mountain plateaus accessible only to intrepid Sierra Club types, and the Mojave Desert is as sterile as the Great Salt Lake. The dry, flat wheat areas in the northeast are suggestive of western Washington. The wide Central Valley between the Coast Range on the Pacific side and the Sierras on the east is the heartland of California agriculture. In reality, it is two valleys: one watered by the Sacramento River to the north, the other the drier San Joaquin Valley at the south. This valley, into which the entire Appalachian mountain range would conveniently fit, produces every known crop of the temperate zone, with the exception of tobacco. Thus California's cotton production, centering in Kern County, ranks second only to that of Texas. Only Iowa leads California in livestock production, and only Florida is ahead in citrus fruits. Artichokes come from Castroville, the "Artichoke Capital of the World"; lettuce from the Salinas Valley; table grapes from Delano; domestic wines (85 percent of U.S. production) from the Napa and Salinas valleys; oranges, lemons, and grapefuit from the orchards of urban-impacted southern California; and dates from Riverside County.

More than any other region, the agricultural enterprises of California are dependent upon environmental modifications wrought by the hands of man. The Central Valley Project, an engineering enterprise unparalleled in the Unites States, has built dams, aqueducts, tunnels, and even reversed the flow of rivers to transport the waters of the rain-drenched north to the parched areas of the south. Without irrigation, much of the San Joaquin Valley would be as dry as Nevada.

Since the days of the original Spanish land grants, large-scale agriculture has been more prevalent than in any other region of the United States. The average farm in the Central Valley contains nearly 1,000 acres, and the average invested value is a gargantuan $327,000. Smaller farms continue to disappear, although in California small farms aren't necessarily poor farms if they produce high-return items such as table grapes. The number of units fell off 50 percent between 1950 and 1970; more than any other state, huge factories in the fields, such as the Kern County Land Company in cotton, DiGiorgio in grapes, and United Brands, Purex, and Bud Antle in lettuce, monopolize land and production. Acreage far in excess of the one percent national average is owned by corporations.

If agriculture in California is more of a boom industry than in any other part of the country, there are still acute problems. Concomitant with large-scale operation, California farming is mechanized with a vengeance—tree shakers drop walnuts and olives into waiting cloth receptacles, and ripe citrus fruits are sucked from trees into pneumatic tubes. California cotton production grew astronomically because its technological efficiency far outpaced that of the older growing areas of the southeastern states. Tomatoes, melons, and asparagus have been bred especially to make it possible to harvest them mechanically. Still, for the delicate and tiresome tasks of picking lettuce or harvesting and pruning table grapes, traditional stoop labor is required. Drawn from recently arrived immigrant groups—first the Chinese and Japanese, later Filipinos, Okies, and now Mexican-Americans—the wage labor in the fields of California has for more than half a century been the most exploited, underpaid, and defenseless segment of the American working force. Only in the last two decades, through the patient and dynamic efforts of one of the great labor leaders of our time, Cesar Chavez, has any progress been made in overcoming the long-standing cultural and economic discrimination that refused to regard the humble people who labored in the fields of California the same as those employed in any other large-scale industry. As of this writing, the heroic struggle of the United Farm Workers continues irrespective of concerted political offenses directed against it, attempts of the Teamsters' Union to undercut and destroy it, and a liberal temporary immigration policy that keeps the reservoir of cheap labor filled.[13]

Economically viable California agriculture may be fighting a losing battle with the inexorable population expansion of the state's urban areas. A few years ago it was estimated that the bulldozers of real estate developers were burying 3,000 acres of orange groves each day in Los Angeles County alone. Land values are escalating. Skyrocketing real estate assessments and the tax bills to pay for the schools, roads, and police protection drive down the often thin profit margins of neighboring farmers. Thus land is sold off and more tracts are built, not only in the citrus groves of the south but where there were once vineyards in Napa and Sonoma counties.[14]

Appropriately, our survey of the geographical landscape of American agriculture has moved from east to west, finally to terminate in California—there are those that say that what happens in California points the way to the American future. If this presages giant agricultural industries functioning in an artificial man-made environment, reaping the fruits of nature with intricate mechanical gadgets, juxtaposed against gregariously expanding and demanding metropolitan conglomerates, then the pastoral images of Jefferson and Goldsmith are as antiquated as the odes of Horace, and the problems of social adaptation more portentuous than even Marx or Weber contemplated.

Farm Peoples

Peopling of the vast agricultural hinterlands of the United States roughly followed the geographical contours. However, the conventional urban wisdom that categorizes all rural communities as homogeneous enclaves is wrong. Neither is it correct to imagine the nation's farms and villages as stable and unchanging little islands in time. Rural townships were never so ethnic as the wards of great cities, but there have been definite ethnic settlement patterns in the countryside, traces of which still persist. Moreover, rural America has traditionally been on the move. For example, in two widely separated rural townships (one in Iowa, one in Illinois) fewer than 40 percent of the people who lived there in 1850 were still present ten years later.[15]

Beginning in the early nineteenth century, declining rural New England was the nucleus of a vast exodus that carried its inhabitants and its influence across much of the northern United States. The inland areas of Vermont, Connecticut, and New Hampshire were the pivot points of the migration. The first New England outpost was in the glaciated rivers and lakes country of upper New York and northern Pennsylvania, linked to the older settlement of the East by the Erie Canal and later by a network of railways. This "Burned-Over District," as it was called, became a second jumping off point, as New England natives poured into Connecticut's Western Reserve in northeast Ohio, moved across into southern Michigan, and skipped over

Indiana to found New England-type colonies in northern Illinois, southern Wisconsin, and Iowa. One enthusiastic chronicleer even purports to trace the long arm of New England all the way to Oregon.[16] Emigrant New Englanders brought along some well identified cultural baggage that continued to mark their presence and influence. Arriving early, they chose their locales prudently, situating usually in richer, glaciated areas. Impressionistically, they seem to have contributed more than their share to the economic and political elites of the areas where they settled. Turner[17] reports that one-half to two-thirds of the delegates to the Wisconsin Constitutional convention of 1846 were born in New England or in the outpost counties of western New York; in a similar convention in Iowa the same year, one-third of the members were of New England birth. Salmon P. Chase of Ohio, Lincoln's secretary of treasury and chief justice of the Supreme Court, was born in New Hampshire, as was Lewis Cass of Michigan, Democratic presidential nominee in 1848. Stephen A. Douglas came from Vermont, and a road marker near West Townshend in that state marks the birthplace of the founder of the Taft family dynasty of Cincinnati, Ohio. The mobile Yankees carried along an interest in education; literacy rates were characteristically high in areas where they settled, free public schools abounded, and some of the best of the liberal arts colleges of the Midwest —Oberlin, Beloit, and Knox are examples—were founded by transplanted New Englanders. And they brought religion, a pietistic, devout Calvinism that usually took shape in Congregational or Presbyterian form. A few, however, were Anglicans; some were converts of Methodist revivalism. Yankee devotionalism carried over into secular concerns. Compared to other areas, those with high New England influence were more passionate in their support for abolition and in the crusade for prohibition. One plausible reason for the Yankee dedication to education was to offset the spread of Roman Catholicism, perhaps a reflection of the nativist sentiments that flourished in New England itself, as its cities and factory towns swelled with the influx of Catholic Irish.

In the years after the Civil War, Yankee-settled areas were bastions of Republican party strength. For example, as late as the period 1920–1948, the leading Republican county in Ohio was Fulton, a rural county bordering Michigan in the state's northwest corner. The county's history, written back in 1888, said this of the county seat: "The distinctive faith of New England Congregationalism has been prominent in the religion of the citizens. . . . A number of its leading families are from the land of Puritanism."[18]

A second ethnic pattern interwoven into rural America has been that of the lowland Scotch, most of them migrants from areas where they had been earlier colonized in Northern Ireland, hence the designation "Scotch-Irish." Some 200,000 Scotch-Irish and 250,000 Scotlanders had arrived in United States by the end of the colonial period, when they made up 15 percent of the white population.[19] As late as 1930, the census reported 1.5 million first and second generation Scots and Scotch-Irish. The original mecca for the group was William Penn's receptive colony, but from there, even before the Revolution, they and their descendants had poured down the Cumberland Valley, populating the Carolinas and Tennessee. Typically, they constituted in Turnerian terms the "cutting edge of the frontier." They were the first to settle on the fringe of the wilderness, and many of the legendary pioneers—Daniel Boone, Davy Crockett, and Andrew Jackson, for example—were Scotch-Irish. A student of Tennessee politics, who has examined the names of all members of the state's legislature from 1820 to 1840, reports finding few names that could not be identified as Scotch-Irish.[20] In fact the Scotch-Irish were so characteristic of the South that one writer suggests that such euphemisms as "southern white," "hillbilly," or that in current vogue, "Appalachian," actually identify Scotch-Irish cultural proclivities that still survive.[21]

Like their Puritan counterparts, the Scotch-Irish were pietistic Calvinists, often virulently anti-Catholic and anti-liquor, although the faith was expressed through the less institutionalized and more free-wheeling Methodist and Baptist denominations. They remained avid prohibitionists (in theory if not always in practice), but religious scruples against the institution of slavery had disappeared among the churches of the South by the 1840s.

If people of Scotch-Irish descent dominated the South, they were anything but a stationary population. Kentucky was settled primarily by Virginians. Mobile Carolinians migrated across the mountains and populated Tennessee; that state in turn was the source of large numbers of migrants to Texas and Arkansas. For example, both Andrew Jackson and James K. Polk, the two most prominent of Tennessee-based political leaders, were born in North Carolina. Sam Houston and Davy Crockett both came from Tennessee. This pattern of east to west migration was replicated in the Cotton Belt. Former Georgians and Carolinians made up the bulk of Alabama's population, and from that state came the pioneers who pushed into the Mississippi Delta lands and east Texas.

Time more or less stood still in the valleys and hollows of eastern Tennessee and Georgia where, well into the twentieth century, descendants of English and Scotch-Irish settlers clung to a tough, flinty Calvinism, traditional folkways, and folksongs, some of which had their origins in Elizabethan days. Isolated from the cotton and tobacco lands, these mountain whites retained an independence that expressed itself in opposition to slavery, to the Confederacy, and in subsequent allegiance to the Republican party. Still, in mid-twentieth century, some of the mountain counties of Tennessee were the strongest bastions of the Republican party in the nation.

In a related migratory sequence, and one that persists to the present day, scores of southerners, many of them mountain whites from the coal mining areas, moved northward into the driftless unglaciated areas of southern Ohio, southern Indiana, downstate Illinois, the hilly regions of Missouri, and some to the southern tier of counties in Iowa.

The dominant Scotch-Irish and earlier English colonial heritage of the South was little suffused by the inputs of other nationality groups. As an illustration, in 1850 only 2 percent of the residents of the South Central states were foreign born, and 85 percent of these lived in Louisiana. The German element, prominent in the Mid-Atlantic and North Central states, was represented only in a cluster of about fifteen counties in the Edwards Plateau of Texas and in a small colonial offshoot of the settlements in Pennsylvania in western Maryland and the Shenandoah Valley. As W. J. Cash reminds us, southern planter, mountain white, aristocrat, and upland poor white all spring from an identical ethnic and cultural background—the divisions between them were economic. He goes on to argue that only the presence of the large black population served to unite all white men, irrespective of economic status, and prevent the fact of class differences from becoming the realization of class consciousness.[22]

The principal non-English speaking element among early rural settlers were migrants from the divided small states and principalities that make up modern Germany. Germans came in a continuous stream from the colonial period to the early twentieth century and represent the largest infusion of any nationality group into the United States. Like the Scotch-Irish, the first German mecca was the Mid-Atlantic states, particularly Pennsylvania; but unlike the Scotch-Irish, Germans tended to choose less rugged, more valuable land (usually already cultivated). Spreading outward from the Lancaster plain, settlements dotted the fertile interior valleys of western Pennsylvania, followed the glaciated lands across into Ohio where large German communities took root in the oak openings (fertile plains surrounded by forest) in the northern part of the state, and extended through northern Indiana and Illinois into Wisconsin, Iowa, and Missouri. Later, German migrants pushed to the very edge of nonarid lands. Large colonies of Volga Germans, long settled in Russia and leaving only when their exemption from service in the Czar's army was withdrawn, peopled the wheat lands of the western Dakotas and parts of Nebraska and Kansas. Germans constituted the major foreign group in most of the farming Midwest. In rank order, states with the largest percentage of German foreign born in 1900 were Wisconsin, Missouri, and Texas, but this discounts the even greater number of second and third generation Germans in New York, Pennsylvania, Illinois, and Ohio. Franklin County, Missouri, and Jefferson County, Wisconsin, were 80 percent German in 1900. In Kansas, in 1880, Germans who made up 5 percent of the population were the largest foreign-born group. The heaviest concentration was in Ellis County and included Lutherans, Catholics, and Volga Germans; the large settlements in McPherson and Marion counties added a substantial Mennonite population to these groups.[23]

More so than the Yankees or Scotch-Irish, the linguistically different Germans tended to cluster in homogeneous communities and maintain a cultural distance from other groups.

Unlike other immigrant groups, the Germans were divided by religion: Protestants from northern Germany, Catholics from Bavaria and the south. Differing in theology, history, and moral standards, German Catholics and Protestants seldom mingled in the same rural community, and their differences often carried over into American politics.[24] Most village and countryside Catholic parishes in the Midwest today are still likely to be German.

German Protestants were usually Lutheran, but they gradually divided into several synods. Some gravitated into the United Brethren and the Evangelical Association, two German pietistic denominations founded in America; others were caught up in the Methodist revivals of the 1830s and 1840s. Visible beyond their small numbers were those who migrated as religious groups: the ascetic Amish, the less conservative Mennonites, and several among the Volga Germans. The fact of German distribution throughout the Midwest and the canny penchant of sectarian groups for selecting quality farmland is attested by the wide scattering of Amish settlements: the largest, harassed by tourists, in Lancaster County, Pennsylvania, with other sizeable communities in Holmes and Madison counties, Ohio, northern Indiana, and central Iowa. Scandinavian migration to America, largely a post-Civil War phenomenon, peaked in the 1880s. It was concentrated in the forest and lake country of Minnesota and Wisconsin, an area not unlike the Swedish and Norwegian homeland. Nonetheless, scattered Norwegian, Danish, and Swedish communities were to be found in Michigan's Upper Peninsula, Iowa, Nebraska, and the Dakotas. The sociologist E. A. Ross conjectured in 1914 that 40 percent of Minnesota's population was by descent Scandinavian. Both Swedes and Norwegians were historic Lutherans, often militantly anti-Catholic, but there were differences between the two major Scandinavian immigrant groups. Norwegian Lutherans, influenced by various evangelical revivals in Norway and America, were more moralistic than other Lutherans. They condemned drinking, card playing, and working on the Sabbath. Members were more prone than other Lutherans to join in various secular crusades such as abolitionism or prohibition. The Swedes assimilated more rapidly; as linguistic separation faded in the second generation and the population dispersed, loyalty to the Lutheran faith rather than nationality was the major integrating force in the group. Not so the Norwegians: linguistic loyalty remained strong until World War I; leaders of the church condemned Americanization, and Norwegian enclaves could easily be identified in large numbers of Wisconsin, Minnesota, and North Dakota counties well into the twentieth century. Among all groups of various national origin residing in the United States, Norwegians had the greatest proportion residing in rural areas: as late as 1940 half of all Norwegians in the Midwest lived on farms or in villages of less than 2,500.[25]

Danish migration to the United States, although substantial, has been little studied or observed. Settling in the same areas as other Scandinavians, Danes joined their churches, quickly abandoned their own language, and rapidly became assimilated Americans. Only a few homogeneous Danish communities, such as the one in Audubon County, Iowa, can be easily pinpointed.

The Finns, who migrated later than other Scandinavians, were considered an out-group, stereotyped as tough, radical, and harddrinking. Some were farmers in the wintry plains and forests of northern Minnesota and the Dakotas. Others were lumberjacks or laborers in the iron mines of Michigan's Upper Peninsula and northern Minnesota. Finns were represented far beyond their numbers in radical political organizations: there were socialist halls and cooperatives in many Finnish communities, and the group was the numerical mainstay in the Communist party's small membership in the Midwest during the Great Depression years.

Several assorted groups with small numbers of rural residents round out the portrayal of the ethnic makeup of the farm population. Dutch Protestants settled in the area around Holland and Kalamazoo in southern Michigan and in Sioux County at the northwest corner of Iowa. Bohemian (Czech) farmers made up a second wave of settlers in Nebraska, taking up lands originally occupied by other groups. Later immigrant groups were but little represented in the countryside. Jewish farmers were almost unknown save for a few truck farmers in a borscht belt in New York's Catskills and chicken raisers in such far removed places as Petaluma, California, and Vineland, New Jersey. Nevertheless, many small county-seat towns in the farm areas had a handful of Jewish families, often proprietors of retail establishments, particularly the ever present Army-Navy store. Italians took to fruit and vegetable growing in several areas of the urbanized East, and still today one may occasionally find Italian names on mailboxes of large dairy farms in metropolitan milkshed areas. Many California wineries were founded by Italian families. Some of the substantial landholders in the truck farming areas of southern California are Yugoslav immigrants. The Japanese truck farmers in the upper Sacramento Valley and around Los Angeles were among the most successful in California before internment during World War II deprived them of their lands. Some of the most recent of newcomers, the urban-based Puerto Ricans, join the daily trek from city centers to the fields of New Jersey where they do the tiresome stoop labor the fruit and vegetable crops require.

Fitting together the ethnic history of rural areas for comparative purposes points up distinct group differences in regions of concentration, rate of acculturation and assimilation, status, and political affiliation among the principal groups. New Englanders, Germans, and, to a lesser extent, Scotch-Irish overlapped in the area loosely defined as Middle West. On the other hand, the South was almost exclusively settled by Scotch-Irish and, of course, the one group of involuntary migrants, the blacks. Scandinavians concentrated in the dairy regions of the Lake states, extending in lesser numbers south into the Corn Belt. Impressionistically, New Englanders, Germans (except for Catholics), and Scotch-Irish fused rapidly and intergroup differences faded. Studies by Paul Kleppner and Richard Jensen have demonstrated the extent to which issues such as prohibition exacerbated intergroup differences, aligning pietistic New Englanders (usually Congregationalists, Presbyterians, or Methodists) against Catholics and, to a lesser extent, Lutherans. The issue even divided several ethnic groups along religious lines—the Norwegians are an example. Politically, New England areas tended to be Republican; so did German and Scandanavian settlements, except when divisive issues such as prohibition or the language issue intervened. The Scotch-Irish, of course, made up the solid Democratic South, but political allegiances in other areas are more difficult to characterize as the group's identity mingled with the core culture. Status differences among these groups are difficult to delineate. Judging from Turner's old but comprehensive studies, buttressed by whatever impressions may be gathered from the distorted county histories of the late-nineteenth century, New Englanders were disproportionately represented in the small town elites of lawyers, doctors, editors, and clerics. An ethnic analysis of history fails its purpose if it becomes a quest for antiquarian survivals; to stress ethnocultural distinctions among the populations that remain on the farms and in the villages of the late-twentieth century would ensnare us precisely in that trap. As dramatic as differences were in the 1890s, and as convincing as evidence drawn from voting returns even into the 1930s may be, the demographic and technological revolutions since the 1940s have subsumed the traditional cultures of rural America as much as it has subsumed the traditional farms.

Any description of the population of the rural portions of the continent remains incomplete so long as one views only the family farms of Ohio, Iowa, or Minnesota or the main streets of southern and midwestern villages. Down the back roads, in remote hinterlands, or in out-of-the-way shantytowns on the outskirts of many a farm town may be found evidences of poverty more stark than in the crowded slums of major cities. As has been noted, racial and cultural minorities, traditionally oppressed because of color or language, constitute a substantial portion of the nonurban poor.

American Indians, heavily concentrated in the states of the arid Southwest, graze their cattle or sheep over the dry grasslands of designated reservations. Others have been shunted off into the least productive lands that remained after the needs and desires of the powerful and influential and more affluent had been satisfied. The best of the Indian lands were bartered away or taken away long ago.

As we have noted in chapter 1, at one time the overwhelming portion of black Americans were sharecroppers and wage workers in the South. With the collapse of that system and the lure of better economic opportunities in the cities and in the North, one of the great migratory movements of modern times has transformed much of this once southern rural population into a northern urban one.

Mexican-Americans constitute one of the most recent emigrant groups to the United States. In 1960, one of every eleven Californians and one of every seven Texans were

Spanish-speaking. Although this population is principally urban (79 percent in 1960), they make up a disproportionate amount of farm wage labor, picking the grapes of southern California, doing stoop labor in Texas, even harvesting cherries in Michigan. Sixteen percent of the Spanish-speaking population of Texas is employed in farm labor, 41 percent in California. A few of these are migrant farm laborers who join with blacks, poor whites, and Puerto Ricans to follow the crops in three broad streams: one, northward from Florida to New Jersey; a second, north from Texas into Michigan and Minnesota; a third, up the Central Valley of California. More of them, however, are shack people, living on the outskirts of farm towns like Delano, California, or hanging on to a humble half-acre homestead in southwest Texas, New Mexico, or Arizona.[26]

Traditional rural America, as it existed up to the great metamorphose of the last quarter century, was diverse in geography, diverse in population. Surprisingly few studies of American farms and villages have given attention to their ethnic makeup.[27] This lack has produced a myopic view of rural politics, overlooking often intense and deep-seated ethnic and religious rivalries, such as that between German Catholics and Protestants. More important, it has left out a dimension in American ethnic history. If there ever was an American melting pot, a concept modern urban-based sociological studies increasingly question, the place to look might be the American countryside. The white, Anglo-Saxon, Protestant core culture was fused at the time when the United States was preponderantly a rural nation. The major groups contributing to the century-long process of populating the farm areas of inner America were the English, Scotch-Irish, Germans (except Catholics), Scandinavians, and Dutch. They shared religious, racial, and physical contiguities. Thrown into interaction with each other, with varying degrees of rapidity, language differences disappeared, religious distinctions were blurred. This is not to argue that complete structural assimilation—the absorption of individuals of different ethnic, religious, and nationality backgrounds into a common set of peer group relationships—occurred. The discussion here has, after all, stressed differences, not similarities. Certainly conscious distinctions, particularly religious, always existed in village and countryside. Nonetheless, a beyond the melting pot hypothesis is more difficult to apply to rural America: assimilation and acculturation, given the commonalities of the groups involved, proceeded more swiftly and surely than in the nation's cities.

If the white, Anglo-Saxon Protestant (WASP) group can be regarded as an ethnic entity, it was one forged in the countryside, and there it sustained its greatest strength. Even now the prototype of the WASP is a small-town Protestant churchgoer, with the Midwest or the rural South as his heartland. Accordingly, much of the rural-urban conflict that has periodically surfaced in our history may mask sharp ethnic and religious differences. Finally, the vacant farmhouses, the shuttered country churches, the dying or transformed villages may mark the destruction of the one cultural base that belonged to white Anglo-Saxons, just as surely as the bulldozer, the urban developer, and the parking lot, or the elimination of sharecropping, have both physically and culturally uprooted other groups.

And so we conclude again on a note of disjuncture. The demographic and collateral technological revolution that swept the countryside after 1945 uprooted its people and dispersed its cultures. The children and grandchildren of Scandinavian or German Catholic traditional farmers are parts of the homogenized populations of cities, faceless suburbs, and transformed small towns. Geographical differences remain, for weather and climate still determine crop patterns, but even these must be qualified. Each great urban area has its sizeable milkshed area that constitutes the major agricultural enterprise on the lands that surround it. If crop specialization increases, it is not because of physical conditions, but because rapid nationwide transportation facilities make it possible. Any distinctiveness that remains in small towns is due to what remains from the past, not what is being created in the present. If one judges simply by the most visible indication, namely, the architecture, the streets of a town in Monroe County, Pennsylvania, are difficult to distinguish from those of a town in Lac qui Parle County, Minnesota. And what urbanite, driving off an interstate highway into any one of the handy roadside auto service centers could tell whether he was in Oregon or Tennessee? This process of cultural homogenization of the rural village and the absorption of the countryside as an outpost of urban society becomes clearer as our points of reference become specific and concrete.

Notes

1. Since 1958 almost 15 million acres have been shifted from farming to nonfarming use; the most substantial decreases were in cropland and "other use" categories. Forest acreage increased. Lloyd E. Partain, "Enough Land for Tomorrow," *USDA Yearbook, 1970,* p. 191.
2. (New York: W. W. Norton & Co., 1962 [1935]).
3. George K. Lewis, "Population Change in Northern New England," *Annals of the Association of American Geographers* 62 (June 1972): 307–22.
4. Turner, *The United States, 1830–1850,* p. 101.
5. Ibid., p. 213.
6. *The Political Economy of Slavery* (New York: Random House, Vintage Books, 1961), pp. 106–53.
7. This interpretation has been challenged in a recent controversial and provocative book by Robert William Fogel and Stanley Engermann, *Time on the Cross* (Boston: Little, Brown & Co., 2 vols., 1974).
8. Merle C. Prunty and Charles S. Aiken, "The Demise of the Piedmont Cotton Region," *Annals of the Association of American Geographers* 62 (June 1972): 283–306.
9. John Fraser Hart, "The Middle West," *Annals of the Association of American Geographers* 62 (June 1972): 266–67.
10. E. Cotton Mather, "The American Great Plains," *Annals of the Association of American Geographers* 62 (June 1972): 237–45.
11. Ibid., pp. 254–57.
12. Robert Durrenberger, "The Colorado Plateau," *Annals of the Association of American Geographers* 62 (June 1972): 211–36.
13. An extensive literature deals with the organizing efforts of the United Farm Workers. For a pessimistic interpretation, see

Winthrop Griffith, "Is Chavez Beaten?" *New York Times Magazine,* 15 September 1974, p. 18; see also Ronald B. Taylor, "Something Is in the Wind," *Nation* 220 (22 February 1975): 206–9. For background, see John Gregory Dunne, *Delano: The Story of the California Grape Strike* (New York: Farrar, Straus & Giroux, 1967); Mark Day, *Forty Acres: Cesar Chavez and the Farm Workers* (New York: Praeger, 1971). The passage by the California legislature, in July 1975, of a law to regularize union election procedures promised to ease the bitter jurisdictional dispute between the United Farm Workers and the International Brotherhood of Teamsters. One immediate consequence of the law was that unionization had at last come to the fields of California. Although, in early 1975, only 25 percent of the state's agricultural workers were unionized, in the early elections only 10 percent voted against having any union. By October, the UFW had won 54 elections, the Teamsters 61, although both had won the right to represent about the same number of workers. Disputes concerning intimidation of workers and improper attempts to influence the voting marred the initial elections. Observers speculated that more than half of the elections held during August and September 1975 would be challenged either by the UFW or by the Teamsters. *New York Times,* 14 September, 22 October 1975.

14. Neal R. Pierce, *The Pacific States of America: People, Politics and Power in the Five Pacific Basin States* (New York: W. W. Norton & Co., 1972), pp. 81–85.

15. Allan G. Bogue, *From Prairie to Cornbelt* (Chicago: Quadrangle Books, 1968 [1963]), p. 25.

16. Stewart Holbrook, *The Yankee Exodus* (Seattle: University of Washington Press, 1968 [New York: Macmillan Co., 1950]), pp. 223–41.

17. Turner, *The United States, 1830–1850,* p. 50.

18. Lewis C. Aldrich, ed., *History of Fulton and Henry Counties, Ohio* (Syracuse, N.Y., 1888), p. 428.

19. Charles H. Anderson, *White Protestant Americans* (Englewood Cliffs, N.J.: Prentice-Hall, 1970), p. 34.

20. I am indebted to Ms Dale Holman, completing a dissertation on antebellum Tennessee politics, for this information.

21. Frank Barna, "The Frontiersman as Ethnic: A Brief History of the Scotch-Irish," in Otto Feinstein, ed., *Ethnic Groups in the City* (Lexington, Mass.: D. C. Heath & Co., 1971), pp. 155–64.

22. *The Mind of the South* (Garden City, N.Y.: Doubleday & Co., Anchor Books, 1954).

23. J. Neale Carman, *Foreign Language Units of Kansas: I. Historical Atlas and Statistics* (Lawrence: University of Kansas Press,

1962). This little known compilation is the most comprehensive study of ethnic distribution of any state of which I am aware.

24. See Paul Kleppner, *The Cross of Culture: A Social Analysis of Midwestern Politics, 1850–1900* (New York: Free Press, 1970); Richard J. Jensen, *The Winning of the Midwest: Social and Political Conflict, 1888–1896* (Chicago: University of Chicago Press, 1971); Frederick C. Luebke, *Immigrants and Politics: The Germans of Nebraska, 1880–1900* (Lincoln: University of Nebraska Press, 1969).

25. Anderson, *White Protestant Americans,* p. 61.

26. Julian Samora, ed., *La Raza: Forgotten Americans* (Notre Dame, Ind.: University of Notre Dame Press, 1966).

27. The major exceptions are the political studies of Paul Kleppner and Richard Jensen cited in n. 24.

CHAPTER THREE

From Community to Society

Suppose that you are on the summit of Blue Mounds, Wisconsin, overlooking the great stretch of dairy country to the east, south, and west. Farm industrial plants, each with its close-set home, embroidered with trees, form distinct patches all over the landscape. But at distant intervals much larger patches appear. You say, "There is the village of Blue Mounds; yonder is the village of Mount Horeb; over there is Barneveld." What is the relation of these villages to those farm plants? Are the villages communities by themselves? Can you safely treat them socially as complete units? How are they related to one another? What is the real meaning of these picturesque human clusters?

... Would it not be well, before imposing a redirected civilization upon the country man, to examine more minutely the larger movements of his ordinary life?

—Charles Josiah Galpin, *Rural Life*

These families, who had formed the backbone of the village life in the past, who were the depositaries of the village traditions, had to seek refuge in the large centres; the process, humorously designated by statisticians as "the tendency of the rural populations towards the large towns," being really the tendency of water to flow up-hill when forced by machinery.

—Thomas Hardy, *Tess of the D'Urbervilles*

Each individual is unique; every individual incorporates part of that which is general. This contradiction—both parts obviously true—neatly expresses the problem any case study confronts. I can make no claim that the two historical examples that follow reflect in microcosm the general patterns of social change that have convulsed American rural life, but I can make a claim that these case studies contain within them *some* phenomena that have touched all of rural society. Moreover, an attempt can be made to sort out those phenomena peculiar to a particular place and those reflecting general patterns, for social theory can help us here. For example, the stages of development that appear in the narrative of an Ohio township over a long 150-year time span are not arbitrary impositions on the data. There are differences, not place- or time-specific, that point to an early pioneer period when the area was isolated and developing an indigenous social framework, and population turnover was high. This can be distinguished from a second period when the area, although still isolated, was linked through improved transportation with regional and national economic processes. As internal economic functions tended therefore to stabilize, turnover rates declined. The contrast is striking with the present when the same area has been almost totally absorbed into a metropolitan, specialized, technologically advanced culture. The central role of transportation linkages as transforming agents is apparent.[1]

The case studies that follow attempt to illustrate and give substance to the impact of change on the life patterns of ordinary people. Neither has any prominent characteristics that would separate it from any of a hundred townships or counties in the United States. I find that generalizations that form the necessary starting and ending points of historical research often seem banal and obvious when baldly stated, but they assume concreteness when they describe in sometimes homely detail how specific people lived and died in Scioto Township, Ohio, or Bedford County, Pennsylvania.

On the surface, the two case-studies are different. One is a single township; the other, focusing on a county-seat village, has to be broadened to encompass the entire county of which the borough is the center. Economically, one was almost exclusively a farming center, and the other, more complex, combined agriculture with small-scale manufacturing and extractive industries; thus, we purposefully touch upon two functionally different types of rural communities. Both are considered in a long-term perspective that spans 150 years, which involves a sacrifice of depth for breadth. Both were originally isolated backwaters, and if their mutual process of development could be expressed in a few succinct words, it would be that for both the central focus of their history was the struggle to escape isolation, and through transportation and communication ties link with the mainstream of the American society and economy. For one of them the quest was well-nigh one of desperation. Likewise, in neither of them have the processes of development been slow and gradual, because for both the most dramatic manifestations of change have taken place since 1938.

For several reasons, I have tread gingerly in using the elusive term "community." Most sociologists agree that for a community to exist at any specific time or place there must be a consistent and pervading kind of social interaction. To demonstrate with historical data alone that such interaction existed in an Ohio township or a Pennsylvania county at some point in the past is virtually impossible. Any township, for example, was clearly a legal and political community, because this is the one kind of interaction that can arbitrarily be created, whether it is convenient or not. But a bounded political community may have no reality at all as a place where most of its inhabitants went to church on Sunday, did their shopping, or visited friends. Moreover, the patterned interactions that make for a community may exist at one point in time but not at another. If I cannot say with complete confidence that Scioto Township *was* a community in 1880, I can declare with a great deal more confidence that it was *not* a community in 1975.

Scioto Township, Ohio

Scioto Township, Delaware County, situated nearly in the geographic center of Ohio, takes its name from the river that forms part of its eastern boundary. It encompasses about thirty square miles. The river, broad and shallow in the northern reaches of the township, sometimes floods the rich alluvial bottomlands that line its banks, but as it flows southward, it enters a narrow, rocky escarpment, once a channel for drainage from prehistoric glaciers that submerged the entire area. The soil of the Scioto bottomlands was rich and productive. Like most of Ohio, the area was once forested with oaks, hickories, beeches, and maples, all of which had to be cleared before farming was possible. The retreating glaciers left behind scattered limestone boulders and, in a few instances, soggy elm swamps, subsequently burned and after months of smouldering, converted into unusually fertile cropland. One dirt road that crosses the township still bears the name Burnt Pond Pike. The limestone rock deposited by the glaciers and buried beneath the topsoil made quarrying the only commercial activity, in addition to agriculture, that ever flourished in the township.

The Virginia Military District began at the west bank of the Scioto; hence a small portion of the township was a part of the United States Military lands that made up the entire eastern section of Delaware County. Since this was part of the Northwest Territory, the land was originally surveyed in the familiar rectangular grid pattern, each township being divided into thirty-six sections of one square mile each.[2] The Virginia Military District was ceded to the federal government in 1783 and the land sold off in huge tracts to land companies or individual speculators. By 1806 a few settlers had squatted or purchased small tracts on lands adjacent to the river, situated along the Sandusky-Franklinton Military Road that followed the west bank of the Scioto. The cabins of the pioneers clustered near the confluences where tiny streams—Bokes' Creek, Arthur's Run, and Mill Creek —flowed into the Scioto.

The census of 1820, the first following the creation of the township in 1814, listed twenty-eight households and a total population of 182. As the land was cleared, the first crop cultivated was corn, which was ground into grain for subsistence, converted into whiskey, or fed to hogs or cattle. Hogs sometimes were driven as far as Detroit or Buffalo for commercial marketing. Flax was grown for home use. Wheat had been introduced by 1826, for in that year one resident hauled a wagonload to Zanesville to exchange it for salt. Early commercial activities related directly to subsistence needs. In 1807 a sawmill was operating along one of the subsidiary creeks; in 1809 a gristmill, soon converted to the production of corn liquor, was built along the banks of the Scioto. A tanner processed rawhides on a share basis; at least one farmer doubled as a blacksmith, another as a carpenter, another a stonemason. Occasionally corn or whiskey were traded for venison or deerskin moccasins with wandering groups of Wyandot Indians.

Isolated, as were all frontier communities, the township was nonetheless propitious for settlement. Delaware, the county seat, seven miles to the east, could be reached only by fording the Scioto, since no bridge spanned the river until 1835. Franklinton (later Columbus, the state capital) was twenty-five miles to the south over the military road, but through it passed the National Road, the major avenue for communication with the East and the artery into the Midwest for settlers from Pennsylvania, Maryland, and Virginia.

Newcomers who expanded the population to 69 households and 464 individuals in 1830 began to establish scattered homesites in the bottomlands several miles west of the river where an east-west access road had been surveyed in 1819. The cluster of cabins around the gristmill came to

be called Millville, and some of the settlers west on the new
road ambitiously plotted a village of twenty-seven lots,
which they called Fairview or Edinboro.[3]

A tax list prepared in 1826 listed fifty-five resident property holders in Scioto Township; thirty owned real property,
twenty-five owned horses valued at $40 each and cattle at
$8 per head, the only items included in the personal prop-
erty classification.[4] The lists reveal some important facets
of pioneer life. Nearly half of the residents were tenants or
squatters. Consistent with what appears to be the pattern in
all new areas, irrespective of the decade of settlement, the
farming enterprises that constituted virtually the only
sources of livelihood were simple and small. The mean
number of horses per taxpayer was 1.5, the average number
of cattle was 3. The largest personalty holder owned but
seven horses and eleven cows. The vast majority of Scioto
Township pioneers could claim but meager wealth: 44 percent were assessed for less than $100 combined real and
personal property and 27 percent between $100 and $200.
This relative equality among the many should not obscure
the fact that some distinct economic disparities existed: the
largest tax assessment, $1,220, was twice that of any other
individual.

Such a skewed distribution of property holding was not
unique to Scioto Township. Studies of other pioneer communities are sufficiently extensive to at least support the
hypothesis that new settlements were characterized by
small farming operations, meager wealth for the many,
and distinct advantages for a few privileged owners. Alan
Bogue has examined both tax lists and manuscript census
schedules for two townships in Cedar County, Iowa, in a
later period, but at a time when the duration from original
settlement was about the same as in Scioto. The 101 farmers who resided there owned an average of two horses and
six cattle; the average farm acreage was 120, but the maximum holding was 640. "At the outset," writes Gilbert Fite,
"most frontier farmers operated on a very small scale."
Pope County, Minnesota, was settled in the late 1860s. In

1868 most inhabitants cultivated less than 25 acres; a majority of the farmers in Chippewa Falls Township reported owning one or two milk cows. Russell County, Kansas, was organized in 1872. Of the 84 farmers in Center Township in 1875, 60 had traditional quarter acre sections, but the two largest landholders reported 470 acres. Fifty-one owned one or more horses, 55 possessed milk cows.[5]

However, in the 1826 Scioto Township tax list the singly most important historical revelation is that three-quarters of the nearly 20,000 acres in the township were owned by nonresidents, and these tracts were, without exception, the largest. This was the pattern to be expected: it prevailed in most of Ohio and in all other townships of Delaware County.[6] The largest landholding of a resident was 359 acres, the average was 148. On the other hand, the tract owned by Thomas M. Bayly occupied the center of the township and consisted of 2,457 acres. Adjoining was the 1,500-acre tract of Edward Drumgoole. Among the other three whose holdings totalled more than 1,500 acres was Lucas Sullivant, allegedly the founder of Columbus. Obviously, these were land speculators (legend had it that one James Paull had acquired his extensive holding in exchange for a horse at an earlier day) whose nonproductive wealth in land far eclipsed that of the pioneers whose cabins ranged along the riverbank. Two of the nonresident owners were large-scale operators of some notoriety. Thomas M. Bayly (1775–1834), a planter and lawyer from Accomac County, Virginia, was a member of the State House of Delegates at several times during his life and served as a Democratic member of the 13th Congress, from 1813 to 1815. His son, Thomas Henry (1810–1856) was a member of Congress from 1844 to 1856. Edward Drumgoole, Jr. and Sr., were prominent Virginia land speculators and members of a family active in the politics of their home state. They owned considerable land in central Ohio; their business affairs were conducted through an agent in Xenia, Ohio. Bayly and Drumgoole owned no land in Delaware County outside of Scioto Township.[7]

Most of these large holdings were not alienated until the 1850s; even then the sizeable Drumgoole tract passed to a banker and manufacturer from nearby Delaware. No Scioto Township land was ever homesteaded; none of the early settlers were the original purchasers. All of the township's land prior to settlement was held by speculators in sizeable tracts. Several of these were alienated early, but the long delay in opening up the huge Bayly, Paull, and Drumgoole tracts affected the pattern of settlement, the location of villages, even the road network that crisscrosses the township today.

The first social institutions, and the first formally to convey transplanted cultural values, were churches and schools. As early as 1810 a Methodist circuit rider held services in the cabins at the Bokes' Creek settlement. In 1834, twenty-three Presbyterians from nine families chartered a congregation at Fairview and built a church out of hewn logs. A year later a group of Baptists built another log church south of Fairview to accommodate their eighteen members. Methodists sporadically attempted to establish congregations in the township between 1830 and 1860; only two survived, one at Millville, another absorbed by the United Brethren in 1888. At one time or another, from 1828 to 1880, nine separate congregations were established in Scioto Township.

Despite the detailed descriptions of the founding of religious bodies in the various published county histories, the subject remains elusive. It is uncertain whether the attention lavished on the details of religious life reflects the real concerns of early settlers or the piety of the compilers of late nineteenth-century histories. A number of attempts to establish churches failed. The memberships stated for the Presbyterian and Baptist congregations were quite small, considering that the township's population in 1830 was 464, expanding to 877 in 1840 (including children). Accordingly, it would appear a large number of the early residents were not affiliated with any church.[8] Four congregations: the original Presbyterian and Baptist churches, the United

Brethren, and the Millville Methodists, survived into the twentieth century.

By 1824 at least two tiny schools were operating in crude cabins built for other purposes, one of them a cattle shed. Schooling was paid for by subscription; the prospective teacher visited homes selling contracts to provide a child's annual schooling for a fixed fee. In 1837, five schools, apparently tax supported and provided with simple one-room buildings, operated in the township. The census of 1840 reported seven schools with 160 pupils, 113 at public charge.

If statistics from the county history are reasonably accurate and not too much distorted by larger numbers in the lower-age categories, Scioto Township residents had a greater dedication to public schooling than in several large cities or in the state of Ohio as a whole. Among the school age group (5 to 20 years), 47 percent in Scioto Township were in school in 1840, 39 percent in Delaware County, 38 percent in Ohio, and 42 percent in Cincinnati, the state's largest city. However, in the area to be considered in the second case-study, Bedford County, Pennsylvania, only 12 percent in these age groups were in school in 1840.[9]

Retail trade came late to the pioneer community. In 1822 the settlers had to travel to Franklinton for such a basic necessity as ammunition. A small general store opened at Millville in 1836. Most transactions were by barter, furs and skins being the most valuable commodities. A tavern, a mile south where the east-west road forded the Scioto, served unofficially as the area's post office.

Immigrants to Scioto Township, as for most of central Ohio, came largely from Pennsylvania and Virginia. For reasons not certain, German immigrants passed by this area; a substantial Amish settlement was located in Madison County, thirty miles southwest, and several German-speaking Lutheran churches in Union County, bordering Scioto Township on the west, survived into the twentieth century. The first manuscript census to provide information on birthplace was that of 1850. Of the 392 family heads enumerated in that year, 144 (37 percent) were born in Ohio; 88 (22 percent) in Pennsylvania, 57 (15 percent) in Virginia, and 28 (7 percent) in Maryland. New England and Yorker migrants, so prominent in northern Ohio, were represented only by 35 individuals born in Massachusetts, Connecticut, New Hampshire, or New York (9 percent). Of the 15 foreign born (4 percent), 7 were from Ireland, 4 from Canada, 1 each from France, England, Switzerland, and Wales, and none from Germany. No blacks were reported in the 1850 census, but the earlier census of 1820 had noted three black adolescents (perhaps slaves) resident in other households.

Such isolated observations assume meaning only in comparative context. Comparing the distribution of all Scioto Township residents (not only family heads) by origin with that of the state of Ohio in 1850 shows that Scioto was obviously less foreign, more Ohio-native than the state as a whole.

TABLE I

Percentage of Total Population by Place of Origin, 1850[10]

Birthplace	Ohio	Scioto
Ohio	61.5	71.3
Pennsylvania	10.1	8.9
New York	4.0	2.6
Maryland	2.0	2.9
Virginia	4.0	6.3
New Jersey	1.0	.9
Connecticut	1.0	.2
Massachusetts	.9	.5
FOREIGN BORN	11.0	4.4
German States	5.0	0.0
Ireland	3.0	.6
England–Wales	1.6	.6

Although statistical differences are minor, the township had a slight southern and border state cast, reflected in the greater number of residents born in Maryland and Virginia and the smaller percentage from New York and the New England states.

No concrete evidence describes the political persuasion of the earlier settlers, but impressionistic data points to a strong Jacksonian proclivity. W. P. Crawford's 1888 memoir asserts that Jackson's image as the hero of New Orleans and his support of popular suffrage had in 1828 a "great influence in establishing the political views of these western townships [in Delaware County], which they have ever maintained." The observation that the townships in the west of the county had Democratic sympathies is supported by election data, first available about 1900, which show Scioto and several adjacent townships as islands of Democratic strength in an otherwise solidly Republican county.

The pioneer settlement in Scioto Township had expanded to 161 households and 877 individuals in 1840, about a quarter century after the first residents arrived. It was exclusively a farming area; of those listing occupations in 1840, 163 designated agriculture, 16 manufacturing, 1 an undesignated learned profession. Much of the farming was for subsistence, and corn was the principal crop. Two east-west roads now crossed the township, but the old military road remained the only north-south axis. Population was spread thinly over those portions of the area not retained in speculative tracts, but there were small concentrations at Fairview, another to the south of it on Little Mill Creek, and another south of Millville on the Scioto.

A comparison of the various early manuscript censuses permits some inferences about the relative permanence of those who chose to live in Scioto Township. Of the twenty-eight family heads listed in the 1820 census, only fourteen could be accounted for in 1830. Apparently, the missing 50 percent had migrated elsewhere. Mobility subsided in the following decade. Among the sixty-nine family units listed in 1830, forty-nine could be identified in 1840. Of the twenty who apparently moved, only four had listed real or personal

property in the 1826 tax list. Among the fourteen households in both the 1820 and 1830 census, twelve remained in
1840.[11] This data, admittedly fragmentary, points to two
types of pioneer residents in Scioto: the stable ones who
settled, remained, and provided the core of the community,
and transients, probably squatters and tenants, who came
for a few years and passed on elsewhere.[12]

Inward migration is another indicator of stability. Assuming for purposes of analysis that no families moved out,
at least 59 percent of the families present in 1830 were new
since 1820, and 57 percent of the households of 1840 were
new since 1830. However, in-migration slowed in the
decade 1840 to 1850, since only 18 percent of households
were new in that ten-year period.

The pioneer stage of development ended in the 1860s.
Economic and cultural isolation gave way to increased integration into regional and national trade patterns and communication channels. The settlement pattern of the early
period was transformed. The single variable that accounted for the rapid transition was the extension of a railroad into the township. Chartered in the 1850s, the
completion of the route, designed to connect Springfield,
Ohio, to the west with a line running north to south from
Cleveland through Columbus to Cincinnati, was delayed
because of financial problems, and trains did not operate
until the 1860s.

Built without concern for the location of the township's
tiny settlements, the right-of-way followed a high ridge
across the southern portion of the township and bypassed
both Edinboro and Millville. The station stop, near the Little Mill Creek settlement (a store and about six houses), was
named Ostrander, after the engineer who surveyed the line,
and it rapidly became the township's economic and social
nucleus. The hamlet at Edinboro so completely disappeared that only a cemetery marks its location. Millville
(renamed Warrensburg) never became anything more than
a few houses, a general store, a church, and a school.

Scioto Township's population reached its peak in the census of 1880, numbering 1,667 persons (see table 2). In the

manuscript record, 241 of the township's inhabitants listed their occupation as farmer. All were men, as were the 62 farmhands, many of them sons of resident farm families. While farming was the predominant productive enterprise, it was not the activity that occupied the working hours of most inhabitants. Three hundred forty-two individuals, all women, listed their occupation as keeping house, and even more, 383, were in school. Of the 47 other occupations recorded, nearly all related directly to the dominant family farm economy, and all but an esoteric handful carried out their work within the boundaries of the township or Ostrander village.[13] The only persons whose occupations required specialized nonmanual skills were the 3 physicians and the 3 telegraph operators. Only three residents were in school outside of the township: 2 in medical school, 1 a law student. Not even a minister for any of the township's churches was listed as resident. Of the 8 schoolteachers counted, one was male, all the others daughters of local families in their late teens or early twenties.

TABLE II

Population of Scioto Township, 1820–1970

Year	Population	Year	Population
1820	244	1900	1,595
1830	464	1910	1,650
1840	877	1920	1,533
1850	1,126	1930	1,443
1860	1,579	1940	1,379
1870	1,542	1950	1,304
1880	1,667	1960	1,585
1890	1,655	1970	1,598

Eighty-three percent of the residents in 1880 were Ohio born; the balance was scattered over several adjoining states, with the 4 percent from Pennsylvania being the largest. Two percent were foreign born. However, the amalgamated nativity pattern of central Ohio that mixed together migrants from Pennsylvania, the South, and New England, identified in the 1850 census, is again obvious in the listing of the place of birth of parents of Scioto Township's residents in 1880. Forty-eight percent had fathers born in Ohio, 13 percent in Pennsylvania, 8 percent in Virginia, 6 percent in Maryland, 5 percent in New York, and 9 percent were foreign born. The pattern was replicated for mothers of residents: 53 percent Ohio born, 7 percent foreign born, with Pennsylvania, Virginia, Maryland, and New York the other major states of origin.

The following summary recapitulates data on place of origin of the residents of Scioto Township:

TABLE III

Population Origins, Scioto Township

	Heads of Household, 1850 (N = 392)	Parents of Residents, 1880 (N = 1,650)	
		Father	*Mother*
Ohio	36.7%	48%	53%
Pennsylvania–New Jersey	25	14.4	14.6
Virginia, Maryland, Tennessee, Kentucky, North Carolina, West Virginia	23	22.5	14.6
New York–New England	9	5.7	2.8
Foreign Born	4	9.0	7.0

Several conclusions follow: Migrations after 1850 tended to reinforce the distribution present in that year. New England was sparsely represented at all times. Scioto township's population, despite its predominant Pennsylvania origin, had a southern-border state cast.[14]

Ostrander village was a shipping and commercial center that served the farming enterprises of the surrounding area and integrated them into the national economy. For a short time the line through Ostrander was the main route of the Cleveland, Columbus, Cincinnati, and Indianapolis Railroad; in 1891, two passenger trains in each direction stopped every day. Lumber and livestock were shipped to nearby cities, some as far away as Buffalo. Several small industries along the railway processed raw materials produced in the area: a sawmill manufactured not only lumber but made wagon spokes from native ash and hickory, and each fall pressed apples into cider. Sawdust was used by the icehouse nearby to preserve ice, cut each winter from Mill Creek. Three brick and tile kilns operated near the village. A grain elevator was built next to the station and a creamery and flour mill close by. Judging from occupations of individuals in the 1880 census, Ostrander in that year had a drugstore, a hardware store, a general store, one or two blacksmith shops, a carriage and wagon manufacturer, a gristmill, a grain dealer, a hotel, a road contractor (he employed a crew of about ten transient Irish-born laborers), two physicians, several carpenters, a plasterer, a sawmill, a saloon, and the railroad station. At least fifteen distinct commercial functions, most of them related to agriculture, were being performed in the village.

The commercial activities in 1908 were: three dry goods and grocery retailers, a restaurant and meat market, a furniture and undertaking establishment, a monument dealer, a druggist, the locally owned Ostrander Banking Company, a hotel, a saloon, two blacksmith shops, a cement block and fence post dealer, two hardware stores, the post office, and the railroad station. Three physicians practiced in the township. If this list is reasonably accurate, a total of twenty distinct commercial functions were being carried out. The village even boasted an opera house, accommodating 350 persons and located in the second story of the main business block.

In 1879 the township had been divided into eleven school districts; each school was housed in a one-room structure. In that year the school session lasted twenty-four weeks and was taught by ten male and eight female teachers. Only three teachers completed the entire term. Of the average 263 monthly enrollment, 69 pupils were above age 16.[15] Ap-

(Courtesy Mrs. Fay Bouic)

The railroad depot, Ostrander, Ohio.

---

parently the only high school was in Ostrander, taught by one teacher.

By the 1890s, countryside churches had disappeared; three of them, the Presbyterian, Baptist, and United Brethren, had removed to Ostrander, and in 1908 the first two each had a membership of about 100. A Methodist congregation met at Warrensburg.

The large holdings of nonresidents had disappeared on the township plat map for 1900. Following the pattern of early settlement, the countryside was dotted by small farms of about 100 acres;[16] the largest farm in the township contained 235 acres. Neither does the plat map demonstrate the checkerboard pattern of land holdings the land survey leads one to expect in rural America. Property lines angled off in a bewildering variety of lines, sometimes straight, sometimes following the contours of roads and water courses. The boundaries of the old speculative holdings could also be detected. Often individual holdings were not adjacent.

(Courtesy Mrs. Fay Bouic)

Looking west on Ostrander's main street about 1900.

Farming was diversified. Corn led as the major cultivated crop by a considerable margin over oats and wheat. Of the livestock herds grazed, fed, and marketed, the largest number were sheep, followed by swine and cattle. The morning and evening milking were unceasing rituals; so was churning butter. Women folk often tended gardens and looked after the chickens.

No published agricultural data for minor civil subdivisions such as Scioto Township are available. However, for Delaware County in 1860, corn was by far the leading field crop, followed by oats and wheat in much lesser amounts. There were more sheep than any other livestock, next swine, then cattle and milk cows. The major product marketed, however, was butter. There were no significant changes by 1880, except that wheat, not oats, was now the second largest field crop. Chickens must have been running all over the place: there were 123,000 in the county in 1880.[17]

An 1899 Delaware County directory lists the real and personal property valuation of residents of Scioto Township. One hundred thirty-four of 288 listed owned realty; diversifying of economic functions and increased participation in larger commercial networks had not substantially altered the pattern of property distribution. Over 60 percent of those listed claimed real and personal property of less than $1,000; the median fell between $700 and $800. Yet two property holders claimed farms and personalty valued between $7,000 and $8,000; the largest valuation, over $9,000, was that of the nonresident owner of a limestone quarry located at the point where the railroad crossed the Scioto.[18]

Two overlapping jurisdictions administered public affairs. The township elected three trustees, a clerk, two constables, and sixteen supervisors. Ostrander, incorporated in 1875, had a mayor, clerk, and six-member town council. Only fragmentary evidence indicates the presence or absence of any political controversy or the partisan persuasion of officeholders. Two of the three township trustees indicated in their biographical sketches in the county history that they were "ardent Democrats." The first mayor and clerk who assumed their offices after Ostrander was incorporated both designated themselves as Republicans. One member of the council characterized himself "an ardent worker in the prohibition cause," but one of his colleagues was the village's saloonkeeper. The political preference of the mayor who succeeded in 1879 was no where stated, but his son, born in 1864, had been named Vallandigham.[19] In every electoral contest for which it was possible to obtain minor civil subdivision data for Ohio, from 1900 to 1930,[20] the township returned a majority Democratic vote, thus defying the traditional Republican loyalty of Delaware County. This included a 61 percent vote for William Jennings Bryan when he was losing Ohio in 1900 with 45 percent of the vote and Delaware County with 41.5 percent.

Scioto Township was never prosperous, and Ostrander never became a thriving village. In the decades after the railroad was completed, its farm products and lumber integrated it into a national market. By 1900 some of the limestone from its quarries found its way to the steel mills of

Pittsburgh and Cleveland. But, culturally, Scioto Township was one of many isolated backwaters of the American countryside, perhaps not unlike the rural community in Iowa where the eminent rural sociologist Carl Taylor was growing up at the same time. In the years before he was sixteen, he ventured from his country neighborhood only three or four times a year to make a trip to the county seat, seven miles away.

The annals of Scioto Township produced no famous personages to add significance and color to the intimate details of the personal lives that were lived there. From fading photographs, records on gravestones, newspaper clippings, and the anecdotes of old timers, one can selectively collect impressions that give some vague substance to the quality of life that went on. Here are some stories the gravestones tell:

—SMART

> John, died November 2, 1851. 43 years, 4 mos., 10 days.
>
> Sarah, daughter of John & A, died November 12, 1851, 7 years, 3 mos., 18 days.
>
> William R., son of John & A, died November 12, 1851, 11 mos., 5 days.
>
> Joseph, son of John & A., died November 19, 1851, 13 years, 8 mos., 16 days.

—ARMSTRONG

Infant	1896
Lurley	1898–1900
Hannah	1900–1901
Ross	1904–1905
Cleo	1916–1918
J. L.	1871–

> Minnie, his wife, 1879–1946 (Daughters of the American Revolution)
>
> Lawrence L., February 23, 1918–September 16, 1944 Ohio Pvt. 39 Inf. 9 Div. World War II

These were some memories etched vividly enough to be recalled fifty years later:

—The curious boys who clamored up into the loft of a barn on the Marysville road to see the grisly remains of the farmer who that day put a shotgun in his mouth and pulled the trigger. The boys were sorry they came.

—The ill-tempered little girl who, to avenge some childhood pique, tied her neighbor's pet dog to the morning train.

—The matronly lady in her sixties who returned to Ostrander each Memorial Day to put a bouquet on the grave of the teenage fiancée who asked her on his deathbed to promise never to marry anyone else. She kept her promise.

—Tom Maloney, superintendent of Ostrander High School for several years before 1924, was probably the best the school ever had. He was firm, tough, and sometimes roughed up obstreperous and defiant older boys to enforce discipline. Some say this cost him his job, but, too, he was a Roman Catholic.

Yet for all this, there was no "Scioto Township Death Trip,"[21] and to deliberately choose samples such as these as typical of life there is to distort history as grossly as the panagyric county histories of the late nineteenth century. Life in Scioto Township was a melange of the tragic, the joyful, the trivial, and occasionally the heroic.

—On hot summer days boys of the village skinny-dipped in the Sheep-Hole in Mill Creek—just as their fathers and grandfathers had done.

—Edward Hill, town drunk, once a soldier in the 80th Ohio Volunteer Infantry, riding home on his mule after a night of customary carousing, reached into his pocket, threw away his bottle, said "Never again!" and never did. Elder Hill, a wizened little man who lived to see almost a century of summers, was the mainstay of the Presbyterian Church and solemnly presided at the annual Decoration Day rites. He was the township's last surviving Civil War veteran.

—Each fall the Ostrander reunion was held at Manville's hickory grove. Chattering farm ladies spread out the covered dish dinner over long plank tables that rested on sawhorses. The high school band played; maybe someone gave a political speech, and prideful parents pushed reluctant offspring through the ordeal—for performer and listeners —of speaking a piece.

Scioto Township's population, which peaked in 1880, began a linear decline that was not arrested until 1950 (see fig. 1). Already by 1910, only the Jerkwater, consisting of a few freight cars and a passenger coach in which no one ever rode, passed through Ostrander every other day. Most of the roads were graveled now, and the auto trip to the county seat wasn't too difficult. All the one-room schools disappeared, to leave finally only an elementary school at Warrensburg and a combined elementary and high school at Ostrander, one of about a dozen such township schools in Delaware County.

Ostrander's business block about 1920 contained a livery stable, two grocery stores, two restaurants, two barbershops, the bank, a drugstore, the opera house, a poolroom, a bakery, a small hotel, a machine shop, the railroad station, and the new grain elevator that towered over the village. At least one physician practiced. Hence, about fifteen economic functions were being performed. The saloon was gone (prohibition had come); so were the blacksmith and carriage shops. Then, on 13 July 1925, a fire destroyed the central block of the village's business section: only the livery stable, the bank and the hardware store across the street, the station, and the grain elevator were spared. Most of the destroyed buildings were never replaced.

In the 1970 enumeration, Scioto Township's population of 1,598 remained nearly the same as in 1960—about equal to the maximum population achieved nine decades earlier. The residents were serviced by a branch bank, a filling station, a post office, a restaurant, a barbershop, a grocery store, and a general equipment chain store that had taken over the old elevator site. There was no physician in the township. For supermarkets, medical service, hardware supplies, or the movies, the county seat is less than fifteen minutes away by car. Warrensburg's old general store was abandoned long ago and is deteriorating rapidly. The railroad tracks were dismantled five years ago. An older house in Ostrander can be purchased for $9,000; a new one might cost $24,000, but there are few of these. The major new residential buildings are trailer-type homes. But regardless of the size or vintage, a television aerial sprouts from most rooftops. "I don't know about a third of the folks in town; new people seem to drift in and out," the president of the village council confessed. Some, attracted by cheap rents and purchase prices, were manual laborers who commuted for forty minutes each day over wide paved roads and down the expressway to work in a furnace plant or valve-and-press factory in suburban Columbus. Others were employed in light industries that had grown up in Delaware; some clerked in the stores and supermarkets there. Retired people were an important segment of the village population—at the annual dinner for senior citizens in 1973, forty-five women and eight men were present. An analysis of the age distribution of the Scioto Township population, comparing its distribution with the national population for those censuses where such information is available, produced results skewed toward younger age cohorts—for example, below 5, 106 in 1830—but in 1930 and 1940, distinctly skewed toward older cohorts—for example, above 65, 105 in 1940.[22]

Only one of Ostrander's businesses in 1973 (the general equipment store) functioned to service farmers, for there was little need. Driving up and down the dusty roads, one soon loses count of the weed-grown yards and rotting houses with broken windows that mark the sites of abandoned farm homes. A few houses have a fresh coat of paint but the farm buildings behind are unused; perhaps a commuting renter lives there. Not many fields, however, go uncultivated.[23] Those not used for pasture are sown with corn or soybeans, which are marketed for cash, not used on the farm. Operating farms are apparent by their trim new outbuildings, often made of aluminum, and the two or three tall silos that store corn for the cattle and dairy herds. Few farmers keep chickens any more;[24] only a few maintain gardens. One resident farmer estimated that the average township farm was about 1,000 acres.[25] His own operation is a good example: his 150 cows are milked by modern equipment; one of his sons holds a master's degree in dairy science from Ohio State. His investment in equipment is more than $100,000, including an air-conditioned tractor. All his milk is sold to distributors in Columbus. The absorption of family farms into larger units, a nationwide phenomenon, has been a gradual process in Scioto Township. Most large operators are from families whose names appear in the 1880 census or the 1899 directory. More prosperous or more innovative, they bought out the farms of small owners or those up in years, and often they rent on a crop-sharing contract. Corporate farming is unknown.

The number of farms in Delaware County as a whole declined from just 3,073 to 2,647 between 1910 and 1945. Then between 1945 and 1969 this number was halved to 1,389; of these only 757 were full-time operations, with gross sales over $2,500. More Delaware County acreage was sown with soybeans (42,503) than any other field crop, but more bushels of corn were produced from the 35,805 acres planted. The major source of farm income in 1969 came from livestock and livestock products, dairy products being the largest, followed by hogs, sheep, and cattle. Cash sales of grain were almost equally important income producers.[26]

Second homes of residents of Columbus occupy areas of the townships just south of Scioto; the suburban fringes of Ohio's fastest growing metropolitan center already touch the borders of the township. One of the old stone quarries has a parking lot, a few gaudy concession stands, and a sign over the entrance that advertises the Aqua Ski Club. A tract parallel to the old railroad right-of-way was, in the summer of 1973, fast taking shape as the Mill Creek Golf Course. In the late sixties, rural land in Scioto was selling for $300 an acre; in 1973 it had spiralled to $700, and some had been sold for $1,000.

The elementary school at Ostrander has eight grades. Older students are bussed fifteen miles away to Buckeye Valley High School, one of four consolidated schools in the county. The driver from Ostrander drives his seventy-two passenger bus 130 miles each school day, and his is one of the twenty-two busses from throughout the county that converge on the school, north of Delaware, every school day.

About fifty people attend Sunday morning services at the Ostrander Baptist Church, the only one of the four in the township with a resident pastor. Students from a nearby seminary service the others; two of these meet only twice a month. Those who greet each other there are friends and neighbors of long duration—few newcomers participate. Sunday evening youth meetings succumbed to television watching several years ago.

Only a few older people remember the Ostrander reunions. No one was much interested in keeping up the annual Memorial Day observances after Elder Hill was gone.

The budget for Scioto Township is prepared by the Delaware County auditor. Real property owners pay a 3.6 mill tax that supports road maintenance and law enforcement in the township. Ostrander residents pay an additional .5 mill for the village's street lights. There is no justice of the peace; the mayor's court has ceased to function. The position of town marshall is vacant—no one wants it. The mayor is a retail clerk in Delaware and has held office for as long as anyone can remember. The six member council meets once a month (in recent years there has never been a contest for the office) to consider such issues as the dog problem or how to stop a few disruptive hot-rodders who occasionally speed through the streets late at night. The three member township board of trustees also meets monthly to sometimes adjudicate quarrels arising from dogs in sheep herds or settle claims for damage to roads and fences by heavy farm equipment. All the trustees, the two township members of the Buckeye Valley school board, and most of the city council are long time residents.

The distinctive Democratic voting behavior of Delaware County's western townships faded in the 1930s. Occasionally in state contests, Scioto would vote more Democratic than the county norm, but the wide spreads of 15 to 20 percent, characteristic of the first three decades of the twentieth century, have disappeared.[27]

On a hot July day few cars traverse the roads of the township; near Warrensburg a few noisy trucks roar in and out of one of the operating limestone quarries. There is minimal activity even around the operating farms. And the sleepy quiet of Ostrander seemed not disturbed at all by the prying historian, with an out-of-state license and a non-American wife, who peered curiously down streets and conscientiously counted television aerials.

Some summer nights small crowds assemble at the ball diamond behind the schoolhouse where Ostrander competes in the "Heart of Ohio" league and where one of several church-sponsored Little League teams play. On fourth of July the village springs to life. Twenty-five or thirty antique cars and some locally decorated floats parade through the streets. The Concord and Scioto Township fire departments hose each other down in a soggy water-fight. The churches and the Boy Scout troop sell concessions and food, and the estimated 4,000 people from the three or four counties who attend go to the horse show, attend the baseball game, and watch fireworks in the evening. Oldsters slip away for the annual retired people's banquet.

For thirty years the Army Corps of Engineers, responsive to the water needs of the expanding Columbus metropolitan area, have weighed the possibility of a dam on Mill Creek. Most of the southern portions of Scioto Township would be flooded and adjacent lands converted to recreational use. A dike east of the town would preserve about two-thirds of Ostrander—the part north of the grade where the railroad used to run.[28]

Scioto Township and Ostrander village can stand as a surrogate in some vital respects for countless rural townships and small towns that cover most of the geographical expanse of the United States. The physical terrain—the rivers and creekbeds, the few gentle hills, the scattered limestone boulders—is the same, and a few anachronistic institutions survive from the area's past, but that which was once a pioneer community is fast becoming a blue-collar suburb.

Economic and cultural isolation, never complete, since complete isolation is impossible, was dissipated first by the railroad, then completely eliminated by the automotive revolution of the last four decades. Once a functioning economic entity, existing to serve needs of an agricultural population, Ostrander village meets only peripheral needs now, as its residents speed in all directions for work, for basic economic demands, for schooling. The township's political and socializing institutions have been absorbed into more comprehensive areal units, as the integration of its government and school exemplifies.

Scioto Township has been profoundly affected by the urban surge that characterizes twentieth-century American social history. Its cultural and economic bounds extend far beyond even the distance to the nearby county seat. Its dairy products are sold in Columbus; its workers find jobs there. In fact, this proximity alone explains why the township gained in population between 1950 and 1960 and has remained stable in the face of the migration of population out of rural areas. Demographic studies have shown that most small towns that have avoided population losses are within a fifty mile radius of some standard metropolitan area. The census bureau now classifies the whole of Delaware County as a part of the Columbus Standard Metropolitan Area. Ironically, that which has preserved Scioto Township may destroy it—if the plans of the Corps of Engineers ever materialize.

There are some survivals. One might wish to know how many of those retired in Ostrander are long-time township residents. I would suspect most of them are. One might wish to explore the hypothesis that the commuting workers who choose to live in villages or the countryside, miles from their place of employment, are themselves products of farms and villages in other parts of the nation. The traditional community is most manifest in the churches, and it is no anomaly that they are the institutions most resistant to change. Long-standing practice, in-group loyalties, doctrinal belief ("No one but a Baptist can get to heaven," avowed one dedicated believer), have beaten back the logic that long ago would have centralized the struggling and competing congregations in the village. Protestant religious institutions, unlike political and educational organizations, lack the centralized authority to achieve integration, despite resistance.[29]

The decline of the township's long-standing deviance from the traditional Republican hegemony in its parent county, a topic one might wish to subject to more penetrating examination, can stand here only as one more bit of evidence of the decline of any distinctiveness that separates Scioto Township from the culture that prevails all around it.

Bedford County, Pennsylvania

"Bedford—A Nicer Place to Stop," reads a signpost a few miles before Exit 11 on the Pennsylvania Turnpike. A close look shows that the paint is peeling. Bedford has been a place to stop, more than a place to stay, ever since 1758 when soldiers of King George III slashed a crude road over the mountains and built a stockade along the Raystown branch of the Juniata River to supply provisions to the troops doing battle against the French and their Indian allies.

For those who chose to stay in Bedford Borough and the county that surrounds it, prosperity or stagnation has always depended upon the decisions of those outsiders who blazed military trails, plotted railroad and highway rights-of-way, or built two different turnpikes, a century apart. For a good case study in location theory and a good illustration of how critical and how tenuous Bedford's links to the mainstreams of culture and commerce are, one might climb up the fire tower on the crest of Will's Mountain, just above Bedford. Off to the east, Evitt's Mountain extends on a north-south axis along the horizon as far as one can gaze, and in it there is just one break—"The Narrows," the natives call it—cut out centuries ago by the shallow streambed of the Raystown branch. This was the pass through which

General John Forbes led his Indian fighters back in 1758, and every major transportation link that has sustained Bedford directly or indirectly ever since squeezes through the same mountain defile.

Besides Will's and Evitt's mountains, two other wooded spurs of the Alleghenies cut across the 1,000-square-mile county at a northeast-southeast angle, and they widen into hill-encircled coves that bear the names of long-forgotten settlers. Morrison's Cove to the north of the town has flat plains like those of Lancaster County; here a colony of German Dunkards settled on some of the best farmland in the region. Milligan's Cove, south of town, is a narrow, rocky valley with forested hills that has supported only a few tanneries, a gristmill, and one of the several resort hotels (located close to several sulphur and mineral springs) that have always been important ancillary businesses in the county. The Raystown branch flows northeast through the county to join with its parent stream near Huntington. The creeks and rivulets in the southern portion of the county drain down to the Potomac across the Maryland border, which forms the south boundary of the county.

The settlers who made their homes in Bedford County in the late eighteenth and early nineteenth centuries were, as might be expected, mostly Scotch-Irish and Germans. Many came from the settled eastern parts of the state, but a significant number worked their way up through the village of Cumberland from Maryland and Virginia. In the German-settled areas the countryside and village churches were usually Dunkard (Church of the Brethren), Evangelical Lutheran, or two late-blooming offshoots of Lutheranism, the United Brethren and German Reformed. Many of the Scotch-Irish and some of the Germans became converts of Methodist revivalism, and this was to be the largest single denomination in the county. One local history mentions in passing the presence of a small Catholic population, but the burying ground of St. Thomas parish in Bedford contains the graves of 100 or more Irish, most of them proud enough of their heritage to have recorded for posterity their place of birth in Ireland's County Kildare or Tipperary. To the west of the town a weed-grown Negro cemetery contains about 200 graves.[30]

The dramatic waves of settlement associated with later frontier areas passed over Bedford County. The first census enumeration to publish detailed information on place of origin, that of 1880, revealed over 90 percent of the county's inhabitants to be Pennsylvania born. Only 2.4 percent were foreign born, and the largest single group of immigrants were the 650 individuals who gave Maryland as their birthplace.

In 1790 Bedford County claimed over 13,000 residents. Bedford village had been laid out in neat grid squares centering around the old stockade in 1761. By 1771 the borough was the county seat for an area that encompassed all of western Pennsylvania including present Allegheny County. In 1794 President George Washington tarried there for two days while he inspected the troops assembled to put down the insubordinate Whiskey Rebels a few miles to the west. Between 1810 and 1840 a brick courthouse, several churches, and a burying ground, built in the center of Bedford, formed a distinctly New England kind of town square, around which residents built trim and sturdy brick homes that would not look out of place in old Sturbridge Village.

The boundaries of the county assumed their final form only in 1850. (Population statistics from earlier censuses are therefore not comparable.) In that year the county's population was 23,052, that of the little county-seat town, 1,203.

As the pioneer farmers cut back the timber up the hillsides and cultivated the bottomlands at Friends's or Morrison's coves, the principal crop sown was rye. Given the hilly, forested terrain, much of the land was unimproved or usable only as woodland pasture. The problems wrought by inadequate transportation, which were to be manifest all through Bedford's history, were already apparent in the eighteenth century. Given the primitive nature of the roadways, it was far easier to transform the bulky grain into whiskey, then load the barrels onto flatboats and float them down the river to Huntington. At least twenty-five distilleries were reported in the county in 1792.

At the time of the Civil War, however, a pattern of agriculture was emerging that would persist with surprisingly little variance for nearly a century. In 1860, the 2,037 farms in the county averaged 183 acres in size, but only 47 percent of the land in farms was improved, compared to 61.5 percent in the state as a whole. Now the principal field crop was corn, then oats, rye, and wheat in quantities considerably smaller. The corn and oats were probably used as winter feed for the nearly 60,000 milk cows, cattle, sheep, and swine that grazed or rooted on the hillside pastures. The major commercial product, as on most Pennsylvania farms of the day, was butter (probably home churned). Bedford County's total production, however, was a driblet compared to that marketed from the state's major dairy counties, Montgomery, Chester, Delaware, and Bucks, which surrounded Philadelphia. Probably most of any year's farm output went for home consumption. Some 7,285 horses, an average of more than three per farm, pulled the plows across the cornfields and the mowers and rakes across the sloping fields of hay.[31]

While Bedford was primarily a farm county, unlike in Scioto Township agriculture was not the only economic activity. The natural resources of the mountains and valleys spawned not only farm related manufacturing such as sawmills and gristmills, but also tanneries, small coal mines, and iron forges. In 1860, 147 manufacturing establishments, gristmills being the most numerous, employed 409 persons. And down in a lonely hollow south of the town, one entrepreneur bought up some land and built a small resort hotel, and thus established the beginnings of a business that one day would come close to dominating the county.

Some of the villages among the mountains were tiny industrial centers. History has given scant attention to the small countryside factories, many of them extractive, that were important components of nineteenth and early twentieth century industrialism. At the time of the Civil War most of the virgin pines had been exhausted for the building of homes and barns; oak timber was hauled down the mountains to be made into railroad ties at crossroads sawmills. The valuable black walnuts had been depleted. The heavily forested hills provided bark for at least six leather-producing tanneries; the largest, at Bedford, consumed seventeen thousand cords of wood yearly in the 1880s.

The coal and iron industries were far the more important. The Broadtop coalfields in the township of that name extend across the county's northeast boundaries into neighboring Blair and Fulton counties. The deposits in these isolated mountainsides, connected neither with Pennsylvania's bituminous mines to the east nor the anthracite deposits to the southwest, combine the qualities of both, although the ore was generally of inferior grade. Tradition has it that even before 1800 coal mined at Broadtop was washed in creeks, skidded down the mountains on wooden sledges, and loaded into flatboats at the village of Riddlesburg on the Raystown branch. Deposits of various types of iron ore were scattered on farms and on mountainsides throughout the county. By 1830 a blast furnace at Hopewell could produce five to ten tons of ore in a good week. Another furnace operated at Everett, seven miles east of Bedford. Furnaces of the Kemple Coal and Iron Company at Riddlesburg drew fossil and other type ores from Wills and Dunning Mountains; a daily yield in the 1880s could be as high as thirty-six tons. Before the enterprises faded in the late nineteenth century, about five furnaces produced iron ore along the stream courses in the northeast corner of the county. Ambitious developers sunk pits into the mountains in quest of richer and better ores. They didn't find them. Even if they had, the low quality minerals from Evitt or Dunning Mountains were of scant importance in an economy where the rich ores of the Mesabi met the coal of Kentucky, West Virginia, and southwest Pennsylvania in the booming steel mills of Pittsburgh and Cleveland.

Precursor of a business that would outlive the village industries, Dr. John Anderson, in 1806, bought up the acreage around a gristmill, a mile and a half south of Bedford, where the water that gushed from the mineral springs was reputed to have remarkable diuretic and cathartic qualities. His original twenty-four-room Bedford Springs Hotel was expanded twice before 1824. Guests could drink the water or plunge into it (a choice of hot or cold), and spend intervening time bowling on the neatly trimmed greens or strolling the gentle serpentine paths through the adjoining hills. The enterprise was a brilliant success, for within a few years three other spas were operating within a radius of a few miles. This was despite the fact that to reach the resorts visitors from the south had to travel the Chesapeake and Ohio Canal to Cumberland and then transfer to surreys that took more than a day to complete the journey north. Tourists from Philadelphia and the East could come by canal and riverboats from Harrisburg to Hollidaysburg, where carriages waited to convey them on a two-day trip south to Bedford Springs. No records reveal how he made the trip, but James K. Polk stopped by for six days in 1849, and one habitual guest, James Buchanan, liked it so well he kept coming back for twenty-six years.

The population of Bedford Borough and County expanded between 1860 and 1890 at a pace more rapid than at any other period in the area's 200-year history. The borough grew from 1,247 in 1870 to a peak of 2,242 in 1890, and varied only by a few percentage points in every succeeding census until 1930. The county's population swelled from 26,763 in 1860 to 39,468 in 1900, then declined in each decade until changes in the 1930s inaugurated a new and different epoch. During this period of expansion, the number of farms expanded from 2,037 in 1860 to 3,240 in 1880 and 3,615 in 1900. The pattern of diversified family farming evident in 1860 still persisted; wheat, a cash grain that had to be marketed off the farm, was, however, now the principal field crop.[32] During these same decades the village industries of the county experienced their short-lived boom and railroad spurs from the major lines to the north and south thrust tentatively into the county.

Transportation was the key. Geography had made of Bedford County a remote mountain backwater; the most important facet of its history was the long battle to transcend such fate. If the wheat and butter from the valley farms were to be marketed in Philadelphia or Pittsburgh and the ores and minerals from the mountains to flow into the mainstreams of commerce, capital had to be found that Bedford County could not generate, and political influence had to be exerted more than the county could muster.

Remote Bedford County had a distinct self-interest in the keen battles over internal improvements that convulsed Pennsylvania politics after 1820. As Philadelphia's commercial dominance slipped away to New York, with its Erie Canal, and to Baltimore, with the Chesapeake and Ohio System, the state marshaled its resources in defense. Legislators from western counties, however, shared no great concern for the economic fortunes of eastern manufacturers. Grain from the southwest counties could find access to markets through Cumberland, Maryland. Representatives from Bedford and surrounding counties displayed little enthusiasm for canal building schemes, such as the one for the Main Line that would combine rail and water transport for a circuitous route from Philadelphia to Pittsburgh. That it bypassed the southwest was of no small importance. Then, in the 1850s, when the powerful Pennsylvania Railroad interests managed to halt plans of the Baltimore and Ohio to extend a line across Pennsylvania from Cumberland to Pittsburgh, disgruntled western legislators threatened an abortive scheme, termed the "Pittsburgh lunacy," to dissociate from the state and form a new commonwealth.[33]

State encouragement of turnpikes was a different matter, because the passages across the mountains had improved but little since the days of General Forbes's trailblazers. The early toll roads were exclusively private ventures, but the state soon extended a helping hand. In a patent move to win the votes of western legislators, the charter of the Second Pennsylvania Bank, approved in 1835, required that the bank purchase specified amounts of stock in various western turnpike companies. Among the eleven companies specified in 1835, three passed through Bedford. By 1838 the toll road network joined Bedford to through routes to Philadelphia to the east and Hollidaysburg to the north.

Stagecoaches, wagoners, drovers, and hucksters plied the routes and stopped for food and lodging at the taverns and public houses located only a few miles distant. Pitt Street, the main east-west route through Bedford, has at least three public houses still standing that date from this period. Turnpikes might stimulate a marginal travel business in remote communities, but as efficient conveyers of raw materials and manufactured goods of Bedford and other counties, they were a failure. They were also a disaster as financial ventures. To buttress the shaky businesses, Pennsylvania made them part public enterprises through buying up shares of stock. It was one of the unwisest investments the state ever made; all of the holdings were liquidated in 1843 at substantial losses and many of the companies, including those that passed through Bedford, went bankrupt.

The fact that the major railroads passed Bedford by left a mark on the borough and county that took many years to erase. The Baltimore and Ohio, denied access to Pennsylvania, ran through Cumberland on its way to Wheeling and made of that city, founded about the same time as Bedford, a commercial center five times as large. The lines that would eventually consolidate as the Pennsylvania Railroad followed the old Main Line, passing through Huntington, Hollidaysburg, and Altoona, forty miles north of Bedford. Altoona, which didn't even exist when Bedford was the proud county-seat town of all western Pennsylvania, became the commercial and manufacturing center of the region.

In the political battles that raged in Washington, D.C., and in state capitals throughout the nation during the criti-

cal period when the iron horse replaced the canal and turnpike as the communication key that would unlock markets,
build industrial cities, and underwrite national prosperity,
Bedford County was a remote arena, its concerns insignificant in national perspective but absolutely critical for the
future development of the borough and county. Bedford's
fate by 1854 seemed to be that of a remote mountain backwater, bypassed by the major avenues of commerce. For
forty years, businessmen, legislators, and the newly formed
Agricultural Society struggled persistently to undo this
fate. Ambitious plans and lofty hopes were plenty, concrete
achievements few.

In 1855 a spur off the new Main Line penetrated southward to tap the coalfields at Broadtop. The Huntington and
Broadtop Mountain narrow gauge railway passed through
Saxton village, which developed as a little mining community, then continued on down to Hopewell and Riddlesburg,
where it promoted the evanescent prosperity of the little
forges and blast furnaces there. One county history notes
cryptically that the railroad was developed by "eastern capital," evidence enough that this was no project sponsored or
looked upon with great favor by local enterprise. On a national scale, the impact of so little a coal-carrying railroad
was insignificant. For Bedford County, it was spectacular.
Isolated Broadtop and Liberty townships in the county's
remote northeastern corner, untouched by the turnpike
network, had, in 1850, 632 and 522 residents respectively.
Twenty years and one railroad later, Broadtop's population
had swelled 158 percent and that of Liberty Township (Saxton), 147 percent. The county's aggregate growth rate was
28.7 percent, Bedford Borough's only 3 percent. In 1900
Broadtop was the most populous of the county's twenty-five
townships and had the greatest number of foreign born
inhabitants.

The rail line was extended a few miles southward to tap
an ore deposit at Mt. Dallas, close to the present village of
Everett. Then, in the most ambitious transportation project
Bedford's citizens ever mounted, enough local capital was

subscribed to extend a single track from Mt. Dallas to Everett, then, in 1871, through the narrows into Bedford. Continuing southward through the county, the little line connected with the Baltimore and Ohio at Cumberland. Spurs connected to some of the aspiring ore mines in the mountains and excursion trains carried increasing numbers of tourists to the exclusive resort at Bedford Springs. But like the connecting lines that passed through Scioto Township, 300 miles west, this was a peripheral operation in a day when even the major lines were over-expanded and over-capitalized. Eventually the little line was purchased by the Pennsylvania Railroad.

During one short intoxicating period, however, Bedford seemed destined to become a railroad terminus to rival Altoona or Cumberland. Some of the nation's most powerful financiers, competitors of the powerful Pennsylvania line, long dreamed of a rival South Pennsylvania road that would slice through the mountains over a route the Pennsylvania had rejected, connect Harrisburg with Pittsburgh, and from there reach out to tap the markets and industries of the Midwest and West. William H. Vanderbilt bought rights to a South Pennsylvania route in 1881, and construction began two years later. On one memorable July morning in 1884, Vanderbilt and a fellow promoter, Andrew Carnegie, stopped by the Bedford hamlet of Breezewood, a place too insignificant even to appear in the state atlas, to inspect the work that had been started on the long tunnel through Ray's Hill, one of nine on the route through Bedford that would be necessary. Even the financial wizardry of a Vanderbilt and a Carnegie combined were insufficient to overcome the problems of an over-extended, bitterly competitive industry. When the road was 60 percent completed and $10 million in construction costs expended, the plan was abandoned and the South Pennsylvania sold at auction in 1890. (Fifty years later the unused right-of-way was incorporated into the Pennsylvania Turnpike.) The railroad history of Bedford ended in 1873 when a spur of the Pennsylvania connected the town with Altoona to the

(Photograph by William Clark)
Bedford, Pennsylvania, summer 1975. The Route 30 bypass is in the foreground. The railroad parallels the bypass near the buildings on the left. Evitt's Mountain forms the background, with the "Narrows" at the left corner of the photograph.

northwest, part of a plan that aimed to carry ores from mines near Cessna, a crossroads town north of Bedford. The ores lasted only a few years.

Circumvented by the major transportation arteries, Bedford's growth slowed in the 1890s and the borough and county way of life stabilized into a pattern that prevailed for more than three decades. The county had a thousand fewer people in 1930 than in 1890, and Bedford, a sleepy county-seat town with about the same population in 1920 as in 1880, supported such small businesses as a wholesale grocery firm, a wholesale peanut distributor, a keg factory, a couple of flour and planing mills, all located along the railroad spur north of the river. Many of its residents lived in big stately federal period houses half a century old; several of the hotels and boardinghouses along the main street were vestiges of turnpike days. Bedford Academy, the private school that had provided the town's only education, became a public graded high school around 1890.[34] The white spires of the Methodist, Lutheran, and Reformed churches punctuated the village skyline. The Methodists and Catholics had the largest congregations, but the various denominations of Lutheran affiliation and derivation had even more communicants. The town came to life on Saturday night when the three blocks of the shopping area filled with farmers from the nearby townships, who came to visit, take in a movie, and pick up supplies that the crossroads stores in the more than twenty-five hamlets in the county couldn't provide.

Agriculture remained the county's principal economic enterprise. As late as 1920, 3,310 of those employed were farmers, while 1,404 worked in manufacturing establishments. The number of farms had increased from the 3,240 in 1880 to 3,615 in 1900 and 3,627 in 1910. This last year was the peak, because the decline to 3,462 in 1920 and 3,184 in 1930 marked the beginning of a falloff that still continues. In 1910 the average size of a Bedford County farm was 129 acres, an average that remained virtually without change through 1930. However, only 73 acres were improved land (56 percent compared to 47 percent in 1860). The major crop was corn, followed by oats and wheat in smaller amounts —the surge in wheat marketing of 1880 had subsided. Of the tillable land, a large amount was left in pasture, the biggest part being sown with timothy. Virtually all of the field crops were fed to dairy cows, for, as in 1860, the production and sale of milk and home-produced butter exceeded the scope of any other farm enterprise. The farms in 1910 were broadly diversified. Swine and sheep numbered about two-thirds the county's cattle population; poultry flocks averaged out to more than 52 birds for each farm. Subsistence needs consumed a sizeable portion of each year's output. Livestock, mostly swine and sheep, valued at $489,000, were marketed in 1910, but another $344,000 worth were slaughtered for home use. The only other crop grown in quantity was potatoes. Ten thousand horses, averaging nearly three for each farm, were the major source of power.[35]

In the twenty years between 1910 and 1930, family farming in Bedford County underwent a few changes. Dairying remained the major enterprise, but now most of the output was marketed as whole milk, not as butter. Only half as many horses were present compared to twenty years earlier. Surprisingly, only 800 of the more than 3,000 farms reported tractors, but nearly all had automobiles on the premises. Communications were obviously better, because a third of the farm homes had a telephone. Nevertheless, except for those located in broad valleys, like Morrison's Cove, the farms in the coves and hollows of Bedford County remained lonely, isolated places. Two-thirds of the farms were located on "unimproved dirt roads," a euphemism that can scarcely capture the inconveniences of travel for an automobile, schoolbus, or milk truck in wet or wintry weather through narrow passes and across rivulets without bridges.[36]

Bedford County's coal and iron ore trickled northward over the Broadtop Railway as raw material now, because the little forges and blast furnaces had long ceased to operate. From the little railroad station by the river, butter and milk from the valley farms and a few manufactured products traveled south to Cumberland or north to Altoona. On summer weekends excursion trains brought well dressed tourists, who tarried only long enough to board the surreys or, later, buses that bore them to the spacious, expensive Bedford Springs Hotel or one of the other sylvan retreats by the tonic mineral springs.

World War I spurred production in the coalfields around Riddlesburg and Hopewell; returns from farming improved, although in no way equal to those in the better lands out west. The collapse came quickly. Mining is a volatile business: when coal prices turn downward, marginal producers simply close up to wait out the day when supplies grow short and prices go up again. The vaunted prosperity of the twenties never touched the coal mines anywhere, let alone the marginal Broadtop fields. By the thirties, the mines were practically abandoned; there was a brief revival during World War II but that was the last time any coal has ever come down from the hills of Bedford County.

The coast-to-coast Lincoln Highway, crossing southern Pennsylvania from Philadelphia through Lancaster, historic Gettysburg and Chambersburg, passed down Pitt Street in the middle of Bedford. As automobile traffic picked up in the late twenties and thirties, the old hotels were refurbished; in summer many of the big old homes sprouted tourist signs, and lodgers could spend a night for two or three dollars. The old fieldstone taverns, where the stage coaches traveling the toll roads had stopped a century before, had quaint appeal to the passing motorist. Out in the countryside little mom and pop filling stations, with overhanging porticos out front and a sandwich shop at the side, were built just a few feet back from the two-lane highway. Trucks penetrated up the hollows to pick up the big ten- or twenty-gallon milk cans that farmers left in the milk house or set out by the mailbox early each morning. The age of the automobile was bringing Bedford tangentially into a mainstream of the nation's commerce.

The rich political data available for any Pennsylvania county makes possible a more comprehensive analysis of Bedford's electoral behavior than space allows or the present analysis demands. Traditionally a Republican county, the political pattern was not a consistent one, and there were differences rooted far back in history among the nearly fifty separate voting units into which the county was divided.

Before 1896, the two major parties were highly competitive in the county. In 1856 the Know-Nothings walked away with most of the Whig votes, and perennial Democratic visitor James Buchanan carried the county and the state. Most postwar elections were decided by thin margins: Samuel J. Tilden carried the county in 1876 with 52 percent of the vote, although Rutherford B. Hayes won Pennsylvania. James G. Blaine won by 51 percent in 1884, and Benjamin Harrison was victorious by 53 percent in 1892. Margins widened after 1896 when national politics began a new epoch. William McKinley swept the county by 57 percent; Herbert Hoover won comfortably in the depression election of 1932, and even Alfred M. Landon squeaked out a slight plurality in the Republican rout of 1936. The only Democratic presidential candidate to win the county since 1896 was Lyndon Johnson in 1964. Catholic presidential candidates were anathema to Bedford County voters—no nominee was shellacked so badly as Al Smith, who garnered only 17.7 percent of the county's vote in 1928; John Kennedy won just 32.5 percent, although Democratic registration was at 46.4 percent.

Inside its boundaries, the country was not so homogeneous. Before 1896, the conflicts of the Civil War years seemed to be reflected in county politics. The strongest Democratic boroughs and townships, some casting nearly unanimous ballots, were in the south, where the streams drain down to Maryland and commercial ties were with Cumberland. Even Bedford Township and Borough were slightly Democratic. With a few baffling exceptions, boroughs and townships in the county's northern tier, including the rural industrial centers around Riddlesburg and Hopewell, were Republican. After the railroad came and the mines flourished then faded, this pattern was altered. Broadtop Township voters could not countenance Al Smith, but one division returned a plurality for the Socialist candidate, and repeated the performance again in 1932. The old mining areas, although vastly changed since the thirties, have been Democratic centers since that time. In 1968 the county's registration was 59 percent Republican; Richard Nixon carried by 69 percent, but he lost Pennsylvania. In recent years, although an occasional political fight may develop, most local offices have been occupied by Republicans, except where law requires minority party representation.[37]

Breezewood, Pennsylvania, where archaic jurisdictions with weak zoning laws meet aggressive commercial expansion. A modern Bedford County dairy farm is at the left.

Whatever fame old Bedford might claim for its frontier stockade—a resting spot for Washington or a summer White House for Buchanan—the most important thing that ever happened there was on the day the Pennsylvania Turnpike, passing 2½ miles north of the town and transecting the whole county, opened in 1938. Bedford was not only saved by the turnpike, it was reshaped and recreated. Although it is a platitude to say that that which can create can also destroy, it is nonetheless true.

If the motorized traveler of today knows anything at all of Bedford County, it is likely because of Breezewood, a microcosmic example of the ubiquitous service centers for autobound urbanites that have multiplied wherever exit ramps lead away from the expressways or freeways that have pierced across the fields and mountains of rural America. Their impact on the nonurban economy is no meager one: the 266 tourist-related businesses of Bedford

County earned 15.6 million dollars in 1973 and provided jobs for at least 2,000 of its residents. Breezewood, near the lonely spot where Vanderbilt and Carnegie checked out the progress on their abortive South Pennsylvania Railroad ninety years ago, lies nearly midway on the turnpike at the strategic point where Interstate 70, the route south to Baltimore and Washington, intersects. Wheeling down the exit ramp, the summer motorist plunges into the "Million Dollar Mile" (actually only 300 yards long). Should he be able to divert his attention for a moment from the activities of his numerous motorbound colleagues or the roaring diesel trucks, he may see about him the concrete results of careless and nonexistent zoning laws and the consequences that follow when archaic jurisdictions confront economic expansion of a magnitude vastly beyond their competence. There are at least 17 gasoline stations, 9 restaurants, and 21 motels—depending how far back from "the strip" one counts. Blazing multicolored signs celebrate the virtues of Exxon, Shell, Kentucky Fried Chicken, and "authentic" Pennsylvania Dutch plaques. There are 750 motel rooms; although one cannot be precise, Breezewood on a summer night may accomodate up to 4,000 overnight guests. Every now and then a bit of authentic Bedford County topsoil breaks the sea of concrete behind the service stations—it's the place you walk your dog. Nearly every billboard advertises some national franchise, but most of the managers and employees would be listed in the rural nonfarm category that now makes up the vast majority of the county's population.[38]

Ten miles west, "Turnpike City" is a smaller-scale tourist complex that has grown up around the end of the Exit 11 ramps just outside of Bedford Borough. Of its six motels, the two most pretentious are owned by national syndicates. Most major national brands of gasoline are represented by spire-like billboards that reach high enough to be read from the turnpike. Route 220, which passes south into Bedford, is lined with ramshackle garages with spare tires and assorted truck parts strewn along their fronts and sides.

There are a few big truck terminals, obviously operating below capacity.

Bedford itself was sliced in half in 1970 when a Route 30 bypass was built on an elevated route that follows the riverbed across the town—not the original one, for the old Raystown branch was diverted for the convenience of the highway engineers. The tackiness of many American downtowns is alleviated in Bedford by the stately early nineteenth-century buildings, most with plaques giving the date of their construction, and by the charming town square. The town's several hotels, some posthouses from stagecoach times, seem not to be flourishing businesses; some have been converted to taverns where workers in the local industries gather to watch Pittsburgh Pirate baseball games. A few of the shops appeal to tourists, but most are small locally-oriented proprietorships: the hardware store, a dress shop, and an Army-Navy store (owned by one of the villages' few Jewish families). The three chain supermarkets are on the town's outskirts. The daily newspaper and two local radio stations confine themselves to the parochial concerns of county residents, and compete with the cable television lines that connect to Baltimore, Washington, and Pittsburgh in an effort to keep local consumers buying in the Bedford retail market. Back from the main street, homes that date from colonial times (a number of ornate federal period structures and some Victorian additions now a century old) are carefully maintained and their immense yards are scrupulously groomed.

The bulk of Bedford County's economic activity takes place within a two-mile-wide belt on either side of the turnpike. Inside these confines, along radial roads around the town, a number of farm fields have been converted to camping spots; a new one opens nearly every year. A state park at Shawnee Lake, a few miles west of town, fills to capacity on summer weekends with families from Altoona, Pittsburgh, and other nearby urban centers, who come to camp, fish, swim, or go boating.

For the more discriminating and affluent traveler, the 150-year-old Bedford Springs Hotel, hidden in a beautiful wooded cove south of the town, has about it a decor of crinoline, old lace, and lattice work, and it exudes a quality of tasteful, proper opulence. James Buchanan might still recognize it, although the bowling greens that were out front are parking lots now, and on the fields to the south is an 18-hole golf course. On a Saturday night in August, the guests from Cleveland, Washington, Baltimore, and nearby cities in Pennsylvania, who can afford the $50 to $100 daily tab, stroll in fashionable evening dress through half-deserted corridors and amble through delicately lighted ramps and walkways among the gardens to the health-giving springs. At Bedford Springs' only remaining competitor, a less pretentious, rustic hotel ten miles away, I could find neither a traveler's car nor a solitary visitor on this same weekend.

The pulsating auto-borne tourist trade, which is Bedford's economic lifeblood, skipped a beat in the winter of 1974, and raised the discomforting possibility that the profits it produces might be as transient as the travelers who provide them. While motor-conditioned suburbanites grumbled about the contrived "gas shortage," the stopover villages of Breezewood and "Turnpike City" suffered a major depression. Several service stations closed for lack of gasoline, and save for urgent demands to national suppliers who seemed miraculously able to come up with an emergency allocation, all of them might have shut down. A 20 percent reduction in the traffic down the exit ramps left counter stools half empty at lunch time, and the motels, which operate only at 40 percent capacity in winter, had even more spare beds. Only half the normal winter staff kept their jobs.[39]

That a long-term energy shortage may be impending, and that inflated costs of operation may therefore cool Americans' long love affair with their automobiles, are topics best ignored in Bedford or any other rural community linked to the metropolitan economy principally as a roadside traveler's service center. It is much more comforting to listen to glowing reports like the one authorized by the Appalachian Thruway Association's Economic Development Council in 1973: the report multiplied the tourist dollar by a factor of 2.36, the reputed income in the local economy of the traveler's turnover dollar as it was expended for everything from paychecks to electricity for the neon signs. This somewhat dubious figure, the eager promoters speculated, will double in ten years when Route 220 through Bedford becomes a part of a great North-South freeway system that will stretch from Georgia, up the mountain chains, and all the way to Canada.[40]

Important as it is, the turnpike, for Bedford County, means more than the dollars the tourists produce. When traffic multiplied after World War II, "Turnpike City" became a hub for the big trucks that sped across the state. Several immense terminals and repair stations of major shippers occupied the huge garages that overlook the row of motels. By 1963, one thousand of the big rigs thundered through each day, and the industry provided jobs as drivers, mechanics, and service personnel for nearly three thousand people. Then, about a decade ago, toll-free Interstate 80, shortening the distance from Pittsburgh to New York, was opened seventy-five miles north. Some 21 of Bedford's truck terminals promptly moved away, and the county has been scrambling to attract new industry ever since. Low tax rates, cheap industrial land, and the absence of unions have been the major lures, and a Bedford Development Council has mounted a vigorous nationwide advertising campaign.

Motor transport brings in the raw materials and ships out the finished products of the light industries that have chosen to locate in Bedford and the vicinity. The county's best catch so far was when the Hedstrom Company decided to move from Fitchburg, Massachusetts, in 1965, largely because of a poor labor relations climate there.[41] Whether the climate in Bedford County will remain favorable for long is not clear: a referendum of the National Labor Relations Board, conducted at Hedstrom in March 1974, opposed organizing a chapter of the International Association of Machinists by a vote of only 125 to 113. Located in a flat, rambling building that takes up about half as much space as its parking lot, Hedstrom manufactures children's play equipment: strollers, bicycles, and tricycles that are retailed through Sears Roebuck, Montgomery Ward, and occasionally under Hedstrom's own brand name. A railroad spur skirts the plant, but most commerce flows in and out by truck.[42] Standard Register, close by, employs 200 men and women who make paper products for the computer industry. Kennemetal, the oldest of the new industries, makes precision bits and augers for the mining industry, employs 400 persons, and relies exclusively on motor transport. Besides these, Bedford Township houses a huge warehouse that supplies the souvenirs that deck the shelves of Howard Johnson's roadside eateries throughout eastern United States. In addition, there is a small plastics factory and a plant that makes pin-mill wood products. Three farm equipment and feed dealers have headquarters along the railroad spur. Hedstrom, which fills about 500 freight cars each year, is the major user of the railroad. The bankrupt Penn Central abandoned all traffic on the route from Bedford to Cumberland after a flood in 1972. The company has recently petitioned to abandon the route north to Altoona, the last rail link into Bedford.

The county's population expanded slowly, jumping from 37,309 in 1930 to 40,809 in 1940, the decade the turnpike opened; growth stabilized through the war decade, then crept upward by another 2,000 in the fifties when the trucks were rolling into "Turnpike City" and the jerry-built concessions were growing around Breezewood. There was zero growth in the sixties, and the number of people in Bedford Borough dropped by more than 10 percent. Out of the county's thirty-eight townships and boroughs, twenty lost population. The place in the county growing most rapidly is Snake Spring Township, through the narrows just east of

Bedford, where developers have built some modern split-level homes on cul-de-sacs not far from the sites of Kennemetal and Hedstrom.

The overwhelming proportion of the county's inhabitants are rural nonfarm residents (81 percent in 1970). Since Bedford Borough is the only urban center of more than twenty-five hundred persons, the future includes those who live in villages like Everett, Schellsburg, or Saxton, the new suburbanites in Snake Spring Township, as well as those who live in the country and commute to work in Bedford, Huntington, or Altoona. Should anyone doubt that a rural county can have so few "farmers," a few hours driving along the winding roadways back away from the tourist mainstream quickly proves the point.

Up in Broadtop Township there are only half as many residents as in the boom times before the twenties; population loss was 17 percent just in the decade of the 1960s. Riddlesburg, Hopewell, and Saxton show no sign whatsoever of ever having been the sites of blast furances and an active coal mining industry. Hopewell's single business establishment is a run-down tavern. Two power plants, one nuclear, are located up near the Fulton County line; many men who live in Saxton drive the trucks that bring in coal for them all the way from Somerset; wives and daughters during the summer months commute down to Breezewood to clean the rooms and serve meals in the motels and restaurants. Land in depressed Broadtop is the cheapest in the county; plots of land have been subdivided, and trailer homes, some with neat flower and vegetable gardens, are spread out along the riverbank. I don't recall seeing a single farm in the township.

The 2,993 farms noted in the 1930 Bedford County census diminished to 1,741 in 1960, and to 1,292 in 1970. We need, however, to look more closely. In the enumeration of employment in the 1970 census, of the 1,802 enployed workers who lived in a rural farm residence, just 786 (44 percent) claimed agriculture as their calling. In a county 92 percent rural, only 7 percent of the work force engaged in farming, and more than half of these worked just part-time. Still, up in Morrison's Cove, DeKalb, or Agway hybrid corn grew tall and healthy in tightly planted fields in the summer of 1974, and herds of big black and white Holsteins grazed on pasture lands near the old red barns and two or three tall new fiberglass silos. Corn and timothy, the latter drying in windrows in mid-August, covered the fields of fertile Pensyl Hollow, west from Bedford on Route 30. One big dairy farm dominates the area, does all its own processing, and sells from its own premises all the milk products it can turn out. Like their predecessors a century ago, this twilight generation of Bedford County farmers are milk producers. Probably the most successful among them is Ken Mowry from the north part of the county. Among his 150 registered Holstein's on his ultra-modern farm is Princess Corinne, an immense 1,600-pound supercow who produces more than 50,000 pounds of milk a year, greater by 5,000 pounds of output than any other cow known to history.[43] Dairy farming, however, is fading away. One of the major distributors, Sealtest, closed its local collecting center in 1963; since then Bedford's remaining milk producers hire a collector who stops every other day to siphon the milk into his tank truck and speed it over the turnpike to Philadelphia. Huge white-faced Herefords, the nation's prime beef cattle, are nearly as numerous as the milk-producing Holsteins, for farmers have shifted to the less demanding and usually more profitable beef production; also one can raise Herefords and hold a job in a factory as well. The cattle are fattened on corn and silage, then sold at one of several auction points in adjacent counties. Since most grains cultivated in the county are used for feed, not sold, soybeans are almost unknown. Diversified farming is part of history now; during two days of driving through the farmlands of Bedford County, I saw only one farm that still raised chickens. Falkland Farms, near the hamlet of Schellsburg, the largest single farm in the county, raises Herefords that are internationally famous. The owner divides his time between his Pittsburgh residence and his spacious Bedford County estate, for his would be classified a family farm.

By contrast, the Beegle farm in Friends' Cove, where I dropped in on a Sunday afternoon, consists of 150 acres that have been in the family for 100 years. On the 50 tillable acres they raise hybrid corn, oats, barley, and wheat. The fifty dairy cows graze the hillside and woodland pastures from May to November, then are confined in the barn for the winter and subsist on a diet of oats and silage. Milk processors buy fluid by bulk, so most farmers prefer the productive Holsteins that yield up to eighty pounds apiece daily. Nevertheless, Mr. Beegle keeps a few Jerseys, knowing full well that their yield, although higher in butterfat content, is only forty to fifty pounds. His Jerseys are the descendants of the herd his grandfather kept. Even for an operation of this small scope, two tractors and a farm truck were parked out in the barnyard and machine shed. Alongside was a hay rake, a baler, two wagons, a crusher-separator for the hay, a big ten-foot mower bar that attaches to the tractor, a chopper for the silage, a manure spreader, a small combine for the barley and oats (owned cooperatively), and a little two-drill planter for the corn. Mr. Beegle hires custom harvesters for the corn and wheat. Just off the milking room a shining clean aluminum refrigerated tank, periodically checked by the State Department of Agriculture, preserves the raw milk between pickups, and an automatic spinning blade prevents the cream from rising to the top. All the hybrid seed and fertilizer used come from one of the three feed and equipment distributors in Bedford. Mr. Beegle applies nitrogen fertilizer to the corn four times during the season, but the distributor brings in his own equipment to spray the crop with insecticides and pesticides.

Mr. Beegle, a handsome white-haired man near sixty, runs the farm pretty much by himself, hiring help only at planting season. Twenty-five cows are milked at five thirty each morning and again at five o'clock in the afternoon.[44] His eldest son is away at college, planning a teaching career. Another son works at Kennemetal; he isn't sure, but he might keep up the farm as a part-time operation some day.

When land is sold in Morrison's Cove or Napier Township it usually remains farmland, but elsewhere old farmhouses are vacation homes for families from Altoona or Pittsburgh.[45] Others have become country residences for town dwellers who rented or purchased the houses left over when farms were consolidated. Pastures and woodlands are subdivided and stationary trailer homes or prefabs erected, which become residences for commuters to the factories of Bedford or the travel businesses in Breezewood. Up in the hilly northwest corner of the county investors from Washington, D.C., have built the Blue Knob ski resort, and already a few vacation condominiums are on the market, with more contemplated. Outside developers who sell to urban buyers are creating a land abuse problem that threatens to become serious. A member of the District Soil Conservation Board complained of a Maryland developer who bulldozed a road through a hardwood forest making right angle turns, crossing streams, and going straight up and down hills. "He then sold land tracts to unsuspecting buyers who will have to live with that haphazard road in the future. Anyone knows that a road straight up one hill and down another will eventually wash away." Developers, he added, sell land without proper roads and facilities, then walk away and leave the problems to the local taxpayers, many of whom are old-time residents.

Water supplies from the mountain springs have been judged adequate for some years to come, but disposal of wastes from tourist complexes, industries, and new suburban developments pose a more serious problem. Engineers cooperating with the Pennsylvania Department of Environmental Resources found the soils of Bedford and adjacent areas "severe to hazardous" for on-lot disposals—that is, cesspools—with a high probability of ground water pollution or contamination. Confronted with land abuse by developers and mismanagement of road and disposal facilities, the county commissioners insist that all they can do is urge township and borough supervisors to enact laws to protect themselves. The Soil Conservation Board is an advisory agency and the State Department of Environmental Resources has limited enforcement powers, cautiously applied when conflicts with local jurisdictions portend.

The county recorder of deeds estimated that land sales in the county increased 15 percent between 1972 and 1973, and prices were escalating. After the inflationary spirals of 1974, one resident estimated that industrial land might cost $1,000 per acre (cheap by urban standards), good farmland, $600, acreage for a vacation home near Bedford, $1,000 to $1,400 per acre and up—in depressed Broadtop, $700 to $800.

Long ago, C. J. Galpin, skeptical of the sharp dichotomy between "rural" and "urban," coined the alternate term "rurban." From the time it was a frontier settlement, then an outpost for marginal farming, manufacturing, and mining, then an early traveler's service center, isolated Bedford County's fate has always hinged on the links that bound and integrated it into an urban world. The rurban places like Bedford, from Georgia to Oregon, are stopping places, centers for light industry, production centers for a few prosperous farmers, second homes for the wealthy, and play areas for the rest of us.

Just how tenuous such a status can be is epitomized by an advertisement in the *Wall Street Journal* of 26 June 1973. Underneath a picture of four husky young men gathered around a tractor, with a silo in the background, the text read as follows:

> Your industry needs what these boys learned on the farm.
> They learned how to work. Hard!
> And since modern farms are as mechanized as most factories, these former Bedford County, Pennsylvania, farmers are as at home with a drill press as they are with a tractor ...
> Located right on the Pennsylvania Turnpike, Bedford County has the location you need ...
> Help these men turn their unemployment checks into paychecks. And help yourself to the hardest working labor force in America.

The ad, of course, didn't need to mention that there were no labor unions in Bedford. If the advertisement brought any immediate successes, they haven't been apparent. The county's unemployment rate has always been among the highest of the forty-eight labor market areas in Pennsylvania. In 1971, with 10.7 percent of the civilian work force without jobs, it was the second highest in the state; in February 1975 it was first. In June 1975, 12.1 percent were unemployed, compared to 9.6 percent in Pennsylvania, and Bedford ranked ninth among the forty-eight areas. The county is one of three of the labor market areas listed as having persistent unemployment.[46]

Notes

1. James C. Malin, "The Turnover of Farm Population in Kansas," *Kansas State Historical Quarterly* 4 (November 1935): 339–72, posits three demographic epochs in the settlement pattern of new areas: a frontier period, roughly twenty years, when population turnover may be as high as 65 percent over any decade; relative stabilization, when the turnover curve flattens; high stabilization when turnover attains an equilibrium at about 20 to 30 percent. Malin specifically concludes that the age of the settlement, not the specific period in the nineteenth century when settlement took place, is the critical variable in analysis of population turnover.

2. Marion Clawson, *The Land System of the United States* (Lincoln: University of Nebraska Press, 1968), pp. 44–47.

3. Sources for the description of Scioto Township include W. H. Perrin and J. H. Battle, *History of Delaware County and Ohio* (Chicago: O. L. Baskin and Co., Historical Publishers, 1880 [Evansville, Ind.: Unigraphic, 1973]), pp. 482–91, 720–40; James R. Lytle, ed. and comp., *20th Century History of Delaware County, Ohio and Representative Citizens* (Chicago: Biographical Publishing Co., 1908); *Modie's Centennial Atlas and History of Delaware County, Ohio* (compiled and published by F. Burr Modie, Columbus, Ohio, 1908). I am especially indebted to Mrs. Margaret Main Bouic of Ostrander, Ohio, who made available to me the unpublished results of her lifelong interest in the history of the area and the genealogy of its families. This included her transcriptions of the population schedules for the federal censuses for Scioto Township in 1820, 1830, 1840, 1850, and 1860. I made all computations included here and transcribed the population schedules for the 1880 census. Mrs.

Bouic's collection also includes seven articles by W. P. Crawford, "Recollections of Pioneer Life in the Western Part of Delaware County," *Delaware* (Ohio) *Democratic Herald,* 6 January, 9 February, 23 February, 8 March, 5 April, 17 May, and 31 May 1888, and an unpublished paper by Loren Moseley, "A History of Scioto Township and Ostrander, Ohio," prepared for presentation to the Delaware County Historical Society. The collection also includes a record of all burials in the several cemeteries in the township, compiled by Mr. and Mrs. Carl Main. I also utilized the *1826 Auditor's Tax List, Delaware County, Ohio,* also compiled by Mr. and Mrs. Main (1955). A mimeographed copy is held by the Historical Society of Pennsylvania, in Philadelphia. Mrs. Anna Pabst of Delaware kindly made available a series of Scioto Township plat maps. Specific references to these materials will be omitted.

4. Since households increased from 28 in 1820 to 69 in 1830, it is likely some were not property holders, hence not included in the 1826 tax list.

5. Allan G. Bogue, *From Prairie to Cornbelt* (Chicago: Quadrangle Books, 1968 [1963]), pp. 241–42; Gilbert Fite, *The Farmers' Last Frontier, 1865–1900* (New York: Holt, Rinehart and Winston, 1966), pp. 46–47. The thorough data contained in Merle Curti et al., *The Making of a Frontier Community: A Case Study of Democracy in a Frontier County* (Stanford: Stanford University Press, 1959), is not strictly comparable because of different categories and different frames of reference.

6. Paul W. Gates estimates that in Ohio in 1810 twice as much land was owned by absentees as by residents. "Tenants of the Log Cabin," *Mississippi Valley Historical Review* 64 (June 1962): 29 n.

7. The information concerning Bayly is from U.S., Congress, House, *Biographical Directory of the American Congress, 1774–1961,* 85th Cong., 2d Sess., p. 529. An extensive collection of Drumgoole papers are a part of the Southern Historical Collection, Library of the University of North Carolina. Of the various local historical sources from Delaware County, only Mr. Crawford's 1888 memoir makes any reference to the holdings of these land speculators. They are, nonetheless, patently obvious from the land plat maps.

8. One might wish to know more about a Christian Union Church, organized in 1865 by individuals who favored peace not war, lasted a few years, and then disappeared leaving behind only a sentence or two in the county history.

9. Using data in the 1840 census, I compiled the total population of several localities between the ages of five and twenty. This

category obviously overlaps expected ages of school attendance both at the beginning and the end, but the categories chosen by census enumerators of 140 years ago are difficult to alter, and of course the measure is applied uniformly in all areas.

10. Family heads rather than total population were utilized in the first tabulation—applying to Scioto Township alone—because the large number of children under ten, all born in Ohio, produced misleading results on the sources of migration. However, for comparative purposes, data for the entire state is available only for the complete population, so these figures represent all age groups and hence are distorted toward the Ohio-born population.

11. In estimating rates of emigration, I have compared not only the three manuscript censuses, but have used the cemetery records to eliminate individuals who died in the intercensual periods. This mobility rate is consistent with the findings of Bogue, *From Prairie to Cornbelt,* p. 315, and James C. Malin, "Kansas: Some Reflections on Culture Inheritance and Originality," *Journal of the Mississippi Valley American Studies Association* 2 (Fall 1961): 8–11.

12. The generality of the pioneer stage described here is limited to areas east of the wheat areas and Great Plains. The kind of subsistence generalized agriculture of Ohio and the Midwest was not possible there. This is a point often stressed by James C. Malin.

13. This esoteric handful included a magician, a huckster, two book agents, a tin peddler, and three railroad section hands.

14. Census data, less complete in 1880 than in 1850, can again be used to set these statistics in a comparative frame. Note again they are for a total population.

TABLE IV

Percentage of Total Population by Place of Origin, 1880

Birthplace	Ohio	Delaware County	Scioto
Ohio	72.	85.2	83.
Pennsylvania	4.2	4.3	4.
New York	1.9	2.4	2.
Virginia	1.5	1.9	2.
Foreign Born	12.0	6.5	2.

15. The county history indicates there should be eighteen teachers, but only eight appear in the manuscript census. This is either

because of an error, which I cannot explain, or because the teachers were nonresidents or temporary inhabitants not present when the census was taken in June. Sixty-nine students above sixteen years of age in school appears an unusually high number.

16. In 1880 the average size of a farm in Ohio was 99 acres; in Delaware County, 94. In 1925 the Delaware County average was 95.4.

17. U.S., Department of Interior, *Agriculture of the United States in 1860* (Washington, D.C.: U.S. Government Printing Office, 1864), pp. 112–14; U.S., Department of the Interior, Census Office, *Report on the Production of Agriculture as Returned at the 10th Census* (Washington, D.C.: U.S. Government Printing Office, 1883), pp. 81, 166.

18. *Wiggins' Delaware and Delaware County Directory* (Columbus, Ohio: New Franklin Printing Co., 1899), vol. 4. The directory lists most of the real estate owners whose names could be located on the plat map for 1900. Omissions were few and appeared to be random.

19. Clement Vallandigham was perhaps the most outspoken of Copperhead opponents of the Civil War; he was deported to Canada and, later, was the Democratic antiwar candidate for governor of Ohio in 1863.

20. State of Ohio, Secretary of State, *Election Statistics* [for various years]. Unfortunately in a number of instances minor civil subdivision statistics are available only for offices such as secretary of state, not for governor or president.

21. The reference is to a widely publicized book, Michael Lesy, *Wisconsin Death Trip* (New York: Pantheon Books, 1973). The book contains some truly extraordinary photographs and some excerpts from local newspapers and later novels that are remarkable for different reasons. With no pretense toward objectivity, the pictures and especially the prose excerpts have been chosen in an attempt to convey a sense of a rural life in eastern Wisconsin at the turn of the century as indeed morbid and macabre. One could distort the history of any rural community in similar fashion, but he would forsake entirely the historical enterprise in doing so.

22. If the same percentage of the target area population was in the same age cohort, e.g. 20 to 30, as the national population, the index number would be 100.

23. Total acreage in farms in Delaware County declined only slightly from 1925 to 1969.

24. Only 85 farms in Delaware County kept poultry in 1969.

25. This is questionable. The average farm in the county was 231 acres in 1969 compared to 95.4 in 1925.

26. U.S., Bureau of Census, *1969 Census of Agriculture—County Data, Ohio,* pp. 169–76.
27. Ohio ceased to publish minor civil subdivision voting data after 1958. A cursory examination of rural Ohio voting patterns suggests a permanent shift from Democratic to Republican in the 1930s of many counties and townships where Democratic tendencies, such as those in Scioto, dated back at least four decades. The trend is obscured because of the huge Democratic majorities in metropolitan centers.
28. Three sizeable dams constructed both to supply Columbus with water and control floods on the Ohio River already inundate considerable acreage in Delaware County.
29. There was considerable unavailing opposition to attempts at school consolidation in the 1940s and 1950s. I found no complaints or regrets in 1973, or no objection to the transfer of political functions to county authorities.
30. Sources for the analysis of Bedford County include: E. Howard Blackburn and William H. Welfley, *History of Bedford and Somerset Counties, Pennsylvania* (New York: Lewis Publishing Co., 1906), vol. 1; *History of Bedford, Somerset and Fulton Counties, Pennsylvania* (Chicago: Waterman, Watkins and Co., 1884); Dorsey S. Ling and E. Howard Blackburn, *Directory of Bedford County* (n.p., 1900); Winona Garbrick, ed., *The Kernel of Greatness* (Bedford County Bi-Centennial Commission, 1971). I have omitted specific page references to these sources and to most of the materials drawn from the published volumes of the First through the Fifteenth U.S. Census, which are the sources of all population figures cited. I am indebted to Mr. William Clark, a graduate student at University of Pennsylvania and a lifelong resident of Bedford, who not only gathered much of the material but served as a patient and understanding guide for yet another tourist who came to explore the farms, towns, and byways of Bedford County. He also made available to me his copious file of clippings from the *Bedford Gazette,* which became the basis for much of the discussion of contemporary Bedford County.
31. U.S., Department of the Interior, *Agriculture of the United States in 1860,* p. 213.
32. U.S., Department of the Interior, Census Office, *Report on the Production of Agriculture as Returned at the 10th Census,* pp. 82, 167, 306.
33. Louis Hartz, *Economic Policy and Democratic Thought: Pennsylvania, 1776–1880* (Chicago: Quadrangle Books, 1968 [1948]), pp. 10, 43–44.

34. Hence Bedford Borough's principal school was private until 1890. Several other private academies, largely for outsiders, functioned at several times in different parts of the county. As for public education, the county superintendant of schools reported in 1860 that of the 187 one-room schools scattered throughout the county, 49 of them were unfit for use. Perhaps this is why the percentage of school age children attending classes, reported in n. 9, was so amazingly low.
35. U.S., Bureau of the Census, *Thirteenth Census of the United States: 1910. Agriculture,* 7:450–57.
36. U.S., Bureau of the Census, *Fifteenth Census of the United States: 1930. Agriculture,* 2, part 1, pp. 334, 340, 346, 350, 356, 368, 380, 384.
37. *Smull's Handbook,* published annually until 1922, and, following that date, the yearly *Pennsylvania Manual* give complete voting returns by minor civil subdivisions for all major elections and usually list county officeholders and their political affiliation.
38. *Washington Post,* 11 March 1974.
39. Ibid.
40. Part of the route is completed and contracts have been let for some of the construction in Bedford County.
41. Hedstrom is a subsidiary of a conglomerate, the Brown Group, owners of Brown Shoes.
42. *Philadelphia Bulletin,* 10 April 1974.
43. *Philadelphia Inquirer,* 1 December 1974.
44. The other 25 are heifers kept for herd replacement.
45. The 1970 census listed 578 seasonal farm homes in the county.
46. *1973 Pennsylvania Statistical Abstract* (Harrisburg, 1973), p. 118; Commonwealth of Pennsylvania, Bureau of Employment Security, *Pennsylvania Labor Markets Ranked on Basis of Rate of Unemployed for October, 1974* (6 December 1974); Commonwealth of Pennsylvania, Bureau of Employment Security, *Pennsylvania Labor Market Areas Ranked on Basis of Unemployment for June 1975* (8 August 1975).

CHAPTER FOUR

Family Farming in the Middle West

*In fact, the barn was never painted at all. The good
potato crop never came. It always rained too little to
make good beans, or too much to harvest them. We
never had so many heifer calves that the herd grew
large and made us wealthy. We were always just getting by.*

*Yet there was always hope, always a genuine belief
that things would be better. After all, we were all sharing the same work, dreaming the same dream.*

*And then came the war, and so many things were
pulled apart that were never put back together again.
The fabric of that life tore, and we looked back from
the other side of the rent and wondered how it ever
worked in the first place, how it ever held together.*

—Curtis Stadtfeld, *From the Land and Back*

The traditional ways the soil was made to yield up its products for human consumption, either directly, or indirectly
through feeding to animals, were little different in 1920
than they were in 1820. In fact, change has been so rapid in
the last three decades that the farming practices of 1920
were probably closer to those of 1720 than to those of the
present day.

The American farmer was not dragged unwillingly into
the technological age. Typically, American yeomen have

been inveterate tinkerers and experimenters: the ingenuity of many of the simple gadgets one may see in museums or occasionally still in use on "living historical farms" are proof of that. The important branch of sociology that specializes in studies of innovation diffusion has been developed largely from rural case studies. These observers have identified sharp differences in "adapter categories," from the innovator at one end of the continuum to the stubborn laggard at the other; they have delineated a series of stages in the adoption process beginning with one of awareness and culminating at the point where an individual decides to continue the use of an innovation he has adopted. No evidence shows that farmers have lagged behind other groups—college professors or school boards, for example—in their willingness to innovate; in fact there are indications that the agricultural sector has moved faster than many other segments of society.[1] As one example, rural communities and farm organizations originally feared the noisy and hazardous intrusion of automobiles on dirt roads and country lanes, but as farmers began to perceive the conveniences of motorized transport, the major market for motor vehicles shifted between 1905 and 1908, from the big city to the country town.[2]

In macroview, the impact of technological innovations in American agriculture can be charted on a graph showing linear projection upward, with two great spurts so attenuated they can be termed "agricultural revolutions." Both occurred at times of social crisis which placed extraordinary demands on the farm sector.

The first centered in the years about the Civil War, when prices rose and farm boys left home to go away to war. Its major characteristic was replacement of hand power with animal power. Wrought iron moldboards on plows allowed more efficient scouring of sticky prairie soil. The mechanical reaper introduced animal power at the crucial point in the grain harvest when rapid work was essential to save the crop. Man-hours of labor required to produce 100 bushels of corn or wheat declined sharply from 1840 to 1880, then continued to drop, but at a lower rate, until 1900.[3]

There was potential for another great spurt when farm prices leaped forward during World War I, and when, during the twenties and thirties, an extremely important innovation, the tractor, was widely adopted. Swollen war demands collapsed too quickly, however, into the farm depression of the 1920s and after; with prices falling and rates of mortgage foreclosures going up, there was neither cash nor incentive for extensive innovation.

The second revolution was in the years of World War II and those immediately following. After 1940, when farm manpower grew short again and income shot up, and then after 1945, when swollen international demand held farm prices up, there was actually a backlog of scientific research and new production techniques waiting for the innovation adopters on the farm. Thus, in 1930, one farm worker supplied 9.8 persons with food; this rose only to 10.7 in 1940, then swelled to 14.6 in 1950, 22.8 in 1957, and 45.3 in 1969. Between 1950 and 1968 output per man-hour in agriculture rose twice as fast as that in manufacturing.[4]

Tarpleywick, Van Buren County, Iowa

Sociologists would have no difficulty classifying as traditional family operations the farm in Van Buren County in southeast Iowa, where the eminent rural economist Henry Charles Taylor was growing up in the 1880s, or the farm in Mecosta County in central Michigan, where the gifted writer Curtis K. Stadtfeld lived as a boy in the 1940s.[5] I cannot assert that they were typical, any more than Scioto Township or Bedford County. The farming practices and quality of life were similar to those that prevailed in much of the East and Middle West, but had few parallels with sharecropping in the cotton South or cattle raising on the plains. Nevertheless, the two expert and sensitive narrators who have described these pinpoints in space and time, one an agricultural economist, the other a perspicacious writer, make these two places a good base point from which to attempt to guage the transforming effect of technological change on the work and lives of simple people whose names don't often appear in the pages of history books.

Tarpleywick, 410 acres of prairie land, was the larger and better of the two farms—more than three times the size of the average Iowa farm in the period from 1880 to 1900. The Stadtfeld place consisted of 120 acres of land auctioned off cheaply to farmers after lumbermen of the mid-nineteenth century had stripped the land of its most valuable asset, the virgin white pines.

Both were diversified units producing a little bit of most everything to meet the family's subsistence requirements, with a little surplus left over for cash marketing. Livestock was the principal product at Tarpleywick; so the major field crop had to be corn—sown on seventy-four acres in the traditional three-year rotational pattern. In addition, the land produced wheat, oats, flax, sorghum, and Irish potatoes; and fifty bushels of apples were picked each year in the three-acre orchard. Nine horses furnished the animal power, and the livestock in 1879 included ninety pigs, eight milk cows, cattle for marketing, sheep for wool and mutton, and the ever present chickens. A garden provided fruits and vegetables for household use. From the Mecosta County farm came dairy and poultry products, beef and pork, and fruits and vegetables, largely for the family's needs. Corn, hay, and oats were necessary to feed the livestock, and Curtis Stadtfeld's father always sowed the sandy back forty in potatoes, hoping some day to turn a handsome profit from one of the most difficult of commodities to cultivate and the most erratic to market. He succeeded in this just once.

Diversity is more than what is produced; it is a matter of how things are done. The traditional farm was an integrated and efficient craft unit. If we could have taken a guided tour around the farm lot at Henry Taylor's birthplace with his dour and silent father, Tarpley, here is what we might have seen:

The pivot point of the 410 acres was the unpretentious white clapboard house. Inside, the ceilings were low and the rooms seemed crowded. The nucleus for activity was the kitchen and the adjoining dining room—a radius determined by the heat that could be thrown off from the wood burning stove. Somehow, the odor of the kerosene, used to start the morning fire or fuel the lamps of evening, always lingered through the house.

A well with a cast-iron pump and a cistern, both outside, provided the water. Other wells, dug at several points on the acreage, furnished the livestock, and a windmill piped water to tanks for the cattle in the back sections.

A red building, the closest one to the house, was the smokehouse; a huge copper kettle, which served many uses, sat in the middle, and hams and sides of bacon dangled from the rafters. Since the smokehouse was mostly a storage place, it doubled as the farm's workshop; odds and ends that could serve as replacement parts covered the tables, and tools hung on the wall. The big loom at the south end of the smokehouse was where Mrs. Taylor wove flannel and rag carpets. One hundred feet from the north end of the house, at a necessary but uncomfortable distance, was a little yellow structure identified by any number of rural colloquialisms—my favorite is "Chic Sale."

Close by stood the hen house. In the sexist vernacular of the day, poultry care was regarded as woman's work. When chicks were hatched in the spring or, in a later day, delivered by mail in cardboard boxes, 200 or 300 at a time, they grew quickly. The males were sorted out and marketed as fryers, and by fall the roosterless flocks would begin to produce five to six sterile eggs per hen each week. The chickens grew up in a special brooder house, towed each year to a different spot to give the chicks a new enclosed space to run, free of any diseases left behind by last year's flock. The menfolk moved the brooder house and cooped up the hens in the fall, but the daily tedium of watering, feeding, cleaning, and gathering eggs belonged to women and children. The poultry and eggs that sold earned pin money for the women, money never taken too seriously in the days when bookkeeping was casual and cost accounting unknown. That was why Curtis Stadtfeld was surprised, while looking over his father's old account books for 1935, to find that the cash income from poultry and egg sales nearly equaled that for the dairy herd.

Fifty feet east of the hen house was a corncrib wagon shed which Henry Taylor called his father's "ever-normal granary." Most of the corn crop to be fed to cattle and hogs over the winter was stored in temporary pens made of fence rails, but prudent farmer Taylor, to carry over sufficient supply from good years to finish off the hogs in the event of a poor growing season, built a double corncrib. A roof covered the two halves, and there was plenty of space between to drive a farm wagon. The cribs rested about two feet above the ground on posts capped with tin pans to prevent rats from scurrying up into the granary.

Further east and little bit north began an enclosure containing pigpens, sheds for cattle and sheep, the horse barn, a carriage house, and a big combination hay and sheep barn, all making up the barn lot. Anything but haphazard, the arrangement and construction at Tarpleywick, or any other traditional farm, were the results of untold generations of trial and error experimentation. The limestone basement of the horse barn could accommodate sixteen animals in stalls on both sides, with a feed room between. The barn was built on sloping ground so that a horse and wagon could drive into the mow above, where the feed grains and hay were stored. Sheds for winter shelter for the cattle and sheep were simple affairs, often with a straw roof but always open at the sunniest south side. Only a few brood sows were kept over the winter; they remained out in the open usually, but a special shed with pens adjacent sheltered them from the bitterest cold and provided comfortable farrowing pens when the spring pigs were born.

The distinguishing feature of any farm was its largest structure, the immense barn. No one has much noted the architecture of farmhouses of the East and Midwest, but lavish books of color plates recall nostalgically the contours and designs of the barns. Serving as vast warehouses, the large mows above were filled, by fall, with hay (hauled loose, not in bales), straw, and corn fodder. The small grain crops stored were needed for winter feed: horses ate oats, chickens wheat, cows needed oats and barley, as well as corn. Great mounds of wheat straw or corn fodder were required for bedding livestock (which also entails absorbing the moisture from manure). During the long winter months, feed and straw were shoveled from the mow directly down to the box stalls or stanchion rows where the dairy cows and cattle lined up.

The half-acre garden across the road was so arranged that it could be plowed, harrowed, and cultivated by horses. The lettuce and onion beds, however, had to be cared for with hand tools. Everything grown there was for family consumption.

The woodyard over by the smokehouse was a small, vital center for household production. In autumn, apples were boiled down to thick and spicy butter in the huge copper kettle. The orchards at Tarpleywick produced twenty gallons each year. Hog killing, in December, required help from friends and neighbors. During a long, strenuous day, the hogs were slaughtered and bled, each animal was soaked in boiling water, and then the carcass was hung head down from a tripod. The skin was scraped smooth and white. After dinner, hams, shoulders, side meat, and fat were extracted. The fat was heated gently in the kettle, then scooped out into earthen jars, with the lard stored down in the cool cellar. Any lean meat remaining was ground in the sausage mill, caught up, and tightly wrapped in pieces of intestine. Hams and shoulders were soaked in brine for salting, then, after an appropriate waiting period, taken to the smokehouse where a slow fire, with green, smoky hickory branches on top, burned in the same copper kettle. As the meat cured, the men and boys took up the next woodyard task: logs that had accumulated through the year were sawed, split, and chopped down to convenient size for the kitchen stove or the fuel-devouring heating stove. By the end of February, a pile to last the kitchen for the whole next year stood twenty feet high, and the woodshed was crammed as a supplement. Two other production activities took place in the woodyard. On some winter days, water was poured over all the ashes that had been collected from the cooking and heating stoves and carefully stored in a V-shaped hopper. This leached out the potash to produce lye. When the lye was brought to a boil, fats, accumulated since hog killing, were added: this dissolved into a mushy soft soap; stored in earthen jars, it was sufficient to do the laundry for an entire year. Finally, in the corner of the woodyard stood a row of beehives; it took expert finesse to induce a new colony of swarming bees to enter an empty hive—almost as demanding as extracting the well-filled units of comb honey at the end of the season and storing them away to sweeten the farm cuisine for yet another year.

Last, lift the sloping doors and go down the five-foot-wide staircase (big enough to accommodate barrels and baskets) into the well-stocked cellar. In early winter the first room was filled with barrels of apples, pumpkins, squash, and cabbage from the garden. In a warmer inner room were bins of Irish potatoes, some carrots, and onions. Wall shelves were lined with glass jars of fruits, jellies, jams— as many jars filled as there were days in the year. Also, there were jars of peas, string beans, and tomatoes; over in the corner were several five-gallon earthenware jugs for pickles, and even larger ones for sauerkraut.

Probably no expert ever did a time-motion study of the production processes on a traditional farm. Clockwork efficiency wasn't needed, but a well-stocked cellar and well-filled barns resulted from shrewd and calculated decisions about organization, location, convenience. Traditional diversified farming required a strong back, skillful hands, and a good head; every now and then it resulted in a broken heart.

The word "capital" was foreign to the traditional farmer's vocabulary, and bank accounts were a rarity. Nevertheless, both Tarpleywick and the Stadtfeld farm represented sizeable capital investments; family subsistence came first, but the farms were commercial ventures, and their success depended upon how much income above expenses could be achieved each year.

In 1900 it required $3,000 to start an average farm; in 1930, $8,000; in 1953, $12,000.[6] The largest item of cost was the land. Usually (although not at Tarplewick), the original purchase was financed by a short-term mortgage of five years.[7] In the most comprehensive study of late-nineteenth century farm finance available, Allan G. Bogue sampled four Illinois counties, where he found that more than 83 percent of mortgages in force in 1890 represented expenditures for the purchase of real estate or its improvement. In four Iowa counties, comparable percentages ranged from 68 to 89 percent.[8] Bogue found that most farmers in the counties he studied were at one time or another during their careers involved in trying to pay off a mortgage. Interest rates in Iowa in the 1870s pushed up to the state's prescribed 10 percent maximum, but then dropped during the next two decades, as speculative eastern capitalists increased their investments in Corn Belt loans.[9]

Estimates of the average amount of mortgage debt per farm are difficult to obtain. In 1920, following the rise in land values inspired by wartime prosperity, the average size of all new loans in United States was $4,270, but in Iowa, where land speculation had been rampant, the average new loan was for more than $11,000.[10] Bogue found that of more than 2,600 mortgages negotiated in three Iowa townships, 1852 to 1896, only 3.2 percent were terminated by foreclosure proceedings. Even in the economically troubled twenties and thirties, most farm owners managed to hang on. Thirteen percent of Iowa farm land changed hands due to foreclosure between 1921 and 1933—and that was considered a figure shockingly high.[11]

There were other expenses besides land. Farmers sometimes contracted chattel mortgages with local vendors to purchase draft animals or equipment; these became more frequent after 1920. In 1870 a McCormick reaper cost $200; a small threshing machine, $160—too much outlay for a small farmer but an expense that could often be distributed by sharing use and cost with neighbors or relatives.[12]

Wages in cash or board paid to hired men or the itinerant bummers (migrant laborers), who were already traveling through the Midwest in the 1870s, was another expense. Then, there were taxes, medical costs, veterinarian bills, and, perhaps, payment on an insurance policy to be paid. For simple grocery supplies and basic dry goods, Henry Taylor's mother could obtain them at the country store in exchange for butter and eggs.

Given the mental bookkeeping used both at Tarpleywick and the Stadtfeld farm, the balance remaining after these various out-of-pocket costs had been paid was the profit from the farm. One year in the nineties, Henry Taylor's father told him he had sold about $2,000 worth of products; he didn't add any estimate of his costs, but Tarpley Taylor was able to expand his landholdings, and he was clearly a technological innovator. The Stadtfelds, forty years later, weren't so fortunate: during the one year a good potato crop came in, they bought a Ford V–8, the only new car they ever owned. Their mortgage was never retired.

Marketing livestock at Tarpleywick and selling milk products at Stadtfeld's farm were the major enterprises with which these two farms hoped to turn a profit.

On the Van Buren County farm, about forty brood cows, English shorthorns, the most popular variety in America, were maintained. Known as "red" cattle or Durhams, they were flecked with white or roan in color, and a hefty steer could achieve a weight of fifteen-hundred pounds. Calves, usually born in autumn, were marketed after two and a half years of fattening with pasturage, but they were fed corn for a few months before the cattle buyer came around so they could be sold as fat corn-feds. The aim at Tarpleywick was to sell two carloads of beef cattle each year.[13]

A dozen brood sows, selectively bred so that some litters arrived in the spring, others in the fall, produced about a hundred hogs for market each year in addition to those slaughtered for home use. Hogs were ideal livestock for small farms. It took little capital to go into business, and no farm animal could convert grain into meat with greater efficiency. The gestation period was four months, compared to nine for a cow. Hogs ate corn, the Midwest's most prolific crop, and raising them integrated easily with other livestock operations. But it was risky business, too; many farmers harbored sad memories of an entire pen being wiped out by deadly hog cholera. Breed types were many: the most popular were the Poland China, the Chester White, and the Duroc Jersey.[14] Hogs roamed freely in the summer and were slaughtered at sixteen to twenty months after a period of corn feeding, when a good specimen might weigh five hundred pounds. Originally, buyers paid no more per pound for lean bacon type pigs than obese blubbery lard types, but consumer demands for leaner pork and bacon changed that. Animals were marketed earlier, new breeds introduced, and the fat producing corn diet modified with ground rye, small grains, milk, and other lean-meat producing substitutes. In the days before farm trucks, the fat, waddling creatures were driven to railhead markets on foot, proceeding at the precipitous pace of about one mile each hour.

A flock of about three hundred ewes of French Merino nonpure grade completed the complement of marketable livestock raised at Tarpleywick. Sheared in the spring, ewes might produce six to nine pounds of wool, roans, twenty-five pounds. Ewes that failed to lamb, those not needed for the breeding herd, and the males were fattened on corn, oats, and hay throughout the summer, then sold in the autumn. The sale of poultry products, occasionally some milk, some timothy, and flax seed made up the remainder of the commercial activities at Taylor's farm. No corn or hay were marketed.

Stadtfeld's Farm, Mecosta County, Michigan

Had Dr. Henry C. Taylor, distinguished professor at the University of Wisconsin, credited with being the father of agricultural economics in the United States, dropped in one day at the Stadtfeld farm in Mecosta County, he would have felt at home. To be sure, tractors had replaced horse power, the pigs in the pen were "bacon type" Duroc Jerseys, not Poland Chinas, but the layout was much the same as at Tarpleywick, and the farm practices amazingly similar.[15] But his trained eye would have detected quickly that, from the balance-sheet side of things, the Stadtfelds weren't doing so well.

Dairy cattle, hogs, and potatoes were the combination the Stadtfelds hoped to turn into profit. The three made for a complementary mix. To support a single cow and the young stock to replace her after five or six productive years, four or five acres of summer pasture and another acre in corn and oats for winter feed were required. Potatoes drained soil fertility, and they needed light, loamy earth enriched with manure and plowed-down sod to produce a good crop. Careful rotation with pasture and small grain crops prepared the soil for a year of potatoes, and the necessary fertilizer came from the manure spreader, not from a chemical factory.

The breed of cows a dairy producer selected depended more on personal preference than scientific evidence. The big Durhams might produce six to seven thousand pounds of milk annually, with 4 percent butterfat, and the Holsteins about the same. Many preferred the smaller red Jerseys that produced five thousand pounds of 6 percent milk a year. Since Holsteins tested out at only 3.5 percent, Jersey defenders insisted the breed produced skim milk. The Stadtfelds sold their Durham herd when a cow tested positive to Bang's disease, and switched to Holsteins. Each cow yielded a pail of milk twice daily, and more in the weeks immediately after calving. Dairy cows were programmed to give birth in spring in order to correlate the period of high productivity with the time when the pastures were green and new. Output fell off in winter; then the cows subsisted on the partially fermented nutritious green feed made from the chopped corn that had been blown into the silo in the late summer. Until the 1940s, milking was done

(Courtesy Mrs. Paul Reece)

A family farm in Michigan, 1940s.

by hand; three workers could manage a herd of more than a dozen. After morning and evening milkings, the contents of the big twelve- to sixteen-quart pails were run through the cream separator at the house, and the cream stored in the cool basement to await the weekly pickup by the nearby cooperative creamery. What was left over was skim milk to be consumed at the table, made into cottage cheese, or fed to the ravenous hogs. A ten-cow herd could produce enough good butterfat so that the cream checks arriving every two weeks might total $60 to $80, the major cash income the Stadtfelds earned. Hogs and chickens were not so important on this farm; the Stadtfelds gladly gave them up to concentrate on commercial production of Grade A milk.

Superintending the commercial side of a traditional farm required attention to a number of variables; risks had to be taken, careful decisions made. What breed of cows or hogs was best, considering a farm's size, acreage, fertility, and the demands of the market? If the price of corn was high, should it be marketed as a cash crop rather than feeding it and gambling on what livestock prices might be later? Was it a safe risk to take a new mortgage to add an extra forty acres to the farm?

A stern regime of daily tasks and unyielding seasonal requirements set the pace of activity on a traditional farm and involved all except tiny children or people too old to work. Lest our description of activities that made up the production process be regarded as tedious antiquarianism, it might be remembered that some variant of the work pattern described here involved in any year, say 1880, a majority of the labor force, male and female, of the United States.

First there were the inexorable daily chores, unchanging from season to season. "Eventually," writes Curtis Stadtfeld, "the round of chores becomes a burden, a routine that destroys the spontaneity of life. The farmer who could not afford to get away for a vacation would come, through the years, to regard himself as a slave to the dairy barn. For the milker, there are no weekends, no sick days, no time for carelessness."[16] C. J. Galpin called little country towns like Stockport, Iowa, or Ostrander, Ohio, "team haul" communities; included in their functional economic radius were all the farmers who could reach them and return the same day, not missing the chores.

A normal work week on the Stadtfeld farm was fifty to sixty hours, a bit less in winter, a bit more in summer, and included two or three hours on Sunday. The labor force consisted of two adults (no observer could in any conceivable way exclude a farm wife from the rural work force) and five children of various ages. The family work force at Tarpleywick was exactly the same size; the work day was probably longer, since there was more livestock and no tractors. The Stadtfelds were late risers: their day began at 7 A.M. Rhapsodic recollections often remember the meadowlarks calling on bright, fresh Iowa summer mornings, or the lowing herd winding over the hill on a cool autumn evening in Vermont, but there are no lyrics about the dark predawn hours on sub-zero Michigan mornings! There was milking

An "A" frame harrow.

---

to be done, the cows to be fed, stalls cleared of waste and manure, the pigs slopped. And the same ritual had to be repeated before suppertime in the evening.

The seasonal cycle was set by nature. Nevertheless, a work schedule had to be planned carefully to avoid strain on men and horses in the peak periods of spring and summer. The cycle started to unfold sometime in March, when the snow began to melt, cattle remained in the barnyard instead of huddling by the barn door waiting for feeding, and a few sprouts of green grass appeared in the meadows.

The first field work of the season was to sow oats, timothy, and other small grasses before the soil was warm enough to plant corn. At Tarpleywick, the tenth of April was the time to start the oats; plowing and fitting of land for corn had to be finished by 10 May. Planting followed a strict rotational pattern: part of the oats would be seeded over corn stubble; the 100 acres of corn would be planted on land where the year before there had been 50 acres of timothy and oats, 25 of clover, 25 that had grown corn.

Plowing was unnecessary to sow oats and small grains; the ground was loosened with a corn cultivator and the seed distributed by a hand seeder which, carried by a single man on foot, broadcast the grain as the small crank was turned. Some skill was required to get an even distribution, particularly on a windy day. Some old-timers remembered when all seeding had been done by hand, just as it had been done in Bibical times, and just as it has been depicted in the somber pastoral paintings of Millet. By the 1880s some innovators like Tarpley Taylor experimented with an endgate seeder, a box-like machine whose gears were attached to the rear wheels of a wagon so that as horses pulled it across the fields, seed was whirled out over a space a dozen feet wide. The Stadtfelds were using a hand-seeder as late as the 1920s. As soon as the grain was on the ground, horses pulled a harrow crosswise over the field to cover it. In Civil War days a harrow was a simple A-shaped frame with ten-inch nail-like teeth attached. By Henry Taylor's time, this had been replaced with a section harrow, a lattice-work device in three sections, with nine bars of five or six teeth each.

Planting and cultivating corn were the most demanding tasks on the farm. First the land had to be plowed. Henry Taylor used a three-horse walking plow with a single share; his father, always on the lookout for labor saving devices, bought a sulky turning plow—meaning one could ride it—made of iron except for the tongue and neck yoke. Three horses pulled it. Some creative technology went into improving the tedious task of corn planting. By the old method, a field had first to be marked off in symetrical squares, 42" X 42". This was done with a horse-drawn marker that followed as straight a line as possible across the width, then across the breadth, of the acreage. Then, at the intersections, seeds would be planted with a hoe or, more efficiently, with a hand-planter that looked and worked like a bellows: pressed close down into the soil, the seeds dropped through when it was opened; then as the farmer withdrew the planter, he would step to the next

(Smithsonian Institution Photo No. 64728)

Corn Cultivator. The high wheels straddled the rows of growing corn.

---

mark, closing the hole behind him with a sweep of his right foot. A horse-drawn mechanical corn planter, introduced in the 1870s, made it necessary to mark the field in only one direction. Then, when the planter traversed the field at right angles to the lines, the pushing of a lever back and forth dropped the seed from two boxes, 42 inches apart. In front of the iron wheels, a pointed shoe, tapered at the front, opened the soil for the seed. The two rear wheels were concave, so that as they passed they pressed the soil back toward the center. An innovation ten years later eliminated the lever. A thin wire with tiny knots, 42 inches apart, was stretched tight and straight all the way across the field and wound into an eye on the planter. As the horses pulled the planter, the balls on the wire triggered a release and dropped seeds at the required intervals.

CULTIVATING CORN.

(Smithsonian Institution Photo No. 45230-D)

Cultivating corn, one of the most arduous tasks on the
traditional farm.

(Smithsonian Institution Photo No. 61682-D)

Plowing, Russell County, Kansas.

Rows of corn that were straight in both directions were the mark of a good farmer; they facilitated the tiresome task of keeping the shoots of corn free of the prolific weeds. Sometimes the process had to be repeated five times before the knee-high corn finally overtook its fast growing competitors. The corn cultivator in all its progressing forms was an ingenious instrument, and an operator had to be alert and skillful. Originally, corn was cultivated with a single moldboard plow that dug furrows in both directions across the growing field, passing as close to the tender shoots as possible without burying them under a mound of dirt. The improved tongued cultivator, in use by the 1880s, had an iron frame shaped like an arch, which permitted it to straddle a row of growing corn three feet high. On each side, mounted behind the two bicycle-sized wheels, were double shovel cultivators. With some fancy footwork and a cooperative team of horses, one in front of each wheel, a farmer could straddle a row of corn, manipulate one of the double shovels with each hand, and thus cultivate both sides of the row at the same time. The principle didn't change when Ford and Farmall came out with their little tractors, introduced in the 1920s. The double-shovel corn cultivator was spread-eagled in front of the tractor; the single narrow front wheel and the widely separated big back wheels were designed to straddle corn rows. Once a tractor could cultivate corn, horses were no longer needed on midwestern farms. Nowadays, although technology developed a big eight-row cultivator pushed by a huge tractor, many corn growers seldom cultivate at all. Instead, chemical weed killers do the job.

When May arrived, farmers kept a wary eye on the weather. With too much rain, the pesky buck weed thrived in the cornfields and cultivators stuck in the muddy soil; with too little rainfall, the oats and timothy dried to a yellow color, and young corn plants barely pushed through the hard dry clay. Following corn planting, a few days were set aside for sheepshearing. After that the corn had to be cultivated for the first time.

(Smithsonian Institution Photo No. 45951-A)

Corn Planter. The two boxes containing seeds were 42 inches apart. The trip lever at the left dropped the seeds at marked spots on the plowed field.

Early June, still before the corn was finally laid by, was the time for harvesting clover hay. The mixed clover, timothy, and oats could wait for the corn. (On the plains early summer was the time for the wheat harvest.) The early settlers cut hay with a scythe. Once part of a field was cut, the heavy bundles were tossed with a pitchfork so they would dry evenly. Then the hay was raked and put into haycocks to cure. After a few weeks it was hauled up the ramp into the barn, and men built brawny muscles lifting the heavy loads with pitchforks into the overhead mow.

McCormick's famous combination mower and reaper set off a chain of innovations that substituted animal power and then motor power for the hard work men had done for centuries. The horse-drawn mower was simple enough:

mounted on two wheels, with a tongue out front, a sharp four-foot sickle-type cutter bar protruded to the right. Honed on the grindstone, its razor sharp edge trimmed off the hay to the desired height as the horses pulled it across the field. It could cut six acres in a ten-hour day.[17] A tractor mower, operating on much the same principle, could, by the 1940s, cut twenty-five acres a day with its seven-foot cutter bar. A hay rake looked like a big garden rake with long curved tongs. The mowed grass was left lying until it cured; then the rake, drawn by two horses, would gather it into windrows, and two men followed along to pitch the hay onto the big lumbering hayrick, with its high sideboards, which delivered it to the barn. The heavy work of lifting hay was alleviated when barns were equipped with tracks along the inner roof to which a horse-drawn hayfork could be attached. A huge grapple fork would be clamped around the hay in the wagon; one horse, spurred often by a small boy, could hoist the load to the crest of the barn, where it was carried along the track and dropped at the appropriate spot in the mow. Another task was eliminated when an angled hay-loader was attached to the back of the wagon. This raker-bar loader eliminated the work of two men; it had reciprocating bars with flexible teeth that eased the raked hay from the windrows up the sloping ramp and into the hayrick where a farm lad with a pitchfork evened out the heaping load.

When timothy and oats were cut for seed or when wheat was being harvested, bringing in the grain was a more complicated task. Innovation was more rapid here, because ripe grain was a vulnerable crop—a day too long in the fields and it might be beaten down by heavy rain or pulverized by hail. For reaping, a longer cutter bar with a bearded sickle and a wheel at the end was used. Behind the cutter bar, a big reel, spinning as the horses moved along, knocked the cut grain onto a platform just behind where the driver rode. A rake, synchronized with the reel, made a circular motion across the platform and pushed the bundle of grain off onto the ground. In 1882 Tarpley Taylor bought a new self-bind-

Reaping the grain. The cut grain was knocked onto the
platform behind the driver.

ing reaping machine. It did everything the older McCormick could, but in addition it wrapped the grain in a bundle
and tied it with a knot before dropping it.

With the seed grain cut and lying in the field, it was time
for summer threshing, a peak period on the rural calendar.
Until the 1890s, threshing was by horsepower; then the big
machines were converted to steampower, and the noisy
"put-put" of their engines proclaimed the presence of
threshers for miles across the countryside. Most threshing
machines were owned cooperatively, the joint owners making up the work crew also. Some of the hulking monsters
were run by itinerants who hired out the machine and the
men to run it for the three or four days a farm such as
Tarpleywick required. Whether the power came from the
team of five horses who circled the machine, activating a
series of graduated gears to high speed, or from the long
belt that ran to the steam engine, or, in later years, was
hitched to a tractor, the core of the machine was the separa-

(Courtesy USDA)

Threshing day. Power was provided by the steam driven tractor.

---

tor. It consisted of a cylinder, which whipped the seed from the straw, and the shakers and riddles, which separated straw and chaff from the seeds. To do the threshing required a sizeable crew: four or five men with wagons to bring the bundles to the separator; two men in the field to continuously load the assembly line of wagons; a worker to cut the bonds when the bundles were dropped on the feeding table; two skilled men who alternated feeding loose bundles into the machine's cylinder; a man to measure the grain as it poured out, and to sack it if it was timothy or wheat, or put it on the wagon box if it was oats. Two or three more men with forks pitched away the growing straw pile; another carried the threshed grain to the storage bins. In a cooperative venture, the men and boys might participate in six or seven threshings in a couple of summer weeks. Noontime dinner for threshers was an American folk custom.

After threshing was finished, the seasonal pace slackened a bit. Perhaps there was time for a brief vacation—that is, unless the work that was neglected during the busy summer days hadn't piled up too much. Waste had probably accumulated around the barns and sheep sheds—now was the time to clean them out for fall and distribute manure on the ground that would be plowed for corn the following spring.

Shorter days and the maples slowly turning red and yellow meant not only autumn but cornhusking time. It was an arduous job that could last from mid-October until late November. Corn was usually husked from standing stalks, as at Tarpleywick. On other midwestern farms corn was cut and shocked in the field and then hauled to the barnyard for husking. If a field husker was working alone, his wagon was equipped with a two- or three-foot bangboard on the far side, for the corn was tossed into the wagon without watching, and the horses controlled by vocal commands alone. Equipped with a peg or husking gloves with a peg attached, he would take each ear out of its husk and loosen it from its stem in about three quick motions. One farmer could do two rows at a time; if three worked, two did the double rows on both sides of the wagon, and a third followed behind to complete the row the wagon straddled. A skilled hand could husk fifty-five bushels in a day.

With cornhusking over, the field work for the year was done. Some say the long winter nights and short days were a time for reflection on the farm: time for reflection once hog butchering was done, firewood cut and split, soap made, fences mended, needed repairs to sheds and buildings finished, and the unceasing round of daily chores completed. When March came the snow began to melt. The cattle stopped huddling by the barn door, waiting to be fed. A few sprouts of green grass appeared in the meadows.

Notes

1. Everett M. Rogers, *Diffusion of Innovations* (New York: Free Press of Glencoe, 1962). This valuable synthetic and summary work has been substantially updated and retitled: Everett M. Rogers with F. Floyd Shoemaker, *Diffusion of Innovation. A Cross Cultural Approach,* 2d ed. (New York: Free Press, 1971).
2. James J. Flink, *America Adopts the Automobile, 1895–1910* (Cambridge, Mass.: M.I.T. Press, 1970), pp. 67, 84.
3. Wayne D. Rasmussen, "The Impact of Technological Change on American Agriculture, 1862–1962," *Journal of Economic History* 22 (December 1962): 578–82. For a comparative and corroborating interpretation, see G. E. Mingay, "The Agricultural Revolution in English History: A Reconsideration," in British Agricultural History Society, *Essays in Agrarian History,* 2 vols. (New York: Augustus M. Kelley, 1968), 2: 11–27.
4. Rasmussen, "Impact of Technological Change," pp. 587–88; Kenneth L. Robinson, "Commodity Policies and Programs," *USDA Yearbook, 1970,* p. 123.
5. Henry C. Taylor, *Tarpleywick: A Century of Iowa Farming* (Ames: Iowa State University Press, 1970); Curtis K. Stadtfeld, *From The Land and Back* (New York: Charles Scribners' Sons, 1972). I shall omit page references except for direct quotations. Dr. Taylor, for many years chairman of the Department of Agricultural Economics at University of Wisconsin, completed this, his final book, shortly before his death in 1969 at the age of ninety-six. Another account which would supplement the description of traditional farming given here is Wheeler McMillen, *Ohio Farm* (Columbus: Ohio State University Press, 1974).

6. E. C. Johnson, "Agricultural Credit," *USDA Yearbook, 1940,* p. 740; Everett M. Rogers, *Social Change in Rural Society* (New York: Appleton-Century-Crofts, 1960), p. 199. Some of the reasons I do not include a figure for the 1970s are suggested in chapter 1 and will be discussed in greater detail in the following chapter.

7. The principal way land could be obtained without a mortgage was through inheritance. In some cases—for example, the Stadtfelds—land was purchased from parents and the seller was also the mortgage holder.

8. Allan G. Bogue, *From Prairie to Cornbelt,* (Chicago: Quadrangle Books, 1968 [1963], p. 180.

9. Ibid., pp. 173, 177–79.

10. John L. Shover, *Cornbelt Rebellion: The Farmers' Holiday Association* (Urbana: University of Illinois Press, 1965), p. 13.

11. Ibid., p. 16; Bogue, *From Prairie to Cornbelt,* p. 179.

12. Tarpley Taylor listed the total value of his farm implements and machinery in 1870 and 1880 at about $240.

13. For an extensive discussion of cattle raising in Iowa and Illinois, see Bogue, *From Prairie to Cornbelt,* chap. 5.

14. The quaint names refer to areas where allegedly the breed was initiated: the Poland China supposedly from Canton, China; the Chester White from Chester, Pennsylvania. Tracing the origins of animal breeds is as complex as completing a family genealogy, and apparently some devotees pursue it with the same dedication.

15. For example, Taylor's description of hog killing day (pp. 37–38) is almost identical to that of Stadtfeld's (pp. 13–16).

16. Stadtfeld, *From the Land and Back,* p. 108.

17. R. B. Gray, "Equipment for Making Hay," *USDA Yearbook, 1948,* p. 168.

PART 2

THE GREAT DISJUNCTURE
Since 1945

CHAPTER FIVE

Technology Takes Over

*Technology is based on scientific discovery, chance
discoveries, experience, invention, ingenuity, hard
work and motivation. Men seek profit; they seek recognition of their peers for their achievements; they seek
opportunities for themselves, their families, their
communities. They seek to reduce the burden of stoop
labor. They seek the satisfaction of service.*

*And finally, farmers, scientists, industrialists, ev-
eryone seeks to satisfy an insatiable curiosity. Jules
Verne said, "What the mind of men can imagine, some
man will do."*

—T. C. Byerly, in *Contours of Change*

*My belief is that science is to wreck us, and that we are
like monkeys monkeying with a loaded shell; we don't
in the least know or care where our practically infi-
nite energies come from or will bring us to.*

—Henry Adams to Brooks Adams, 10 August 1902, in
Henry Adams and His Friends.

The coming of a new day in the countryside throughout the
world has traditionally been heralded by the familiar cry of
the cock. Strange, then, that the sound is seldom heard
among the farms and villages of the Delmarva Peninsula
(Delaware, Maryland, and Virginia), because this is one of

the greatest poultry producing areas in the world. About twenty corporations, among them Kane-Miller, Tyson, Ralston-Purina, and Pillsbury, have transformed the farm wife's source of pin money into the most integrated and mechanized industry of any engaged in food production. About 95 percent of broilers and most eggs marketed today are produced in the factories of these corporations or by farmers under contract to one of them.

The process by which a technological revolution was achieved in poultry raising provides a good model for sorting out and identifying the component elements in the greater process of change that, by the mid-seventies, has eliminated all but a few vestigial remains of the traditional farming that went on at Tarpleywick or the Stadtfeld's farm.

It all began with scientific investigation. The first object of interest was the article produced—in this case that most humble of winged creatures, the chicken. The federal government had an important role. Department of Agriculture scientists in the 1930s began attempts to inbreed chickens in the quest for better egg-producing hybrids. A National Poultry Improvement Plan was inaugurated in 1935 to enhance production and marketing qualities through nationwide performance testing. Poultry breeders thus were able to compare different stocks in terms of rate of gain in live weight, efficiency in food utilization, and the attractiveness of the carcass for marketing. The result was that chickens were bred like corn: a variety of crossbreeds, incrossbreeds, strains, and cross-strains systematically chosen to incorporate desirable production characteristics and gain hybrid vigor. Simultaneous research sought a more nutritive diet, employing newly discovered vitamins such as B_{12} and D. By 1950, broilers were being produced that yielded one pound of weight for every three pounds of grain consumed; a gain of 40 percent over traditional farm performance. By 1970, this feed efficiency ratio had been reduced to 1.8. When chickens were marketed live, barred feathers were a mark of quality, but when sold dressed the black pin feathers blemished the appearance. What was needed was a white bird that grew up fast and used feed with high efficiency. Galvanized in the late forties by the compelling slogan "chicken of tomorrow," government geneticists, producers, and processors pitched in. Consumers have that chicken of tomorrow—today.[1]

The next step was to modernize the production process. Commercial production of broilers for meat consisted of a series of stages: development of breeding stocks, hatching eggs, manufacturing feed, maturing, processing, and marketing. Some enterprising innovators saw the possibility of combining some of these: producers began to specialize in poultry raising.

One method was to create poultry factories where chickens would be hermetically confined to a controlled feeding area and fed only prescribed diets of least-cost, high efficiency rations, with antibiotics added. Since the price of ingredients for feeding has been changing impulsively in the 1970s, poultry nutritionists now use a computer to determine the best formula. Confined flocks of thousands of laying hens became common; corporations, such as those with installations on the Delmarva Peninsula, hatched literally millions of chicks daily to prepare for the broiler market. One operator can service sixty thousand birds: in a high rise egg factory he may pass above the cackling flock on a traveling platform, the wheels riding along pipes that convey feed to the caged occupants.

In the pioneer days of the broiler industry each step in the production process was controlled by an independent entrepreneur. Gradually, vertical integration brought all of the stages under the control of a single management, often the feed producer. In this way, production could be synchronized and the produce even marketed to specification. Manufacturers of frozen dinners or of crispy take home chicken required broilers within a definite weight range in order to assure that portions would be equal.[2] Fifty times as many broilers were produced in 1967 as in 1935. Assembly line production cut the price of chicken for consumers so it was

(Courtesy USDA)

In a high-rise egg factory an operator passes above the flock on a traveling platform. He can service 60,000 birds.

no longer a luxury item reserved for Sunday dinner. Poultry consumption in the United States had been stabilized at about sixteen pounds per person annually, from 1910 to 1940; in the early seventies, it was fifty pounds per person.

A related method of integration is contract chicken production. Producer corporations loan independent farmers money to build a chicken shed, and provide him with the corporation's special feed to be supplied to chicks who are hatched in the corporation's incubators. When the birds are matured to market specifications they are removed to the corporation's processing plant, slaughtered, packaged, then shipped off to Colonel Sanders or the supermarket. A farmer-caretaker in 1972 was paid fifty dollars for every 1,000 chickens he raised.[3]

The smooth passage of broilers from egg to dinner table has been interrupted several times by a variable that did not figure in the careful calculations of the integrators. The producers under contract, once small independent farmers, were, in their view, being exploited economically by those who owned their means of production, controlled the capital, and programmed the productive process. The fifty dollar fee was not self-renewing: when a new brood of chicks was delivered to the contracting farmer, corporations might adjust the fee consonant with the market price of chickens. In 1972, chicken farmers on the Delmarva Peninsula threatened court action when broiler corporations proposed cutting growing fees in half. In 1970 a Department of Agriculture study estimated that poultry growers were working at an average wage of minus fourteen cents hourly. That year a group of chicken raisers in nine counties in northern Alabama organized a chapter of the National Farmers' Organization (a midwestern group that had staged a series of withholding actions in an attempt to gain collective bargaining agreements with processors of livestock and milk) and called a strike. "Us folks in the chicken business are the only slaves left in the country," Mr. Crawford Smith, one of the local organizers of the strike effort, declared. "Ralston-Purina even tells me what kind of chicken house I got to have. They call all the shots—they give you a contract for as many or as few chickens as they want and then they pay you whatever they want." For a few weeks, pickets marched up and down in front of the local processor's office. Mr. Smith and his associates could have refused, of course, to sign contracts, but payments on the corporation-financed chicken house still had to be made. The broiler firms insisted that their contracts aided the farmers by protecting them from fluctuating market prices; they refused any negotiations. The picket lines and the strike lasted only a few weeks.[4]

To bring some kind of order and synthesis to the complex changes in the nature of farming taking place, Everett M. Rogers, a rural sociologist, specified the major trends and shifts as follows:

1. American farms are increasingly specialized.
2. American farming is not only becoming more specialized, it is also becoming more capitalized.
3. It is characterized by greater efficiency and productivity.
4. American farms are increasing in size.
5. The functions of farming are changing; there is a trend from the economic function of production to the social functions of residence, subsistence, and security.
6. American farming is increasingly interdependent with foreign markets.
7. Interdependence between industrial employment and farming is increasing: there is a marked increase in part-time farming.
8. One of the most important changes in the nature of farming is the increasing interdependence of farmers upon agriculture-related industry.... A new term—agribusiness[5]—is now applied to the total agricultural economy. [It] includes the manufacture and distribution of farm supplies plus the processing, handling, merchandising, and marketing of food and agricultural products plus farming itself.[6]

We have already anticipated many of these trends and shifts. While it is useful to categorize and organize them, they are obviously intricately related. For example, specialization can take place only when there is a sizeable market and a means to transport the commodity produced to its furthest perimeters at reasonable cost; specialization also bespeaks efficiency, and that requires mechanization. Investments in machinery means expanding enough to obtain maximum unit costs on capital investments in equipment. The necessity for effective capital generating and credit mechanisms is obvious.

The thrust of social change in American agriculture, which has very nearly run its course, is toward integrated agribusinesses, which now utilize scientific research and advanced technology over a whole range of productive activities to minimize production costs, and large-scale advertising to stimulate consumer demand. Raw materials are being gathered from decentralized production stations, which we used to call farms, transported to food manufacturing plants, converted into marketable products, and merchandised through an intricate distribution network.

Complex credit devices generate the capital to sustain the whole operation.

The harbinger of the technological revolution that set in motion the process that has led to modern agribusiness was the tractor. Sparingly used before World War I, tractors on farms multiplied in the twenties and thirties, and the velocity of adoption would have been greater had it not been for the depression. In 1930 about 800,000 were in use, and the number doubled by 1939. In that year, there were still more than 15 million horses, mules, and colts on the nation's farms—by 1959 they were so few the Census of Agriculture stopped counting them.[7] The original tractors were tank-like contraptions of iron and steel, usable only for heavy draft work. Improvements during the thirties replaced the metal wheels with rubber tires, and compact models like the Fordson were developed for use on small farms. Horse-drawn implements (such as the hay-loader and reaper) were quickly and easily modified to its use. Plowing, discing, harrowing, mowing, and, finally, cultivating could all be done by tractor. The big general purpose farm tractor led to the development of the combine, an innovation in the grain fields as important as the McCormick reaper. One machine integrated all the muscle work and cumbersome mechanics that had gone into threshing and transferred the whole operation into the field. Corn and cotton pickers soon followed; tractor power loaded forage into silos and hay into the mow.[8] By 1966, 5.5 million tractors of varying types and sizes were traversing the fields and lifting the loads on American farms; models with air-conditioning and radios, power brakes and steering, and hydraulic lifts were available. Concomitantly, expenditures for power and repairs of equipment increased six times over between 1935 and 1967.

While the tractor was slowly perpetrating a mechanical revolution, scientists of the U.S. Department of Agriculture and those in laboratories on university campuses were sowing the seeds of a takeoff that would change the grains in the fields and the ways they had been planted and culti-

(Smithsonian Institution Photo No. 60690)

Fordson Tractor, 1917.

---

vated for centuries. The impact of the scientists' discoveries
has been felt almost entirely since the end of World War II.

The first major genetic innovation was the development
of hybrid seed corn. Parent varieties with sturdy stocks
were crossed with those of high yield and with others resistant to various plant diseases and insect pests. Output per
acre could be increased 20 to 25 percent by planting hybrids
rather than the usual open-pollinated variety; still higher
yields could be attained if special fertilizers and hybrids
adapted to particular regional conditions were used. Adoption of hybrid seed corn proceeded slowly at first. Seed had
to be purchased each year, since hybrids are not self-
generating; this was another out-of-pocket drain on the
farm family budget. Early adopters soon demonstrated the
innovation's profitability: increased income from greater
productivity more than offset any added costs.[9] Virtually all
corn grown today is of the hybrid variety.

Meanwhile, collateral scientific research was developing other new hybrids. Around 1960 hybrid grain sorghum was introduced. A few years later it was almost universally adopted, and yields increased by 25 percent. The development of new wheat varieties was a greater challenge; dramatic breakthroughs, after years of research by the American scientist Dr. Norman Borlaug, working from field laboratories in Mexico, spurred the Green Revolution that swept across much of the cultivated world in the late sixties. With the disappearance of horses, less acreage was needed for oats; much of it was transferred to what was to become the United States' most rapidly expanding and most profitable field crop: soybeans. Production increased fourfold between 1950 and 1972. Boosting output per acre was a more difficult scientific problem than for corn or grain sorghum. Since it is a legume with a built-in nitrogen supply, the soybean is not very responsive to the nitrogen fertilizers that are the most widely used on American croplands. Close to 85 percent of the increase in soybean production has come from expanding the acreage devoted to it. Science did discover ample and profitable uses for the plant: it provides the most nutritious animal feed available, and new developments presage that human beings will be eating a lot of it soon.

New hybrids alone were not sufficient to obtain higher yields from the land. Even the best of them could not thrive on depleted soil, and they remained vulnerable to weed and insect pests. Chemical nutrients, particularly those containing nitrogen, have replaced manure as fertilizer, and the old system of three-year crop rotation in the cornfields is no longer practiced. Virtually unknown on farms before 1940, chemical soil additives were applied that year at the rate of about seven pounds per acre. This doubled to fourteen pounds in 1950, and seventy pounds in 1970. Chemical weed killers were introduced in the late forties; hand-hoeing, long the tiresome summer occupation of the cotton sharecropper, and the arduous corn cultivation on midwestern farms are no longer necessary. About a quarter of all farms were treated with insecticides in 1964. These were entirely chemical products that were applied mechanically or by the five thousand airplanes that were employed that year in contract crop dusting programs. Some of the successful experiments to develop substitutes for environmentally dangerous nonselective pesticides (compounds that are toxic to a wide variety of organisms) are ingenious and even a bit bizarre. Sex attractants, simulating the chemical processes in a target insect, lure unsuspecting winged or crawling victims to their annihilation. Sterile male screwworm flies are dropped by plane monthly along the Mexican border; since the female mates only once, and the probability is that it will be with a sterile male, screwworm infestation has markedly declined.[10]

The end result has been one of those quantum leaps in output that technologists love to celebrate. Take corn, for example. Before World War II, it was grown in a three-year rotational cycle in 42-inch rows and fertilized with manure; 10,000 seeds were planted on each acre, and the average yield was 38 bushels. Today growers fertilize with 150 pounds of nitrogen, plant 25,000 hybrid seeds on each acre in 20-inch rows, control pests with herbicides and insecticides, and obtain yields averaging 90 to 100 bushels for each acre.[11]

Unfortunately, the balance sheet isn't complete, when only the dramatic increases in production are entered. Lavish use of nutrients increases soil productivity, but at the cost of potential long-range soil deterioration and pollution of water supplies. A leading ecologist asserts: ". . . some of the most serious environmental failures can be traced to the technological transformation of the United States farm."[12] Nitrogen is a particular problem. It is produced naturally in soils by microbial action; most is taken up by growing plants, and in the traditional farm cycle was partially replaced by return of plant debris and animal wastes to the soil and by fixation in the soil of nitrogen from the air. (This is not to argue there was no soil deterioration on traditional farms.) If quantities of nitrogen are artifically applied in excess of what plants extract, residues can be leached from the surface soil and, since nitrates are mobile, find their way into streams, lakes, or the nearest city's water supply. There is another potential debit item. Some ecologists hypothesize that continuous and intensive use of nitrogen fertilizer destroys the natural population of nitrogen-fixing bacteria in the soil; once the artificial product has been generously applied over a long period it will be impossible to go back to the natural process.

In 1970 about twice as much fertilizer was being dumped on fields than would be required if all crops received the applications recommended by state agricultural experiment stations. Inorganic nitrogen is so effective a growth stimulant that heavy applications can push corn outputs per acre up above the 100 bushel mark. Until a few years ago, the cost of the fertilizer was cheap. That is why, for example, Illinois farmers increased applications from 10,-000 tons in 1945 to about 600,000 in 1966. In 1958, 100,000 tons brought an acreage yield of 70 bushels; the application of 400,000 tons in 1965 obtained an acreage yield of about 93 bushels. The law of diminishing returns was operating: 300,000 tons of added nitrogen brought only 23 bushels of increased yield. Since 80 bushels was the economic break-even point for growers, and fertilizer costs at that time were about $20 for each acre, efficiency of use and long-term consequences were of little concern in the ruthless quest for profit.[13] Agricultural scientists rested content for many years with the spectacular production increases their researches had wrought. In the last few years their technologic sanguinariness has markedly diminished.

While genetic research has been most dramatic in botanical fields, success in technological tampering with the breeds and sexes of livestock appears imminent. It has already taken place in the poultry industry. Computer technology has facilitated the necessary performance testing for large livestock populations. Most swine are artificially bred now. Artificial insemination is used widely in the dairy population; sperm of cattle is frozen and preserved, vastly expanding the "services" of a superior sire. So called hybrid vigor—that is, longer survival, more rapid growth, better feed utilization—has been shown to produce a 15 to 20 percent advantage over straight-bred offspring of the same species. Future research promises scientifically induced multiple births for cows and increased litters for pigs; the agenda also includes programming the sex of livestock so that females would be born only from parents from which herd replacements would be desired; all other offspring would be faster growing males that would grow up someday to be a pork chop or a sirloin.[14]

Like the proverbial rolling stone phenomena, the velocity of agricultural innovation increased with breathtaking rapidity after 1945. Hours of labor for the 4 percent of the nation's workers still employed full time in agriculture remain long: 53.9 hours in 1973 compared to 43.1 for nonfarm workers. Productivity gains have been truly extraordinary. Since 1948, output per man-hour has quadrupled in agriculture but only doubled in the nonfarm sector. This increase was due primarily to technological innovations. Between 1950 and 1972, total lands used for crops decreased by 11 percent, but the index of crop production per acre (1965=100) increased from 69 in 1950 to 114 in 1972.[15]

The modern cotton producing operations in the Mississippi delta or east Texas are one example. The traditional methods of "fitting the land" for cotton, harvesting, and cultivating were not too different from those used for corn growing at Tarpleywick in the 1890s. In 1948, 140 man-hours were required to produce one bale of cotton, in 1968 only 25.

The planter begins the season by purchasing seed from certified producers: it comes graded and coated with chemicals to combat against seedling diseases. Then the stalks from last year's growth are removed from the fields by high-speed cutters that look like giant lawnmowers; they chop the old stalks into tiny particles that can easily be plowed under. In the same single operation, fertilizer may be applied and a preplanting herbicide incorporated into

(Courtesy USDA)

A six-row chisel planter which can be used either for corn or cotton.

---

the soil. During the season, four different types of herbicide
—preplanting, preemergence, postemergence, and "lay by"
—are applied. A huge tractor plows the soil deep or shallow,
depending upon the quality of the acreage being tilled.
Rows are automatically bedded and shaped into smooth,
uniform surfaces, ready for the big eight-row precision
planter that can seed one hundred acres in a single day. The
time for planting is determined not by tradition or guesswork but on the basis of advice by scientists, engineers, and
weather forecasters. The cockpit of a planting tractor re-
sembles that of an airliner: a seedbed conditioning tool is
mounted out front, and the planter may be equipped with
applicators for fungicide, insecticide, and herbicide. Conventional weed killers are applied in four or five steps; conventional sweep-type plows may cultivate between the

(Courtesy USDA)

A spindle-type cotton harvester.

rows once or twice during the growing season, applying pesticide simultaneously. Techniques such as these have helped raise the average acreage yields for upland cotton from three hundred pounds in 1948 to more than five hundred in 1968.[16]

Ninety-six percent of the cotton crop was harvested mechanically in 1969, compared to less than 10 percent in 1949. The most widely used method was the spindle-type harvester, from which hundreds of rotating spindles entered the cotton plant and removed the lint and seed from the burs, much the same way a hand picker used to do it. Stripping, a cheaper means, removes in one operation burs, bolls, leaves, and stems, but it can be used only where plants grow taller than three feet. Chemical defoliants, applied in advance, decrease the leaf and stem trash picked up by the picker or stripper. At first, machine-harvested cotton sold

(Courtesy USDA)

A stripper-type cotton harvester.

for twenty-five dollars a bale less than that which was hand picked because cotton gins had difficulty processing and drying the moist and trash-clogged raw material. A lint cleaner was added to remove "pin and pepper" residues, and a "stick and green leaf" machine is standard equipment now. Still, Eli Whitney's venerable innovation, nearly a century and a half old now, was the bottleneck in the operation. Developments since 1958 have produced a new high-capacity gin stand that separates the lint from the seed more efficiently. Older 80-saw stands might process twenty bales in an hour; the new stands, with as many as 120 saws, approach a capacity of thirty bales. The speed-up achieved by the high capacity gin stand rendered obsolete the older method of unloading from conveyance to mill by means of a vacuum tube; four to six men were needed to handle the cotton in the gin yard. Now a truck dumps the cotton into a pit and it is gulped automatically into the gin.[17] It is, therefore, not surprising that small producers and processors have been driven from the field and cotton is disappearing as a crop in the marginal acreages of the Southeast Piedmont.

Automation has eliminated the back-breaking labor once required to get in the hay. Pitchforks rust in the toolshed, and hay-loaders and rakes stand abandoned in the field or have long since been pulverized by the junk dealer. Man-hours required to produce a ton of hay have been reduced to less than a third of that required in 1940.

Tractor-propelled cutter bars, seven feet long, mow the clover or timothy, and self-propelled units with twelve- or sixteen-foot bars are often used over large acreages. Faster and more uniform field drying is facilitated by conditioners and cutters attached to the tractor's power unit. Cut hay is squeezed between pairs of heavy rollers that mash the stem and thicker parts, and then the hay is dropped back onto the stubble in a swathe or in loose windrows.

If long, loose hay is needed for immediate feeding, and the climate is dry enough to assure a low moisture content, huge tractor-mounted buck rakes, like giant pitchforks, hoist up the hay from the windrows. The rake is propelled by a tractor's hydraulic system and dumps the hay into portable cages. Specially designed trailers can move the cages around the fields. One man with a tractor can perform the whole operation.

Most hay nowadays is marketed off the farm, so it must be baled, cubed, or made into pellets that can be shipped easily and facilitate feeding livestock. Baled hay accounts for about 80 percent of total production. An automatic baler, manned by one driver, packages up to twenty tons in an hour, ties the bales, and can be adjusted to vary the size and density of the bale. A bale thrower, attached behind, tosses the big bundles into a wagon. Self-unloading wagons, vertical elevators, and mow conveyors allow a single operator to bale, load, unload, and store the hay. Random stacking of bales wastes storage space, but cavernous haymows of barns built fifty years ago have more than enough room.

Cubing and wafering machines can be used only in low rainfall areas of the West, since moisture content must be no more than a low 10 percent. These machines compress the hay tightly into tiny units, 1¼" X 1¼" in cross section—convenient "bite-sized pieces," for cows. Where hay pellets are produced (in more humid areas), hay must first pass through a dehydrator. The ripe timothy or clover is normally taken from the fields by a forage harvester; it may have a big five to ten ton self-unloading bin attached, eliminating the need for a separate tractor or truck to follow the harvester. After drying, the hay is ground through a hammer mill and steam and water are added to produce a mixture that can be made into pellets; the mixture is then forced through a die by rollers, and knives slash it to desired lengths as the material is pushed out of the dye. The most popular pellets are about ¼ inch in diameter. Those made from dehydrated material are used as feed supplements for poultry flocks; field cured pellets are an efficient way of supplying hay to cattle on feedlots.[18]

Production of beef cattle is the major farm enterprise in the United States. Income from it made up 26 percent of total cash receipts from marketing in 1973.[19] Science has yet to breed an improved steer. The big Herefords, the most popular breed, are still inefficient feed converters, since they consume 6 to 9 pounds of grain for each pound of live weight added (compared to 3.5 to 4 for hogs, 1.8 for chickens). Increased production of beef has come from raising more cattle, not from technological changes in the stock. The number of all other livestock on farms (hogs, sheep, laying hens, milk cows) has decreased since 1945. Consumer demand has spurred the expansion of this large and inefficient conversion of grains and hay into steaks and hamburger. In economic vernacular, beef is "status" meat, and, as the United States has grown affluent, beef consumption has nearly doubled, from 60 pounds per person each year in 1950 to 116 in 1972.

Beef production is a different enterprise than it was in the days when cattle were fattened on midwestern farms on diets of hay and corn for sale in the stockyards of St. Paul or Chicago. The feeding process was the one point in the cycle from farm or ranch to dinner table where more efficient procedures could allow quality control and cut costs. Nowadays, cattle from the open ranges on the Great Plains or the Southwest are shipped to giant feedlots where they are fed specially prepared diets, through automated bins, before they are marketed. Capacities of feedlots range from less than one thousand to over one hundred thousand. When they arrive at the feedlot, cattle, like little boys arriving at summer camp, are vaccinated for various diseases, sprayed, in order to control external parasites, and fed antibiotics. They are rapidly conditioned to low roughage and high-concentrate grain rations. The diet includes urea, a synthetic chemical compound containing 45 percent nitrogen. A pound of it should yield 2.8 pounds of protein in steers; in 1969, five hundred thousand tons of urea were used. Feedlots draw heavily upon valuable, high-nutrient feed grains—corn, soybeans, and the like—and reduce even more the feed conversion ratio: 10 pounds of grain in the feedlot is needed for every pound of live weight added. The length of time cattle will remain on finishing rations in the feedlot depends upon the weight of the animal upon arriving and the desired slaughter weight: the average is about 150 days. The largest feedlots, often owned by feed producers and processing companies, but some by supermarket chains, are maintained at full capacity throughout the year. As one herd is marketed, a new one replaces it. In 1966 more than 10 million cattle, about half the nation's beef production, passed through feedlots on the way to slaughter. In 1968, the 1 percent of the feedlots that have a capacity greater than 1,000 fed 47 percent of the cattle marketed.[20] In 1974, as costs of feed grains reached unprecedented highs, a greater portion of the cattle were held on farms and ranches, and fed pasturage. The result produced beef of somewhat lower quality, although Department of Agriculture spokesmen hastened to assure consumers that there was no taste differential. In order to reduce the record-high expenses of cattle feeding in 1974, suggestions were made to change grading procedures and extend the sale of "boxed beef"—meat cut and prepared in retail portions entirely at the centralized processing plant.[21]

Efficient feeding and quality control come at a price. In 1969, the nation's 107 million cattle, 57 million hogs, 21 million sheep, and 2.1 billion chickens produced approximately ten times more biological waste than the entire human population.[22] Feedlots alone produce more organic waste (maintaining proper scientific euphemisms) than the total sewage from all U.S. municipalities. Concentration of large numbers of cattle and chickens in a restricted area has created a disposal problem of gargantuan proportions. The natural rate of conversion of organic waste to humus is limited: in a feedlot, most nitrogenous waste turns soluble, as ammonia or nitrate. This is evaporated or leached into ground water, or rain may carry it to nearby surface waters. There are recorded instances where fish and cattle have been poisoned downstream from feeder lots.

Disposal was no problem on the traditional farm, where anything wasted was considered a loss: agronomists do not question the high value of manure as a soil conditioner and plant nutrient. Nevertheless, the cost alone of hauling manure from a feedlot is appreciable; and this does not take into account the cost of applying it to some farmer's fields. It is cheaper and easier to distribute nutrients of the same quality, and lesser quantity, out of commercial fertilizer bags.[23] Ecological zealots may take some sardonic delight in noting that, given the current rate of production, our civilization confronts the distinct possibility of being at some finite time in the future buried in excrement.

The capital and managerial requirements for a farm, even of average size, are roughly comparable to those of a small manufacturing plant. Given skyrocketing real estate values, the capital investment in land alone exceeded $125,-000 for an average operating unit in 1974.[24] To underwrite the cost of the technological revolution, the farm debt of $54.6 billion in 1969 was four times greater than the total debt in 1950. Between 1960 and 1968 gross capital expenditures for machinery and motor vehicles rose 82 percent. Production costs—fertilizer, equipment, hybrid seed—take 71 cents of every dollar of gross income. In the autumn of 1974, a farm equipment dealer in Suffolk County, New York, complained that a tractor that cost $2,000 fifteen years ago was priced at $16,000; and that fertilizer that once cost $40 a ton was selling at $100 a ton.[25]

A farm financial revolution has paralleled the one in technology. Farmer and landowner are no longer synonymous; the traditional onus against renting has disappeared. Capital committed to land has been tied down for all time; renting land on an annual basis frees capital for other uses, requires a smaller investment, and allows farmers to operate on a larger scale. Immense segments of the cornlands of the Middle West, the wheatfields on the plains, the cotton acreage of Texas and California, are not owned by the farmers who operate them. Cattle raisers in the West pay rent per head for grazing on private or public lands.

Few farms invest in costly equipment that is needed only a few days for specialized tasks. An efficient farm owns only the flexible machinery necessary for day to day operations: tractors and adaptable plowing, seeding, and tillage tools. Even so, the cost of these for a Corn Belt farmer could be as high as $30,000. Custom services are widely available to perform all the functions necessary for field crop production. It is theoretically possible for a farmer to act as a subcontractor, renting land, and arranging to have it planted, cultivated, and harvested, all the while remaining in his comfortable suburban home, intervening only to extract what profits remain at the end.

Livestock breeding herds traditionally have been financed by short term collateral mortgages, the herd and its increase being the collateral. Recently, dairy and beef cattle have sometimes been rented to farmers. One form of "tax farming," a popular occupation of individuals in high-income brackets, works through brokerage firms which invest their clients' abundant capital in buying animals and renting them to farmers. A farmer thus stocks his herd without a major financial commitment, and the new owner gains the tax advantage of treating income from breeding stock as a capital gain, with the resulting 50 percent reduction in tax cost.

Financing of the goods and services required for a year's production (fertilizer, seed, feed, labor, and so forth) is provided through several complicated means of obtaining production credit. Large-scale farmers do not buy their annual production needs with the earnings of the preceding year's crop; to do so would mean that capital would lay dormant during the slack winter season. Earnings are better put to work in other investment opportunities. Perhaps a producer will obtain a crop mortgage payable at harvest time, particularly if the commodity he raises commands a ready market, such as wheat, cotton, corn, or soybeans. In the cotton states, ginning companies, owned by merchandisers of cotton-lint fiber and cottonseed oil, extend crop mortgages to growers and sell the notes to commercial banks. Vendors of seeds, fertilizer, and insecticides frequently extend dealer credit, without interest charges, to farmer purchasers; the costs of delayed payment are included in the markup. Often the dealer-creditors apply the additives to the fields themselves, using their own equipment and expertise; this guarantees a good crop, insofar as this is possible, and, of course, helps assure repayment of the producer's obligation. Another form of production credit is the advance given to a producer by a shipper-packer or processor with whom the producer has signed a contract. Most broilers, vegetables for canning or freezing, oranges for frozen juice concentrates, and fresh vegetables are grown under contract arrangements. Producers are supplied necessary seed, chemicals, and even handy hints on how best to plant and harvest. A contracting firm may supply the farmer a loan if it is needed, and a contract is useful if the producer needs to borrow from the local bank. In the vegetable industry, the grower under contract is responsible only for bringing the crop to harvest. The processor takes over with the actual harvesting and then trims, grades, and packs the head lettuce, snapbeans, or broccoli for shipment. One type of contract states no price figure, but specifies a minimum share plus anywhere from one-third to one-half of the profits. Another, a flat fee contract, pays the producer a sum covering all production costs, usually paid in advance. The producer is thus challenged to minimize his expenses and earn a profit for himself at the end.[26]

The costly production expenses, the great capital needs, and the necessity for skilled, professional management all underscore just how much the small, diversified traditional farm has become an anachronism. There is no dirth of hard evidence to sustain the point made in the first chapter: farms are growing larger and the big operators supply a lion's share of the market. Since 1950, the size of the "average" farm, uncontrolled for crop or region, increased from 234 to 376 acres. The most recent figures, reflecting the heady spiral of farm prices in 1973, show that the trend toward consolidation is accelerating. Farms with sales greater than $100,000 grew from 55,000 in 1970 to 109,000, three years later. They constituted, in 1973, 3.8 percent of the total operating farms, but earned 34.8 percent of the realized net farm income. At the same time, farms with sales of less than $5,000 made up 53 percent of the operating units in 1970, and 43 percent in 1973. In the latter year, their realized net income made up 6.7 percent of that for all farms.[27]

Is the trend toward bigness an inevitable one that will soon swallow all smaller producers? Are corporate farms soon to replace one- or two-man units? The answer to both these questions is a qualified "no." As the accompanying chart prepared by the Department of Agriculture shows, 80 percent of American farms are owned by individual proprietors or partners; most of the corporate farms are closed family-owned businesses.

The department began to measure the extent of corporate farms, as a class, only in 1968, and their measurements have consistently been challenged as underestimates. Aggregate figures do not reveal that 20 percent of the land in California and Florida, and 28 percent in Utah, is farmed by corporations. Moreover, corporate holdings are skewed by size. Corporations holding ten thousand acres or more accounted for 8 percent of all units, but held 71 percent of corporate owned land. Corporations owning less than one thousand acres constituted 58 percent of all corporations, but held less than 5 percent of corporate land. Then there is a problem of definition: many of the family-owned units noted on the chart aren't family farms at all, because they employ more than 1.5 man years of nonfamily labor.[28] The most recent data available, although somewhat ambiguous, indicates a continued linear rise in corporate ownership. Twenty percent of acreage sold in the six months ending 1 March 1974 was purchased by private or public corporations, up from 10 percent in 1972. Of that 20 percent, however, 18 percent represented purchases by private corporations, which are usually incorporated family units. In 1974, 64 percent of sales of farmland were to individual purchasers.[29]

Contrary to conventional wisdom, the major incentives that led to the increase in corporate farming had little to do with capital needs or economies of scale. The Internal Revenue Code appears to have been a much more important stimulus. As the technological magic of the postwar years pushed up farm output, land values skyrocketed. Changes in the tax laws in the 1950s freed farm operators from short term capital gains assessments and afforded landowners the possibility of achieving a lucrative one-time capital gain. Most of the corporations sampled by USDA in 1968 began their operations after 1950.[30] Other provisions of the Internal Revenue Code, included in the guise of assisting the family farmer, afforded ways in which large operators could distribute profits throughout the operation in order to convert them into lower capital gains categories. The driving force in creating corporate farms was the nonfarm investor seeking tax shelter, quick capital returns, and profits through land value appreciation. Government payments, a function of the historical acreage base, provided financial leverage that was better exploited by large or corporate farms than by small units.[31] Tax reform legislation in 1969 removed many, but not all, of these loopholes.

The argument that only a corporate organization could attract the capital needed to create a new technology fails. There was no shortage of capital in agriculture in the fifties and sixties; the sector was better capitalized than at any time since World War I. All loans of the various components of the federal credit system to agriculture had been retired by 1968. Life insurance companies, the traditional suppliers of funds for farm mortgages, negotiated only 4 percent of the new mortgages in 1970.

Neither does the traditional argument that is historically advanced for integration—the necessity of capturing the advantages of large-scale secondary or coordinating organizations—work in agriculture. By the time corporate agriculture emerged in the 1950s, a complex infrastructure of information networks, dynamic research organizations, and price and production coordination—most of it under government sponsorship—already existed.

Corporate agriculture also faced some personnel problems. The United Farm Workers in the early sixties had begun the long task of raising from quiescence the long exploited agricultural wage workers. Then, there was the elusive force of tradition: auto workers usually don't contemplate ever owning the plant or even a part of it; farm workers just might.

Some corporations that had boldly ventured into farming in the sixties were backing out by the mid-seventies. As for the future, Philip Raup crystallizes the prospects well:

Farm corporations that began operating after 1965 were too late to capture big operating gains from rising efficiency and just in time to encounter inflated land costs, pollution crusades, and organizational efforts among farm workers.[32]

Corporation farming is a red flag issue that has unfortunately deflected some demands for reform that could more

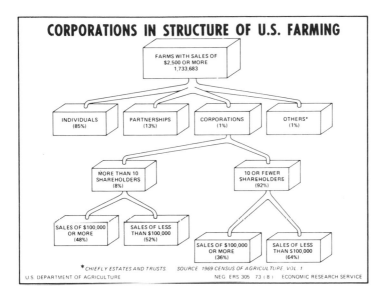

effectively have been channeled against other targets. The form will probably continue and even increase in those industries to which it is best adapted: poultry raising, orchards, cattle feed-lots, and vegetables for canning. A far more important integrating tendency is the rise of the oligopolistic agribusiness complex that amalgamates independent farm producers as one part of a centralized, hierarchical structure that includes supplying production needs, processing, and marketing. This will be examined in the following chapter.

While the traditional small-scale farm may be outmoded, it does not follow that because of their size huge farms are the most efficient production units. Beyond certain perimeters, continued expansion ceases to be an efficient use of resources. Even the most mechanized operation is still governed by a seasonal cycle—the time it takes crops to grow, sows to give birth, or cattle to mature. Poor weather affects large and small farms alike. Many cost items such as seed, fertilizer, and pesticides are the same per unit of production regardless of the size of the farm. Large units obviously distribute costs of machinery across a wider capital base, but it should be recalled that most major functions can be custom-hired. A recent study by the Economic Research Service of the Department of Agriculture hypothesizes that a technically optimum one-man farm, defined as "the man and his complement of tractor and machines," can capture most of the economies associated with size. Enlargement beyond optimum one-man size would not substantially reduce production costs. The study assumes that the operator will rent, not own, land, and the optimal acreage described is substantially greater than that of the average farm today. The example, then, is no typical "small farm" operation. Optimal size for a one-man operation will vary according to geographical location and the crop cultivated; and no matter how it is stated, the costs of operation are still very high. The study hypothesizes eight separate crop farm models. The operator earns a salary for his labor and for his management. Table 5, as an illustration, is the model for a corn-soybean farm in Indiana.

From table 5 it is evident that net income increases at a declining rate as the size of a farm grows. Net income more than triples when a one-half-man operation becomes a one-man operation, but increases by less than half when a one-man operation is doubled to two. Still, the optimum USDA projects is no "mom and pop" operation; neither in any way is it, or can it be, a turning back to Tarpleywick or the Stadtfeld farm.

At the time of this writing, it cannot be determined if the fleeting observations that follow are transient phenomena or perchance harbingers of some eddying of the flows of change of three decades duration. First, after the long years of spectacular gains, output per man-hour in agriculture has begun to decline; it dropped 6.8 percent in 1972 and 4.6 percent in 1973.[33] Second, as might be expected, given the numbers who have left the farms, the downward trend in agricultural employment has slowed. Nevertheless, the Bureau of Labor Statistics projected an anticipated decrease at an annual rate of 4.9 percent between 1972 and 1980. In perplexing contrast, agricultural employment registered a

TABLE V

Indiana: Corn-Soybean Farm* (Tenant-operated)

Item	Farm Size		
	1/2-man	1-man	2-man
		Acres	
LAND	400	800	1,600
Corn	170	340	680
Soybeans	175	350	700
		Dollars	
INCOME			
Corn	27,500	55,000	110,000
Government payment	3,200	6,400	12,800
Soybeans	20,000	40,000	80,000
	50,700	101,400	202,800
EXPENSES			
Land Rent	16,000	32,000	64,000
Machine charges	13,600	20,000	40,000
Hired labor	1,850	3,700	12,400
Other	12,650	25,300	50,600
NET	6,600	20,400	35,800
RETURN TO			
Operator labor	4,600	6,000	6,000
Management	2,000	14,400	29,800
CAPITAL MANAGED			
Land	240,000	480,000	960,000
Machinery	90,000	130,000	270,000
	330,000	610,000	1,330,000

*The farm has 1 heavy tractor and 1 light tractor plus a complete line of corn and soybean machines, including tillage, planters, a corn picker-sheller, and a soybean combine-harvester. With these machines a man can grow 340 acres of corn and 350 acres of soybeans. In addition, there are 107 acres of program set-aside land. The farm operator puts 900 hours of his own labor directly into these crops and hires labor seasonally for crop operations that require 2 men such as grain harvesting and hauling. The 1/2 man farm has somewhat smaller machines and the operator puts in about 700 hours of labor in producing corn and soybeans. The 2-man farm is double the 1-man farm in crop acreage and machines.[34]

small *gain* in 1972, and remained unchanged in 1973.[35] Third, and most surprising, census bureau surveys between 1970 and 1973 revealed that for the first time in the century, rural population grew more rapidly than urban. In that interval, counties with no urban center of fifty thousand or more gained by 4.2 percent; metropolitan counties gained 2.9 percent. The reasons for this reversal are still speculative: among those citied are growth of retirement centers, a leveling off in the loss of farm population, the back to the land movement, and the fact that more rural people are staying where they are rather than facing uncertain job prospects in large cities. These, of course, could be evanescent phenomena—some of the confusing concomitants of a sputtering economy. The magnitudes of gain in rural areas in no way suggest any reversal of the revolutionary population transfers since 1945.[36]

One thing appears more certain. Changes, such as those of the last thirty years that have transformed traditional farming, and which passed by with little notice, will not escape public scrutiny again. Thus, historians of agriculture have devoted most of their research to farmers who are dead and systems which are archaic and have failed to bring a time perspective to the revolutionary changes of the present. As we have noted, agricultural economists and rural sociologists have until recently ignored the problems of relocation and adjustment for the millions of migrants from countryside to city. Much of the popular discussion of contemporary agricultural progress, particularly in reports emanating from the Department of Agriculture, has been suffused with a starry-eyed technological optimism that assumes circumstances are improving so long as lines move upward on production charts. In contrast, these things seemed to be happening in 1975: the consumer price index, even with unemployment rising, continued to go into orbit, with the costs of food products leading the way; the specter of serious worldwide food shortages loomed in the future; technology and "progress" were straining the fragile ecosystem, perhaps to its very limits. Under the circumstances, what happens on the American farm promises to be a major public concern for a long time to come.

Notes

1. Donald R. Durost and Warren Bailey, "What's Happened to Farming," *USDA Yearbook, 1970*, p. 5; T. C. Byerly, "Systems Come, Traditions Go," *USDA Yearbook, 1970*, p. 34; Edward C. Miller and Earl F. Hodges, "One Man Feeds 5,000 Cattle or 60,000 Broilers," *USDA Yearbook, 1970*, pp. 58–59.
2. Miller and Hodges, "One Man Feeds."
3. *New York Times*, 5 December 1971.
4. Ibid., 22 November 1970; 5 December 1971.
5. The term "agribusiness" was coined only in 1956.
6. Everett M. Rogers, *Social Change in Rural Society* (New York: Appleton-Century-Crofts, 1960), pp. 335–39.
7. R. S. Kifer et al., "The Influence of Technological Progress on Agricultural Production," *USDA Yearbook, 1940*, pp. 512–13; Durost and Bailey, "What's Happened to Farming," p. 2.
8. USDA, Economic Research Service [hereinafter abbreviated ERS], *Changes in Farm Production and Efficiency: A Summary Report, 1973*, Statistical Bulletin #233 (June 1973), p. 22.
9. The pioneer research in the sociology of innovation diffusion studied the rate of adoption of hybrid seed corn. The stages of adoption mentioned in the preceding chapter were developed from these studies. See Bryce Ryan and Neal C. Gross, "The Diffusion of Hybrid Seed Corn in Two Iowa Communities," *Rural Sociology* 8 (March 1943): 15–24; Everett M. Rogers, *Diffusion of Innovations* (New York: Free Press of Glencoe, 1962), pp. 33–36.
10. Byerly, "Systems Come, Traditions Go," p. 36; Durost and Bailey, "What's Happened to Farming," p. 3; F. A. Johnson, E. E. Sandman, and Donald R. Shepherd, "Protecting Our Food Resources," *USDA Yearbook, 1971*, pp. 313–18; H. C. Cox, "New Approaches to Pest Control," *USDA Yearbook, 1971*, pp. 308–13.

11. Durost and Bailey, "What's Happened to Farming," p. 3.
12. Barry Commoner, *The Closing Circle: Nature, Man and Technology* (New York: Bantam Books, 1972 [1971]), p. 144.
13. Ibid., pp. 78–90, 114–51, 261–62; Ronald G. Menzel and Paul F. Sand, "Water Quality and Farming," *USDA Yearbook, 1971,* pp. 305–6.
14. R. E. Hodgson and E. J. Warwick, "Animal Product Needs and How to Meet Them," *USDA Yearbook, 1971,* pp. 320–23; *New York Times,* 21 August 1974.
15. Deborah P. Klein and Daniel S. Whipple, "Employment in Agriculture: A Profile," in U.S., Bureau of Labor Statistics, *Monthly Labor Review* (April 1974), p. 31.
16. Part of the increased yield, however, is because of the westward migration of cotton production to the more fertile soils of Texas and California.
17. Rex F. Colwick and Vernon P. Moore, "King Cotton Blasts Off," *USDA Yearbook, 1970,* pp. 39–46.
18. James L. Butler, "Winning the Race to Get the Hay In," *USDA Yearbook, 1970,* p. 52–57.
19. USDA, ERS, *Farm Income Situation* (July 1974), p. 38.
20. Miller and Hodges, "One Man Feeds," p. 58; Byerly, "Systems Come, Traditions Go," p. 36; Melvin L. Colner and Louise N. Samuel, "Competition for Land Resources," *USDA Yearbook, 1970,* p. 207; Commoner, *Closing Circle,* pp. 146–47.
21. *Philadelphia Inquirer,* 15 September 1974.
22. Walter R. Heald and Raymond C. Loehr, "Utilizing Agricultural Wastes," *USDA Yearbook, 1971,* p. 300.
23. Menzel and Sand, "Water Quality and Farming," p. 307; Commoner, *Closing Circle,* p. 146.
24. USDA, ERS, *Farm Real Estate Market Developments,* CD–79 (July 1974), p. 3.
25. Orville R. Krause, "Farm Production Capacity Can Meet Our Needs," *USDA Yearbook, 1971,* p. 279.
26. Warren R. Bailey and John E. Lee, Jr., "The New Frontier of Finance," *USDA Yearbook, 1970,* pp. 10–19.
27. The increase in the number of farms with net sales above $100,000 may reflect higher farm prices rather than any change in ownership patterns. Most of the smaller units are, of course, part-time farms whose operators earn most of their income from work off the farm. USDA, ERS, *Farm Income Situation* (July 1974), pp. 69–70.
28. Philip Raup, "Corporate Farming in the United States," *Journal of Economic History* 33 (March 1973): 275–77.
29. USDA, ERS, *Farm Real Estate Market Developments* (July 1974).

30. Raup, "Corporate Farming," p. 281.
31. Ibid., p. 285.
32. Ibid., p. 290.
33. J. R. Norsworthy and L. J. Fulco, "Productivity and Costs in the Private Economy," in U.S., Bureau of Labor Statistics, *Monthly Labor Review* (June 1974), p. 3.
34. Warren R. Bailey, *The One Man Farm,* USDA, ERS, ERS–719 (August 1973). See also Joel M. Halpern, *The Changing Village Community* (Englewood Cliffs, N.J.: Prentice-Hall, 1967), pp. 116–17.
35. Klein and Whipple, "Employment in Agriculture," pp. 31–32.
36. *New York Times,* 18 May 1975.

CHAPTER SIX

Agribusiness Triumphs

The dynamic forces that are most profoundly affecting the nature of rural life today derive from the industrial city and the metropolitan community; and the most central characteristic of these forces is the economic interdependence that modern technology and industrialization have introduced into the country as well as the city. A situation has been created out of which new kinds of economic disparities and social dislocations have developed. Measures conceived in traditional terms, although helpful, have generally failed to achieve any substantial adjustment. The inadequacy of older institutions and arrangements, even as means to attain the substance of older ideals and aspirations, has become more apparent as the modern situation has intensified. As a result the boundless confidence and optimism by which the agricultural domain of this country was first settled and made productive have been increasingly qualified by bewilderment and pessimism, and the former ideal of progress is giving ground to a new ideal of security. The bewilderment and pessimism are likely to endure until the way seems clear to the attainment of security —until institutions develop that within the modern situation can assure the safety of the more lasting needs and desires of men, even though these appear in altered form.

—Paul H. Johnstone, in *Farmers in a Changing World*

The marketing of farm products on the traditional farm seemed a casual affair. The marketing of farm products in the modern agricultural economy is anything but a casual affair. On farms such as Tarpleywick, itinerant buyers might visit in order to make bids on poultry or livestock, and cattle or hogs might be driven afoot to the nearest market town. In a later day, pigs, sheep, or steers were loaded onto farm trucks and hauled to a nearby country auction barn. Grain crops were sold for cash at the local elevator, perhaps cooperatively owned. Farmers monitored the market like they watched rain clouds. Listening to the noonday radio market reports was as regular a part of the ritual as the daily chores; the figures the announcer rattled off helped in making the decision of when to market and what to plant for next year. Whether prices were high or low, there was persistent grumbling that a farmer always had to sell on a buyer's market, buy on a seller's market. When prices and incomes went periodically into tailspin, farmers didn't take it at all stoically. They had the capacity for stirring up some of the most spirited political ruckuses in the nation's history—the Populist Movement and the Farmers' Holiday Association are examples. Nevertheless, dairy and cotton farmers and livestock and cash grain producers alike were tied to a complex and intricate market structure that stretched from the country elevator or railhead through the urban stockyards and grain terminals to the frenzied commodity markets at Chicago or New York and on into the mazeways of international trade. After 1933, farmers had to adjust to the additional complications of acreage allotments, nonrecourse loans, and price support payments. The transition of the farm from craft enterprise to big business began then, and the process of integration is still going on.

Family farmers, as tradition perceives them, are scarcely involved at all in the modern marketing process, and even the modern technologically advanced farmer may not sell at all—if he is a broiler producer, it is much more accurate to say that he processes. Soybeans, corn, and wheat may be delivered after harvest to the same contract processor who supplied the seeds, fertilizer, and insecticides, and who extended credit for the planting. Beef and dairy cattle may not be owned by the operator who does the feeding and milking. The farms where the major share of produce for domestic consumption and export originate are "factories in the fields," the first steps that are organized, financed, and administered by the processors, export firms, and conglomerates that preside over one of the biggest business operations in America.

The consumer goods on display at the local supermarket have been altered many times over since the raw product left the farm.

Total marketing costs—shipping, processing, packaging, retailing—absorb about two-thirds of every dollar spent on food. As an inviolable rule, the more a food product is processed, the lower the return to the farmer. Thus in 1969 farmers received 67¢ of every consumer dollar spent on eggs, since the product was sold in substantially the same form it was produced. The producer received 50¢ for milk; 22¢ for fresh oranges; 14¢ for 2 loaves of bread. For a cotton shirt, the grower of the cotton received about 7¢ for every dollar in price. Producers of wheat and cotton could give away their entire crop free without creating more than a minor effect on the price of bread or shirts.[1]

The difference between what farmers receive and the retail value of food, is what economists call the "marketing margin" or "farm-retail price spread." In long term, that spread is increasing. Before concluding that increased food prices mean farmers get rich, it should be noted that the price of a typical "market basket"[2] of selected farm foods rose 19 percent in the "pre-inflationary" decade, from 1959 to 1969. In the same interval the marketing margin went up 14 percent.

Changes in the costs of marketing, which include labor, packaging, transportation, and so forth, are for the most part independent of the supply and demand factors that influence farm prices. Accordingly, when farmer's prices drop because of a large supply, most costs of marketing are not affected at all. In 1973, farmers received 45¢ of the consumer's food dollar; by September 1974 they received only 38¢. Here is what the food industry did with the rest: 30¢ went for labor costs, 7¢ for packaging, 4¢ for transportation. Corporate profits accounted for 4¢, and business taxes, interest, and repairs, 2½¢ each. Advertising, depreciation, and rent cost the industry 2¢ each; the remaining 5½¢ went for such miscellaneous expenditures as utilities, promotion, and fuel.[3]

The industries that manufacture, process, wholesale, and retail food have been the principal agents in the organizational revolution that has overtaken American agriculture. Processors and distributors of farm products employ about ten million workers—more than double the number of farmers. If we add those employed in manufacturing and selling farm supplies (the total of all engaged in agribusiness), we have accounted for about a quarter of the entire American labor force. The food industry is integrated both horizontally and vertically. From 1947 to 1967, the number of food manufacturing firms declined by 33 percent, but output per firm shot up 167 percent. Of the thirty thousand plants operating in 1967, nine thousand were owned by companies operating two or more; this one-third accounted for two-thirds of total production and about 70 percent of the industry's profits. Chain supermarkets have driven out the mom and pop grocery stores everywhere, except in remote country towns and crowded city centers—places where large-scale operations are unprofitable. In 1948, 62 percent of all grocery store sales were by firms with annual sales less than $300,000; in 1963, the figure was 24 percent.[4]

Farm to Factory: The Food Processing Oligopoly

Vertically integrated food processors bring under one blanket all the stages involved in the production process: they contract with farmers for the purchase of raw materials; some control packaging plants and shipping companies; others own firms that manufacture farm equipment, feed, and fertilizer. The big supermarket chains are vertical integrators, too. They produce substantial amounts of the bread and dairy products on their shelves, and they contract with farmers for the purchase of fresh fruits, vegetables, and meats.

Of the estimated $77 billion Americans spent for food marketing in 1972, the greatest portion, $28.6 billion, went to processors; $22.4 went to retailers, $17.7 to eating places, and $10.3 to wholesalers.[5]

Businesses that manufacture, process, and pack food include such familiar giants as Ralston-Purina, with its Checkerboard Brand, Kraftco, with its well known varieties of packaged dairy products; but one soon learns that there is more to a name than meets the eye, particularly if it is a brand name. General Foods, one of the industry leaders, supplies not only Maxwell House, Yuban, Sanka, and Postum for coffee drinkers, but also a line of cereals that includes Grape Nuts, Post Toasties, and Alpha Bits. It also retails Birds-Eye Frozen Foods, Calumet Baking Powder, Jello, and Kool-Aid. Those who dine out can do so at a company owned Burger Chef; and those who want to grow their own vegetables, plant their gardens with Burpee seeds, also manufactured by General Foods. Of Campbell's, it might be said "By Their Soups Ye Shall Know Them," for the company accounts for 90 percent of the canned variety marketed in the United States. Not so well known is the fact that it sells bread products under the Pepperidge Farm label. Wonder Bread and Hostess Cup Cakes come from the ovens of Continental Bakeries, a subsidiary of International Telephone and Telegraph. Pepsi-Cola doesn't just provide thirsty customers with a refreshing soft drink; it manufactures Fritos to make them more thirsty. Coca Cola Corporation doubles as the manufacturer of the Minute Maid line of frozen juice products. Procter and Gamble produces not just soap but Duncan Hines Cake Mix, Crisco, and Folger's Coffee. Greyhound doesn't just run busses; it owns Armour and Company, a major processed and fresh meat manufacturer.[6]

Large, horizontally integrated companies such as these have the leverage to penetrate the production process and integrate vertically as well. Through contracts with farmer-producers, processors obtain commodities of predetermined price, quality, and finish on the delivery date they designate. A 1972 study estimated that vertical integrators had absorbed 97 percent of broiler production, 95 percent of vegetable processing, 85 percent of the trade in citrus fruits, 80 percent of seed crops, 70 percent of potatoes marketed, 54 percent of turkeys produced, and 51 percent of fresh vegetables.[7] The percentage figures are an index of the extent to which, for these commodities, production (farming?) and processing are a single operation.

Not only have processors absorbed some of the functions of the farmer-producer, they have reached in the other direction, and functions once performed in the family kitchen are now carried out in the kitchens of huge manufacturing plants. For example, consumers in 1969 bought nearly as many frozen, canned, and dehydrated potato products as they did fresh potatoes. Sales of frozen preprepared dinners (half a billion dollars worth) doubled in the four-year period, 1965 to 1968.[8]

The actual factories that process and manufacture food are elaborate and automated. Company researchers and home economists may design a new food and its container. Economists then test it on the market and estimate sales volume. Engineers design and build the equipment to produce it. Then specialized workers preserve, cook, season, color, and otherwise manicure the product for the nation's dinner tables.[9] In 1964 the food industry spent $135 million for research. Over 90 percent of this went to applied research, often difficult to distinguish from promotion, since it included such activities as motivational research and package design.[10] Only about 4 percent of such innovations ever reach the market shelves; of these, one study estimated over 80 percent were new products in name only—the huge portion were variants and adaptations designed to offset some competitor's brainchild.[11] Fortunately for the food processors, the most complex scientific research in food and agriculture has long been carried out by the United States government.

Processors are sensitive to consumer demand—if it isn't there, they can dip into their sizeable advertising budget to stimulate it. In 1973, the food, beverage, and grocery products industries spent $2.9 billion on media advertising, half of it on television and another $3 billion on promotions such as trade stamps and contests. One of every five television advertisements is for food or drink. Understandably, advertising is thrown disproportionately behind highly processed, higher profit foods rather than those that are less processed and which often have greater nutritional value.[12] A good example is the aggressive promotion of delectable sugar-coated pellets of breakfast cereal, which are highly palatable to the tongues of finicky children but utterly without redeeming nutritional value. Almost universally condemned by nutritionists, the products are nevertheless market leaders.

An efficient transportation system that utilizes refrigerator cars on railroads, heavy trucks that speed over interstate highways, and, in some instances, even airfreight, has reduced ton-mile costs and permitted most processors to enlarge operations, sell in a nationwide market, and reach over most of the continent for their raw materials.

Statistics on horizontal integration reveal a familiar pattern of oligopolistic competition. One measure is the percentage of the market controlled by the four largest firms. These are examples from 1966:

TABLE VI

Industry	Market Share of Four Largest Firms, 1966[13]
Cereal Preparations	87%
Chocolate and Cocoa Products	85
Bread and Prepared Flour	75
Biscuits, Crackers, and Cookies	70
Wet Corn Milling	67

One of the giant food processing firms that spans the entire agribusiness spectrum, from production through retailing, is Ralston-Purina of St. Louis. The company is the world's major producer of commercial feed for livestock and poultry; it markets over 350 varieties with the well known checkerboard label. The company is also the world's leading manufacturer of dry dog and cat food. For the supermarket shopper, Ralston manufactures two brands of tuna fish, Chicken of the Sea and Van Camp, an assortment of cereals sold under Chexbrand or Ralston Hot Cereal brand names, and Ry-Krisp crackers. In 1968 the corporation widened its operations by purchasing Foodmaker, Inc., the operator of some 730 Jack in the Box food carryout installations. The Danforth Foundation, benefactor of numerous educational projects, is named for the company's founder, and in 1973 owned about 8 percent of Ralston-Purina's common stock. Although it was instrumental in bringing about vertical integration in the broiler industry, the company sold all its broiler and egg facilities in 1972.[14] In 1973, the corporation's aggregated pretax earnings were derived from agricultural operations (36 percent), consumer sales of pet foods and cereals (40 percent), international marketing (13 percent), and sales by the carryout food chain (12 percent).[15]

DeKalb Agresearch, Inc., a less well known corporation, with headquarters in the Illinois city of that name, integrates a diverse series of agribusiness operations. DeKalb is a major producer of hybrid seed corn; it shares half of the domestic sales with a competitor, Pioneer Hybrids. Its aggressive research division, with laboratories in United States and five foreign countries, is improving corn and sorghum hybrids, experimenting with hybrid wheat, and working to develop a better breed of hogs. The firm also sells hybrid layer breeders. DeKalb went into the farm marketing business in September 1972 when it purchased Heinold Companies, a brokerage firm that buys hogs at seventy-five different sorting stations, holds them for less than twenty-four hours, then ships them off to the packing house or to a supermarket chain. A branch of Heinold services clients as a broker-agent, buying and selling futures on the Chicago Mercantile Exchange. Among other adjuncts of DeKalb, Sensors, Inc., markets heat detection devices and is experimenting with applications of infrared technology to crop production. Another DeKalb subsidiary, Arizona Feeds, operates feedlots in the Southwest; another, Lindsay Manufacturing, is the third largest domestic manufacturer of irrigation equipment.[16]

That some of the nation's greatest corporations, ranked by revenues and assets, are involved in agribusiness should come as no surprise. Some of them, like General Motors and Ford, with their trucks and tractors; DuPont and the major oil companies, with chemicals and gasoline; and Sears, Roebuck, in retailing, have been there for a long time. The penetration of huge, diversified conglomerates into agribusiness is a relatively new phenomenon; it is almost as new as the big multinational corporations themselves.

Tenneco of Houston, Texas, ranked fifteenth in terms of assets among all U.S. corporations, is such a conglomerate. Their agribusiness activities are subsidiary to major investments in pipelines, oil, and natural gas production. In 1973, these generated 39 percent of the corporation's sales, but 59 percent of its profits. In 1970 Tenneco acquired Heggblade-Marguleas, the nation's largest distributor of fresh fruits and vegetables. The company was modernized, capital was increased, and its products marketed under the brand name Sun Giant. Tenneco already owned Packaging Corporation of America and J. I. Case Company, a major manufacturer of farm and construction equipment. Shortly after it entered food processing, Tenneco bought one of the oldest and largest corporate farms in the United States, the Kern County Land Company, one of the biggest cotton growers in California. Tenneco presides over a vast, integrated farm-to-market enterprise; in its various divisions everything needed at the various stages of farm marketing is manufactured: tractors for the farm, fertilizer for the fields, and packages for the products. Tenneco also controls

(Courtesy USDA)

Neighborliness in the supermarket.

an immense data processing plant and the Newport News Shipping and Drydock Company. Regarded as a solid, conservative company, Tenneco's earnings per share crept up at a modest annual 7 percent during the period between 1963 and 1973. In 1974, bolstered by strong performances in oil and chemicals and a booming demand for J. I. Case machinery, Tenneco's earnings per share were projected at $4.25, up from $2.86 in 1973.[17]

International Telephone and Telegraph, the best known of the multinational conglomerates, acquired, in 1968, the Continental Baking Company, the largest wholesale bakery in the nation, with annual sales of nearly a million dollars worth of Wonder, Hostess, and Morton bread, rolls, cupcakes, frozen dinners, and other food products. Food processing and services accounted for 12 percent of ITT's sales and revenues in 1972, and 1 percent of its profits. ITT-

Continental has been at loggerheads with the Federal Trade Commission ever since its inception. In 1973 the commission ruled that the bouncy aphorisms about the specified number of ways Wonder Bread might stimulate growth processes constituted false and deceptive advertising. Independent of some other unpleasantries visited upon ITT, while the Watergate scandals unfolded in 1973 and 1974, the FTC has charged that the company violated a 1962 order forbidding any more acquisition of baking companies for ten years. Pending complaints accuse the company of engaging in such predatory business practices as cutting prices and concentrating advertising in areas where competition is intense, and in subsidizing below-cost bread sales with high markups on cakes.[18]

Since the days of the Grangers, independent farmers have been banding together into cooperatives, member-owned enterprises that may market products collectively, buy and sell necessary supplies and equipment, provide insurance coverage, and run retail outlets. Patrons are the stockholders and directors, who receive back a portion of the profits as patronage refunds. The Capper-Volstead Act of 1922 gave a green light to cooperatives by providing that the fact of their existence was not a fortiori a violation of the antitrust laws.[19] Cooperatives pay no federal taxes on corporate income, because they are regarded not as profit making businesses but as cost saving enterprises that return the savings they achieve to their members in the patronage refunds.

Today many of the old farmer co-ops are as much agribusiness conglomerates as some of the largest processing corporations. A few are actually rivals. Sunkist Growers, Inc., of Sherman Oaks, California, a cooperative, markets 45 percent of the nation's fresh oranges and 85 percent of its fresh lemons.[20] Agway, Inc., of Syracuse, New York, operates retail outlets, sells petroleum products (its largest volume trade), eggs, potatoes, operates an insurance company, and even owns 7.4 percent of the common stock of Mohawk Airlines.[21]

In an industry that is moving inexorably toward consolidation and integration, the farmer cooperatives have been caught up in the same process. Members have little more involvement in decision making than do corporate shareholders or labor union members. Skilled and trained managers, hired from industry or graduate schools of business, guide the organizations by the only principles that allow a cooperative to function in a competitive world—those of the modern business corporation. Management is often insulated from members, and even from boards of directors. Often the latter tend to represent the largest of member operators; in some instances, the democratic Rochdale principle—one man, one vote—has been modified to allow voting by shares or by business volume. In others, directors are indirectly nominated by management.[22]

Fifteen years ago, a rural sociologist, expressing concern over the bureaucratic takeover of the old cooperative movement, suggested that the message management ought to beam persistently to apathetic co-op members was: "*You* are the co-op. *You* own and control it. Its employees work for *you*."[23] I have chosen two, hopefully, nontypical examples to illustrate the problem faced by co-op members.

It would have been difficult in 1974 for members of the Lehigh Valley Cooperative, in Pennsylvania, or of Dairylea Cooperative, Inc., in New York, to have taken that admonition seriously. The 750 members of Lehigh Valley, who believed they belonged to the largest and, financially, the strongest dairy cooperative in the state, learned in May 1973 that the half-million dollar profit their management reported was in reality a deficit of more than $5 million. The fault was bad managers, not bad farmers. Without the knowledge of the board of directors, the hired administrators, who drew salaries commensurate with those of other corporation executives, had watered the books with $3 million of nonexistent inventory and made illegal contributions to the Committee to Reelect the President, some of which found its way into the Watergate hush fund. The corrupt management was ousted, but the members, not the managers, had to pay the debt by taking a 50 percent cut in their milk receipts in a two-month period.[24]

Across the border, in New York, the eight thousand members of Dairylea were hit in November 1974 with an assessment of $18 million to make up management produced deficits. This was only one problem. A fierce internal battle was raging between the board of directors and the hired manager-executives. Twelve present and former employees were under criminal indictment for filing false reports to cover up the fact that the firm had been watering the milk it marketed in the New York City–New Jersey area.[25]

These blatant examples still leave out the saddest episode in what has happened to the dairy cooperatives, organizations for which some embattled farmers back in the thirties picketed highways and dumped milk along the roadside. In the late fifties, as the age of conglomerates was dawning, various dairy cooperatives, suffering a perennial excess of supplies, banded together to form cooperative federations. The largest of these, Associated Milk Producers, Inc., served forty thousand members, from New Mexico to Minnesota, and controlled about 12.5 percent of the nation's milk supply. AMPI, along with two other big cooperative federations, burst out of corporate obscurity when dramatic revelations in 1973 uncovered the following scenario: On 12 March 1971, Secretary of Agriculture Clifford Hardin rejected a joint plea of the cooperatives to increase milk price supports.[26] On 22 March the co-ops dipped into their abundant—and legal—political contributions fund to pass along $10,000 to President Richard Nixon's campaign for reelection. The next day the president met with the leaders of the cooperative federations. The following day, managers of the dairy co-ops gathered in Chicago for a mammoth "Salute the President" fund-raising dinner; sharing in their revelries was Murray Chotiner, one of the president's longtime political associates. Some further potential contributions were discussed. Just one day later, on 25 March, Secretary Hardin reversed his earlier order and granted the increased supports; simultaneously the president ruled out any prosecution of AMPI under a pending antitrust suit. Subsequently, the dairy cooperatives poured $422,500 into the Nixon campaign coffers.[27] The President was not the only political aspirant who benefitted by donations from managers of the dairy cooperative federations: other recipients included Hubert Humphrey, Wilbur Mills, Edmund Muskie, and a host of Congressional candidates. Former Secretary of the Treasury John M. Connally was, however, acquitted of charges of accepting a milk industry bribe.[28] In August 1974, AMPI settled the long-standing antitrust suit by agreeing to desist from using threats and coercion against nonmembers and refraining from a series of specific practices the Justice Department had branded as illegal. In the same month the cooperative pleaded guilty of making illegal campaign contributions in 1968, 1970, and 1972 and was fined $35,000.[29] Recently the National Association for Milk Marketing Reform, an association of bottlers and cheesemakers, has charged that the giant tax-free cooperatives, partially immune from the antitrust laws, continue to use their bargaining muscle to force milk prices as much as 11¢ a gallon above the federally prescribed minimum (not maximum) price. Thus far, the Department of Agriculture has made no move in response.[30]

The food processing and manufacturing industry is concentrated and controlled by a decreasing number of corporate syndicates; huge conglomerate aggregrates have penetrated it deeply. These characteristics, however, do not distinguish it from any other segment of the economy of the United States—food processing, however, may be more competitive than, for example, oil refining, steel, or automobile production. The food industry turns a smart profit annually, but it is not the most profitable or lucrative American business. Financial prognosticators and investment analysts view it with scant favor. In both 1972 and 1973 average earnings per share of invested stock for companies that manufactured canned foods, dairy products, packaged meats, and packaged foods lagged from 5 to 40 percent behind the average earnings of 425 selected industrials.[31]

Oligopolistic food processing corporations are strategically located in a controlling position all along the conduit from the farm to the dinner table. Behind a galaxy of illusive brand names, they create an illusion of competition greater than actually exists. They wield potential power to box in consumers and influence prices in the segment of the economy that no single individual can avoid every day of his life. Power itself does not corrupt; concentration of power is not sinister. It becomes so only when it is employed in ways that victimize consumers, bludgeon competitors, set artificial prices, and yield unwarranted profits. The fact of concentrated market power is easy to demonstrate; instances of abuse are not. Nonetheless, the activities of the dairy cooperatives and ITT-Continental are clear cases of market exploitation, and demonstrate that the potential for further exploitation of economic power is omnipresent. One particularly blatant example of such abuse of oligopolistic power came to light in August 1975 when five of the nation's largest sugar refining companies, among them Great Western, Holly, and Amalgamated, pleaded nolo contendere to charges of price fixing. Each was fined $50,000. Consumer prices for sugar had shot up 400 percent from January to December 1974. Great Western, a major sugar beet refiner, increased its profit margin 1,200 percent during the year.[32] Axiomatically, the temptations and possibilities of utilizing such power are greatest when the economic climate is stormy. Unfortunately, American history records not a single example of a viable, organized movement of food consumers.

Factory to Consumer: Competitive Food Retailing

The ubiquitous supermarket is a relative newcomer among venerable economic institutions; its rise correlates with the mechanization of farming and increased automobile ownership. In 1920 only one food chain retailed more than $200 million in merchandise; in 1929, six did. By 1974, nine of the food chains were billion dollar businesses. Two giants vie for leadership in this highly competitive universe. It is competitive, however, in a very strange way. The Great Atlantic and Pacific Tea Company, of New York City, long the "General Motors" of food retailing, operates thirty-five hundred stores in thirty-five states and leads in number of outlets. It has lost its leadership both in sales volume and earnings, however, to the rapidly growing Safeway Company, of Oakland, California, which runs twenty-three hundred stores in twenty-seven states, the largest operations being in California and the District of Columbia. Among the other major participants in an industry more oligopolistic than food processing are Winn-Dixie in the Southeast and Kroger in the Middle West.

Anomalously, food retailing is so competitive that it isn't competitive at all. The new supermarkets (a supermarket is defined as a food retailing establishment with annual sales above $500,000) followed the exodus to suburbia in the postwar years. Through economies of size, volume purchases and deliveries, kickbacks from processors and customer-seducing specials, they had few difficulties underselling, then driving out of business, the small individual proprietors—the family farmers of the grocery trade. From that point on the going got rough. As shopping centers burgeoned in suburban towns across America, the number of supermarkets nearly tripled from the year 1948 to 1963, then slowed to a more modest pace of increase—only one thousand a year. A supermarket that, as an average, could count upon a population of eleven to twelve thousand potential customers in a service area in 1954, serviced only thirty-six hundred in 1968. A harassed manager of a new A & P store might find that he had five to ten competitors in a one-mile radius.[33] All these competitors shared the same economies of size and scale, and they bought most of their merchandise from the same processors. Profit margins dwindled from the highs of the early years and have been stabilized at about a 1 percent margin on sales for the past decade. With costs of operation, including sizeable

(Courtesy USDA)

Truelson's Meat Market, Duluth, Minnesota, in the 1870s. Fish and game from the waters and woods of Minnesota were specialties.

items outside inventory such as transportation, rent, interest, and labor costs approximately equal, and with canny shoppers likely to notice gross price differentials on commonly purchased items such as milk, bread, or coffee, price competition in food retailing came virtually to a halt. For example, a survey in Kansas City by the Senate-House Joint Economic Committee in 1974 found 2,969 out of 3,959 items on the shelves of the city's Safeway and A & P stores to be priced exactly the same.[34]

The result has been competition in words but not in deeds, in illusion but not in reality. Attractively priced specials lure customers through the doors; the store cheerfully takes the loss it suffers on the item and compensates by markups on other merchandise, often strategically shelved near the alluring loss leader. Carefully calculated store arrangements place high-profit items along the most heavily traversed aisles at the store's margins or on lower shelves that are convenient to the clutches of spoiled and demanding children. Standard, low markup items are jammed at the center of the crowded inner aisles. Musak soothes the confused shopper as he or she moves through the store where, on the average, eight thousand separate products and brands are shelved. For a few years trading stamps and various games of chance were popular attractants; their passing must stand as the only positive good wrought by food price inflation. A & P threw the whole industry into turmoil, in 1972 and 1973, with an aggressive price-cutting campaign, noneuphonically labelled "WEO" (Where Economy Originates). Despite its valiant efforts, it ended 1973 with a deficit of more than $2.00 per share of stock.

In 1966, the average markup of supermarket over wholesale prices was 21.48 percent, most of which was consumed by business expenses. Pricing and advertising for each chain store are rigorously controlled from regional headquarters. A local manager's duties are confined to shop decor, customer relations, inventory control, and general supervision of personnel. Items most likely to bear the highest markups are frozen foods, butter, ice cream, beer, wine, liquors, dried fruit, paper products, pet foods, snacks, desserts, soft drinks, condiments, and spices.[35]

The forty thousand supermarkets in the United States are as characteristically suburban as power lawn mowers and antiseptic architecture. Speculative developers of the big shopping centers prefer to lease to well-established companies with trade names the affluent and discriminating customers in suburbia will recognize; they usually require that any lessee have an AAA credit rating, obtainable only by businesses with net worth above a million dollars.[36] In poorer, older areas of cities operating costs are 2 to 3 percent higher—just enough to erase the narrow profit margin; land in parking-lot size quantity is hard to obtain, occupancy costs are higher, and sales of high markup luxury items less. The result is that the supermarkets stay away, and those who live at the city's center buy from small local stores and, as a result, pay prices 20 percent higher.[37]

Clamoring for customers and for profits, the competitive food retailing giants earn less per share than is average for Standard and Poor's 425 industrials. The executive director of the National Association of Food Chains estimated, late in 1974, that the industry's return on investment was about 7.5 percent, compared with an average of about 10 percent for all American industry.[38] Profits crept upward in 1974 despite (or because of) price inflation; A & P abandoned price cutting and moved temporarily into the black, although it continued to lose its battle for customers with Safeway. With trading stamps gone and the Musak dulled by the clatter of automatic markers stamping higher prices on the merchandise, the beleaguered superchains became the vulnerable front-line targets for the irate frustrations of inflation conscious housewives and their husbands.

A & P has closed out 1,025 outlets in 1973 and 1974 and has added only 273 new ones. Safeway gained a net of only 43 new stores in 1974.[39] The most active expansion campaigns in food retailing are not by the supermarkets. In 1960 there were about 2,500 convenience stores, with names such as 7-11 and Stop and Shop, operating in the United States; in 1970 there were 13,250. A third of these, the 7-11 chain, are owned by Southland, an integrated agribusiness corporation that also produces processed and canned foods, and candy and dairy products. Located away from the shopping centers, their service is speedy, their hours long, although prices are higher and brand selections fewer. Thus they serve the same functions as the old mom and pop grocery. Consolidation and integration of food retailing didn't, in the last analysis, do away with the mom and pop grocery stores; it just did away with mom and pop.[40]

The big retailers of food products contribute to vertical integration almost as much as the processing companies. For more than a decade most of the chains have marketed baked goods, coffee, and dairy and meat products from their own manufacturing plants. For a number of canned and frozen foods retailers contract with processors for goods that are sold under the retailer's distinctive brand name. Supermarkets send buyers into the countryside to facilitate large volume procurements; many have established their own grading stations and packing sheds. Most contract with farmers directly to obtain products that meet definite specifications: a sizeable portion of supermarket meat, eggs, and fresh fruits and vegetables are obtained in this fashion.[41] Big farm through big processor to big retailer—that's the route even the little pigs take to market today!

American Agriculture and the World Market

The circle must be expanded wider: the products of American farms have never been marketed exclusively in the United States. American agriculture since, at least, 1850 has been enmeshed in a complex international marketing system that has often exercised a determinative influence on the prices American farmers receive for grain and livestock. In the days before government price supports, the international market for heavily exported commodities such as cotton and wheat exercised an automatic control on American farm prices. If the world price was higher than the American, commodities would flow into more lucrative foreign markets; if domestic prices were higher, Canadian wheat or Egyptian cotton might enter the country or, if it was excluded by tariff barriers (which it usually was), would nevertheless force American competitors out of the major markets in England and Western Europe. Morton Rothstein has shown that the spokesmen for Western farm groups were never oblivious to the rich possibilities of the markets of Europe and Asia as outlets for the abundant harvests that America's better technology and more fertile lands produced. It is no anomaly that the Populists were eager supporters of American expansionism in the 1890s.[42]

Urbanized America remains the breadbasket of the world; it has for a long time been the major exporter of food products and the second largest importer. Exports dropped away when world trade stagnated during the depression years, then accelerated in the war and postwar years—1967 was the peak year when $6.8 billion of food products flowed from the United States to foreign markets, constituting 22 percent of the nation's total exports. Then, with the devaluations of the dollar in 1971 and 1973 and other political decisions that stimulated foreign trade, worldwide price inflation, and the growing demand for meat and feed grains in developed countries, the volume and total value of American agricultural exports shattered all previous records. In 1972, $8 billion worth of farm exports left American ports; in 1973, $13 billion; and, in the greatest increment of any single year in history, exports worth $21 billion were shipped in 1974. This required the output of one of every three acres of cropland harvested: exports in 1974 ate up two-thirds of the total wheat production, one half of the rice and soybeans, and over 40 percent of the cotton and tobacco. The returns from these exports made up almost a quarter of the cash receipts from farm marketings and a quarter of total U.S. receipts from exports. Value of exports rose slightly in the fiscal year 1975; higher prices, not greater volume, accounted for all the gains. Volume actually declined by 10 percent. Thus the explosion in volume and value of exports is one obvious reason for the perilous domestic price inflation that began, simultaneously, in 1973.[43]

Exports of farm products are critically important to the precarious international trade and financial position of the United States. An adverse balance of payments in international credit markets has been the norm since the late fifties: cheaper and better electronic equipment, clothing, and autos from Japan, Germany, and Korea flooded the American market (although the foreign firms that manufactured them were often American-owned); the military lavishly poured dollars into foreign economies; and American capital sought lucrative investment opportunities abroad. Despite deficits in credit transactions, through most of this period the United States maintained a favorable trade balance: the value of merchandise exported exceeded that imported. Then this began to falter in 1969. When world prices, particularly for oil, went into a spiral in 1972 and 1973 the United States experienced its first trade deficits in thirty years. The favorable trade balances in 1969, 1971, and 1974 were entirely due to the surplus of agricultural exports over imports; the negative balances in all the deficit years would have been greater had not agriculture always had a surplus. The excess of farm exports over imports in 1974, the greatest ever recorded, offset what otherwise would have been a disastrous trade deficit. Throughout 1975, the United States again achieved a favorable trade balance. The figures for August underscore just how critical agricultural exports were to this balance. The total trade balance was $910 million; the agricultural balance was $913 million, while the nonagricultural ran a deficit of $3 million. The current national policies that seek so vigorously to stimulate export markets for Illinois soybeans or Kansas wheat thus become a little more understandable, if not justifiable.

Before World War II, bulky bales of upland cotton from the delta states and east Texas constituted over half of the agricultural exports. However, as other nations increased production and man-made fibers replaced natural ones, cotton exports fell until they made up less than 10 percent of shipments abroad in 1973 and 1974. In terms of quantity, grain crops, such as rice (60 percent of the crop), wheat, and corn, are the major American exports. Wheat and soybeans, however, are the principal money makers. Demand for the latter as animal feed has increased exponentially in recent years, as consumers in the industrializing nations of the world demand more meat for their dinner tables.

Japan is the leading customer for American farm products, absorbing more than 10 percent of total exports in 1974 (20 percent of the soybeans). Western Europe imports more from the U.S. than any other region (34 percent in 1974); West Germany is the principal buyer. Exports to the People's Republic of China rose from $200 million in value in 1973 to $903 million in 1974, making it the second largest customer in Asia. India, on the other hand, purchased only $245 million in 1974 and received $66.6 million in relief aid, compared to Japan's $3.3 billion of purchases. Thus, American food sold abroad goes in large measure to nations that are industrialized, affluent, and well fed.[44]

Agricultural products flow into export markets through two channels: private commercial sales and government financed programs such as Public Law 480 (Food for Peace). The former has accounted for 81 percent of sales since 1955 and is responsible for all of the gains of the last half decade. Ninety-six percent of the record shattering exports in 1974 were private commercial transactions. The omnipresent hand of agribusiness rests heavily upon the international export trade. Ninety percent of the outflow of America's largest export crop, its grain, is handled by just five concerns: the Cargill Grain Company, the Continental Grain Company, Cook Industries, Inc., Dreyfuss, and Bunge Company, in roughly that order of size and volume. The business world in which they operate is murderously competitive; the companies are secretive, and they watch each other like hungry predators for obscure bits of information that can make the difference between profits and losses. Of the five, only Cook Industries is not a privately held, family concern. With world grain prices skyrocketing, Cook's net income in fiscal 1974 shot up to $46.2 million from $22.7 million in 1973.[45] From its Memphis, Tennessee, headquarters the corporation oversees not only the merchandising and processing of grains and cotton that make up 60 percent of its business, but it also manufactures and sells building materials, distributes fertilizers and pesticides, and runs companies that control termites and sell real estate, insurance, and secondhand computers. A communication link ties its offices to the nation's grain exchanges; teleprinters transmit weather maps covering most of the world; nine agricultural economists, specializing in one particular crop, monitor its worldwide development, from planting to harvest. To negotiate an export sale, Cook and its competitors seek to outbid each other in public tenders, the means by which most foreign purchasers buy, or outmaneuver one another in the more secretive dealings, which big buyers such as the Russians, Chinese, and Japanese prefer. Once a sale is made, the company immediately enters the futures market and hedges the sale by buying as many bushels as it has just contracted to sell. Profits can also be made by means other than the expertise by which the big dealers size up the volatile market. It is reported that Continental, the principal in the Soviet grain sale of 1972, made its biggest gain in that sale through the shipping rates it was able to charge.

The mystery that shrouds the furtive operations of the giant international grain oligopolies evaporated slightly in the summer of 1975 and revealed some unsavory and illegal practices. Investigations by the United States attorney at New Orleans uncovered the fact that Bunge and Cook had shipped grain abroad with weights overstated. Grain of lower grade than foreign purchasers had paid for was shipped and in several instances damaged, and contaminated products were delivered. These frauds had been perpetrated on some occasions by bribing inspection officials of the United States Department of Agriculture. These illegal practices, which had been going on from 1964 to 1973, had apparently earned more than $5 million in ill-gotten gains for the two companies. These were no idle charges: in October 1975, Bunge, after extensive plea bargaining, pleaded nolo contendere to charges of conspiring to systematically steal grain. The company pledged to spend $2 million during the following three years in a self-policing operation to prevent future corruption, and was fined a paltry $20,000, the maximum the law allowed.[46]

Most American commodities sold for competitive prices in the world market of the fifties and sixties. However, for several crops that were in such surplus that foreign markets were essential (wheat, cotton, and feed grains), the world price was lower than the government's domestic support price. In these instances, the government paid export subsidies to shippers in order to bridge the gap. Such policies are an anachronism in today's inflated markets; apparently the last export subsidies paid were to the grain corporations that sold wheat to the Soviet Union in 1972.

On the other hand, the president is empowered to embargo exports of certain commodities if it is determined that supplies are perilously short in the United States. When soybean prices skyrocketed in the turbulent commodities market in the summer of 1973, shipments abroad were temporarily restricted; a quasi-embargo was placed on fertilizer exports when the world price was twice the domestic. In October 1974 President Ford temporarily halted a second massive grain sale to the Soviet Union and ordered the secretive export companies to ask permission before any large overseas sales were culminated in the future.[47] In the face of persistently mounting domestic food costs and the continuing pressures of international demands, strong pressures were being exerted in 1974 for an accentuation of such restrictionist, nationalistic policies.[48]

The second way that exports leave the United States is under government financed sales and in donations of agricultural products to needy foreign countries under Public Law 480, enacted in 1954 and substantially amended in 1966. These shipments, which totalled $23 billion in value by 1974, were an important humanitarian gesture; untold lives were saved in India alone during the famine of 1966. Nonetheless, the original purpose of Public Law 480 was not to alleviate hunger abroad; it was to dispose of a surplus of farm commodities whose storage costs alone were estimated at $1 million daily. The act has never been devoid of political purposes: its application was limited to friendly nations, and shipments had to be terminated to any nation which appropriated U.S. private property or failed to protect adequately American private holdings. In 1973–1974, as changing circumstances caused the virtual phasing out of the program, 42 percent of this aid was channeled to South Vietnam and Cambodia.[49]

Public Law 480 was not a giveaway program. The original statute provided for two types of exports: those paid for with local currencies nonconvertible into dollars, and direct donations to individual governments or to charities for distribution. The first was by far the most frequent and posed some vexing problems. Despite the attempt to sink American counterpart funds into loans for long-range development projects, and even to finance educational exchanges such as the Fulbright-Hays grants, the United States became the unwanted possessor of mammoth accumulations of nonconvertible foreign money. By one estimate, following the emergency shipments to India in 1966, about two-thirds of the currency circulating in that nation was actually owned by the United States.[50] Accordingly, amendments forbade any sales in nonconvertible currency after 1971; beginning in 1965 credit sales rose substantially, with payments being made through long-term dollar credit or with convertible local currency (see table 7).

Amendments in 1966 dressed up the program with a new name, "Food for Peace," which stressed surplus disposal less and humanitarian objectives more. To protect against scarcities at home, the amendments stipulated that no agricultural commodity could be certified for export under Public Law 480 if supplies were inadequate to provide for domestic needs, afford sufficient carryover, and meet anticipated commercial export requirements. By 1967, government concessional sales were diminishing; ironically, despite the name change, political objectives were more important than in the fifties. Shipments in 1974 were the smallest in any year since the act's adoption. The Soviet grain sale of 1972, exploding world food prices and escalating demands for commercial exports, had swept away the American farm surplus and left few reserves to provide food, as concessions or gifts, to the increasing numbers of the world's people who were hungry.[51]

Public Law 480 helped dispose of a portion of a backbreaking surplus; through its convertible credit sales it made a small contribution to alleviating an adverse balance of payments. It served important humanitarian purposes and cost, over a nineteen-year time period, about one-quarter the appropriation the military budget consumed in the fiscal year 1975. The most serious criticism levied against the program was that the dependence upon American food aid deterred underdeveloped nations from embarking upon attempts to enhance their own agricultural output and adopt needed measures to check rampant population growth. Nevertheless, the fact they had been among the major recipients of food aid did not inhibit the spectacular but short-lived success of the Green Revolution in India and Pakistan in the optimistic years of the late sixties and early seventies.

Imports of foreign agricultural products can influence American farm prices, and have periodically stirred intense political infighting. In the peak year of 1951, imports (about $5 billion worth) accounted for 10 percent of total cash receipts from farm marketings. From 1960 until 1970 they gradually crept upward at about a 2 percent annual rate, while imports of nonfarm products increased at an 11 percent annual rate. Then from 1969 to 1974, U.S. agricultural imports advanced 52 percent, to $9.55 billion in value, the greatest in history. (Most of this increase reflected higher world commodity prices.) Imports are divided into two categories: supplementary—commodities that compete with those produced domestically; and complementary—those which do not compete. Supplementary imports made up two-thirds of the total in 1974, compared with an average of 55.6 percent in the decade of the sixties. The three major farm imports are sugar, coffee, and processed meats. About half of the imports, principally complementary products, enter the United States duty free. For the remainder, tariffs average only 10 percent, the result of the reciprocal trade treaties that began in the New Deal years. American farmers are less sheltered by tariffs than farmers of most other nations.[52]

Section 22 of the Agricultural Adjustment Act authorizes the president to impose a quota fee in addition to the basic duty when imports of a particular product threaten to undercut price support programs. Thus in 1974 restrictions were in effect on imports of flour, cotton, sugar, some dairy products, and peanuts.[53]

Sugar was given special status by the Sugar Act of 1934, enacted in depression times when surpluses burdened the American market. Volume import quotas limited foreign

TABLE VII

U.S. Exports Under Specified Government Programs, 1955–1974
(In Millions of Dollars)

Year	Foreign Currency	Long Term Dollar and Convertible Currency Credit	Government to Government Donations for Disaster Relief and Economic Development	Donations Through Voluntary Agencies
1955	73		52	135
1956	439		63	184
1957	908		51	165
1958	657		51	173
1959	724		30	131
1960	824		38	105
1961	951		75	146
1962	1,030	19	88	160
1963	1,088	57	89	174
1964	1,056	48	81	189
1965	1,142	158	55	183
1966	866	181	87	180
1967	803	178	110	157
1968	723	300	100	150
1969	346	427	111	154
1970	309	506	113	128
1971	204	539	138	142
1972	143	535	228	152
1973	6	653	159	128
1974	***	573	146	144
(Preliminary)				
TOTAL	12,292	4,174	1,865	3,080

*Barter: Use of Commodity Credit Corporation commodities for barter or exchange to obtain strategic materials and material needs of foreign aid and assistance programs.

**Other: Mutual Security, AID

***Amount less than $500,000.

Barter*	Total P.L. 480	Other **	Total Specified Government Programs	Percent Total Agriculture Exports
125	385	450	835	26
298	984	355	1,339	38
401	1,525	394	1,919	41
100	981	227	1,208	30
132	1,017	210	1,227	33
149	1,116	167	1,283	28
144	1,316	186	1,502	30
198	1,495	74	1,569	30
48	1,456	14	1,470	29
43	1,417	24	1,441	24
32	1,570	26	1,596	26
32	1,346	42	1,388	21
23	1,271	37	1,308	19
6	1,279	18	1,297	21
1	1,039	11	1,050	18
	1,056	12	1,068	15
	1,023	56	1,079	14
	1,058	66	1,124	14
	946	84	1,030	8
	863	76	939	5
1,732	23,112	2,529	25,672	

M. Louise Perkins, "Fiscal 1974 Exports under Government Financed Programs Moved Below Billion Dollar Mark," USDA, ERS, *Foreign Agricultural Trade of the United States* (November 1974), p. 29.

shipments into the United States, and production quotas controlled domestic production. Certain sugar producing nations were assigned an import quota, hence guaranteed a share of the U.S. market (Cuba was dropped when the United States ceased to recognize the Castro regime). When world and domestic prices hit all-time highs in the winter of 1974, many quotas went unfilled. The act, an anachronism in a world of short sugar supplies, was not renewed, and expired 31 December 1974. Advocates of abolishing the Sugar Act contended that with import quotas removed, foreign suppliers would rush into the U.S. market, causing prices to decline. Major traders were skeptical. Sugar prices vacillate wildly—for example, 12.5¢ per pound, in 1964, to $1.25, in 1967, to 65.5¢, in November 1974. With demand increasing and supplies short, any major expansion of sugar production is unlikely because moneylending institutions are loathe to invest capital in so volatile a business.[54]

Setting Prices for Agricultural Products: The Commodities Market

A complex financial institution, the commodities market, overarches the entire food production and marketing process. The practice of forward buying and selling began more than one hundred years ago as a means to protect owners of large stocks of perishable commodities (for example, wheat or corn) from rapid price changes between the time of purchase from the farmer and sale to the processor. For example, if the owner of a country elevator bought grain in August at $1.50 per bushel and was then fearful of a price decline, he preferred to shift the risk to the processor by signing a futures contract in which the processor agreed to buy at $1.58 in November. The processor was just as unwilling to assume the complete risk, but perhaps in between were individuals with capital and their own assessment of the market who were willing to buy and sell futures contracts in anticipation of profit.

Ideally, the commodities market is a way of distributing the risk involved in trading in products with high price

volatility. In the ideal-type constructions, of which economists are so fond, it is regarded as an equilibrating institution. Commodity traders, by purchasing a grain crop in the
autumn when it is cheap, withholding it, and selling for a
profit later when the price has risen, serve to keep the price
equal throughout the entire year. Obviously, this vital function of commodities trading cannot be discounted—in normal circumstances it does its job well.[55] Nevertheless, the
commodities market is not a neutral institution which simply reflects classic impersonal workings of supply of and
demand for commodities. Given low margin requirements,
the vulnerability of the market to rumors, and short-term
phenomena, when economic conditions are unstable its erratic operations can have a profound effect not only upon
pricing but upon timing of marketing and even choice of
crops to be planted. Market activity has been stimulated to
record highs in participation (and prices) in the economically unsettled years of 1973 and 1974. Both long-term and
short-range changes in farm production and farm marketing were taking place. Under such circumstances, the commodities market, scarcely understood by anyone except
those who participate in it or try to teach students about it,
is deserving of more careful attention.

The trading of commodities takes place in several large
exchanges. At the largest and most important of these, the
Chicago Board of Trade, grains and grain products are
bought and sold. The Chicago Mercantile Exchange is primarily a livestock market, and a number of smaller exchanges, such as the New York Cotton Exchange and the
Kansas City Exchange, duplicate some of the operations of
the major Chicago centers. Until very recent changes were
made, trading on the exchanges was regulated by the Commodities and Exchange Commission consisting of three
members: the secretary of agriculture, the attorney-gen-
eral, and the secretary of commerce. Its staff was small, and
the parent body met infrequently. Even with the recent
changes, however, the great exchanges are largely self-
regulating.[56] Only a licensed broker, who buys a seat, may
participate in the frenzied activity in the pits. Each com-

modity is traded only in prescribed, usually sizeable, quantity (for example the standard contract for wheat is 5,000 bushels). For each commodity traded, delivery is made only in specified months; for example, all contracts in wheat futures call for delivery in December, March, May, July, or September. Bidding is controlled by imposing minimum fluctuations; for wheat, bids go up and down in ¼¢ units; daily limits whereby any commodity may advance or decline are set by the exchange—soybeans, for example, may rise or fall only 10¢ per bushel on any single trading day. Hours for trading are restricted on all exchanges to 9:30 A.M. to 1:15 P.M., Chicago time. Most farm produce, except fresh fruits, vegetables, and tobacco, are traded. Volume on the exchanges rose in 1974 to an unprecedented 27.7 million contracts traded. This was an 8 percent increase over 1973, but still not as great as the 41 percent increase during the period of 1972 to 1973. The estimated dollar value of the commodities so traded was a gigantic $555 billion.[57]

To establish a point of entry into the buying and selling process, some distinctions are necessary. There are two markets for most commodities: first, a cash or spot market where buyers and sellers meet and sales are made here and now; second, the futures market. A dealer in futures makes a contract to deliver or to receive at one of the specified delivery months. A buyer of a futures contract agrees to *purchase* and pay in full for a certain commodity to be delivered in some definite future month. When one sells a future, he contracts to *deliver* a given amount of the commodity at a specific price in a given month. Just to complicate things, the seller owns not a bushel of the product when he signs the contract, and he will probably own none at any time during the transaction.

Crudely simplifying for the nonspecialist, and sloughing off enough detail to appall a specialist, here is a clarifying example.[58] M. Miller contracts in August with B. Baker to deliver to him in January eight carloads of flour at a price that includes the cost of the wheat Miller used to produce the flour, his production costs, and a profit. Miller has no wheat in his warehouse so he buys with a futures contract 15,000 bushels of December wheat (the delivery month) for $1.50 per bushel. He pays his broker a margin, usually 5 to 10 percent of the purchase price, as proof of his good faith. If before December the price goes above $1.50, his broker will demand additional margin. In market parlance, Miller is a hedger. In order to protect himself from the risk of a price increase before he has to deliver to Baker, he, through buying the futures contract, assumes a position in futures, equal and opposite to his anticipated cash position come December. Miller is also termed "long" in wheat because he made a contract to *buy* in his first transaction.

S. Speculator, on the same August day, has decided that because of a likely decline in exports, the price of wheat is going to drop. Speculator therefore requests his broker to *sell* fifteen thousand bushels of December wheat at $1.50, and he, too, puts down a margin of the total price of the wheat he is pledged to sell. He, of course, owns not a bushel. Speculator, then, is short in wheat—his first contract was one to *sell.* Sometime before December, Speculator has to come up with wheat to deliver to Miller or get himself out of (offset) the contract. Actually, the dealings are not so stark: both the contracts of Miller and Speculator are processed through the clearinghouse of the Chicago Board of Trade, which becomes a third party to the contract, guaranteeing delivery of the wheat to Miller and the cash to Speculator at the time of his sale.

Come December, Speculator's prognosis proves correct. Foreign demand for wheat has declined and December futures are down to $1.40. Speculator has a paper profit of 10¢ for every bushel he contracted to sell ($1,500). Accordingly, Speculator asks his broker to buy back the December futures at the new, lower market price and takes his profit.

Meanwhile, poor Miller still has a contract to buy December wheat at $1.50. Has he been beaten out of $1,500 by Speculator? Not quite. Miller, too, calls his broker and tells him to sell the $1.50 contract, and he does take an immediate loss, 10¢ less per bushel than he paid. Having accepted that loss, however, Miller now buys the wheat he needs for the cash (spot) market price of $1.40; he now has cheaper wheat to convert to the flour he is delivering to Baker in January. Considering no other factor, all Miller has lost is the commission and brokerage fee. B. Baker, of course, has to maintain the high price of bread due to the relatively expensive flour he buys, but he can always pass that along to C. Consumer.

The protection afforded buyers, such as Miller, through selling hedges, was the principal reason for futures sales in the first instance; today most such purchasers will hedge. To understand the kind of price insurance hedging is intended to provide, a few more fundamentals are needed. The futures price is always higher than the cash price because of the costs of carrying charges (storing and insuring the commodity) and the interest charges on amounts over the margin. At the time of the sale, however, irrespective of the market, the cash price and the futures price will be the same. Here is an example of another kind of selling hedge where the price of wheat rises.

TABLE VIII

1 December	
Cash Market	*Futures Market*
M buys 5,000 bushels of wheat @ $1.40	M sells 5,000 bushels March wheat @ $1.48¼
1 February	
M sells 5,000 bushels of wheat @ $1.50	M buys 5,000 bushels March wheat @ $1.52¾
+10¢ per bushel	−4½¢ per bushel

In this instance Miller sacrificed 4½¢ because of his selling hedge; this is a chance most prudent buyers will take, gladly accepting the small loss as the price of protection against price declines.

In the real world of the commodities market, operations aren't so simple or prices so low. For one thing, any commodity may be sold six or seven times prior to delivery, and the original contracts may be signed before the crop is even in the ground. A number of supply and demand factors can influence futures prices. As an example, the market in soybeans exploded to record-shattering highs in frenzied trading in the summer of 1973. In the spring of that year farmers were contracting to sell for $3.00 per bushel, and they were happy about it, because this was higher than the government support price. The American crop was adequate, but meat-hungry foreign nations, who needed the "miracle crop" for animal feed, placed record high orders; the world supply of fish meal, the major competitor of soybeans as a nutrient for cattle, plummeted when the Peruvian anchovy catch failed. Since the price of futures is based upon an appraisal today of what the market will be in the future, and prospects for soybeans were extremely optimistic, the price shot upward. Those long in soybeans (mostly speculators) were ecstatic when the futures price by mid-June hit an unprecedented $12 per bushel. Shorts, meanwhile, went desperately scrambling to offset their contracts to deliver at the lower price.

Sugar futures took off in a similar speculative binge in November 1974. In what seemed like the plot line of a James Bond thriller, world supplies were short, the Sugar Act was expiring, and rumor had it that Arab oil money was being funneled into promising sugar futures. To complicate the intrigue, sugar beet production in the Soviet Union declined, Cuba reneged on promised deliveries to the Russians, and the latter were compelled to purchase a substantial amount on the open market—they negotiated a contract with Brazil. Before doing so, however, the Russians judiciously invested in sugar futures. Profits brought about by their own entry into the market more than paid for their Brazilian purchase.[59]

In such a frenetic buying and selling process, there is always the danger of a squeeze. This happens when there is less of a commodity certificated for delivery—an inspector must certify that the stored commodity is acceptable to the exchange and the weight accurate[60]—than the open interest (the total amount of contracts for delivery outstanding). The result is that the longs refuse to sell until the price level is satisfactory to them; and the shorts, scrambling for cover, may have to pay an amount far in excess of what they anticipated.

A year's activity in commodity trading for a grain crop such as corn (the most widely traded crop) begins when farmers start selling even before the May planting. Enough is sold to cover immediate production expenses. These are cash forward sales for harvest delivery to local elevators, who in turn sell to grain merchants. The merchants then are long in corn, and they hedge by selling new crop futures. Farmers hold a substantial portion of the corn crop on farms and in local storage facilities for sale throughout the year and complete selling the old crop just ahead of the succeeding year's harvest.

During the summer, corn for export is sold for fall or winter shipment. These transactions place export firms in short position, so they hedge by buying new crop futures. Processors and manufacturers who have large delivery commitments are usually short cash corn. To some extent, they cover (hedge) through purchases of futures contracts.

In theory, the futures market is the arena where commodity prices are established on the basis of supply and demand factors that are external to the market itself. Predictions about the weather, the crop outlook, export demands, or government reserve policies can produce sporadic price fluctuations. What influence has this on farm marketing and pricing? First, most participants in commodities trading are speculators—the purpose of commodity trading is to make a profit. In an important sense, a hedger is a speculator, too; he is reallocating and conserving capital for profit making investment elsewhere. The prevalence of speculators and the low margin requirements raise the constant danger of overheating—that is, the commitment of excess credit to a process where prices are set by rumors, intuition, and guesswork. This happened to soybean futures in the summer of 1973, and to sugar futures in the autumn of 1974. Second, the prices set in this fashion can influence supplies of commodities. High prices, of course, drain reserves and inventory. Moreover, farmers often decide how much of what they will plant by watching the price of futures. The frenzied trading in feed grains, exacerbated by speculation, is one reason for the temporary plight of American cattle raisers. High feed prices have compelled them to cut back supplies and leave livestock on pasturage rather than stuff them with costly feeds.[61]

"Cowboy Arithmetic": Cultivating the Internal Revenue Service

Commodity markets have a long past: William Jennings Bryan criticized them in his "Cross of Gold" speech. On the other hand, tax farming, or "cowboy arithmetic," as a means of attracting capital to agriculture is as new as the term agribusiness. Oppenheimer Industries, of Kansas City, for example, specializes in investing the excess capital of wealthy corporations or individuals in cattle and other agricultural activities. It accepts neither a client with a net worth less than five-hundred thousand dollars, nor one who is in an income tax bracket below 50 percent. Its specialty is tax saving through depreciation allowances, favorable capital gains levies, and other appropriate loopholes in the Internal Revenue Code. One method, already noted, is to rent cattle owned by affluent clients to farmers for fattening and finishing for market. One apparently satisfied Oppenheimer customer was the former governor of California, Ronald Reagan, who avoided payment of any state income tax in 1970.[62] Cal-Ag, of Palo Alto, California, provides management services that operate more than four thousand acres of farmland in California. The company promises its clients: "The owner of the farm never loses control of the operation, but he doesn't have to worry about day-to-day problems. He doesn't even have to know anything about farming to be a prosperous farmer . . . Cal Ag's experienced farm managers handle everything."[63]

Federal tax records in 1970 showed that at least three of every four individuals with incomes above one-hundred thousand dollars were, in one way or another, involved in farming. Not only were they able to report their profits from agriculture as long-term capital gains, with the attendant 50 percent reduction in the tax bill, but most of them claimed losses in farming that could be written off against taxes on nonfarm income.[64]

The Tax Reform Act of 1969 placed some restrictions upon livestock breeding as a tax shelter. Following its enactment, one firm went bankrupt, and Oppenheimer substantially reduced client investment in its cattle raising program. Any tax advantages resulting from establishing citrus groves were removed. Nevertheless, the act applied only to very large investments (yearly losses in excess of twenty-five thousand dollars) and left a substantial area where investors in cattle breeding could harvest tax advantages. The reform fell short of its declared objective of demolishing tax shelters in agriculture.[65]

Pocketbook to Dinner Table: The Consumer Pays More and More

To stop with a static description of the food marketing system leaves out the important developments of 1973 and 1974 that moved the farm news from the financial pages to the front pages of the nation's newspapers. Most consumers may not be aware of the specific figures detailed in table 9, but they need not be reminded of their consequences. The Consumer Price Index spiraled steadily upward from 127.7, in January 1973, to 155.4, in December 1974, (1967=100), with food prices leading the parade. The increase in food costs during these two years was greater even than that following the removal of price controls after World War II.[66] In the early stages of the escalation an unprecedented consumer meat boycott sought vainly to rally buyer power in protest against rising prices, and in a few places angry housewives abandoned their grocery carts and seized picket signs instead.

If the magnitude of food price increases and the specter of shortages were baffling, there was good reason. The United States, its citizens long acclimated to agricultural surpluses, produced one of the largest grain crops in its history in 1973; more cattle grazed the plains or grew fat in feedlots than ever before. Acreage that was long held out of production by government policy was plowed and planted; the grain reserves that once swelled warehouses and elevators virtually disappeared. The result: not a market glut but the highest food prices in the nation's history.

While the Consumer Price Index crept upward, prices received by farmers rode the inflationary spiral to an unprecedented peak of 208 in August 1973. Newspapers that summer often featured pictures of happy farmers perched on their tractors, expressing their obvious pleasure at the fortunate coincidence of bumper grain and livestock output at the same time that prices were at their highest since the war years. For the first time since the Department of Agriculture began to collect statistics, per capita income in the farm sector ($4,820 per person) was greater than that in the nonfarm sector ($4,270).[67] The differential would have been even greater had not the farmer been caught in the inflationary squeeze, too. Production expenses rose a hefty 19 percent; and in today's specialized economy the depleted dollar buys no more milk in paper cartons or hamburger wrapped in plastic for the farm wife from Iowa than for the suburbanite in Westchester County.

Had modern farmers won prosperity by gouging American consumers? Table 2 partly answers that question. The index of prices received by farmers bears little relation to the persistently ascending consumer price index. For the statistically minded, the two correlate at .42. Farm prices fell off rapidly from their August 1973 high. For livestock and poultry producers, the consequences were disastrous. Spurred by the abnormally high returns in the summer of 1973, herds and flocks had been expanded recklessly. Then,

TABLE IX

The Steady March of Inflation, 1973–1974 (1967 = 100)

Year	Month	Consumer Price Index	Food	Prices Received by Farmers
1973	January	127.7	135.7	145
	February	128.6	136.2	149
	March	129.8	136.6	159
	April	130.7	136.5	158
	May	131.5	137.9	163
	June	132.4	139.8	172
	July	132.7	140.9	173
	August	135.1	149.4	208
	September	135.5	148.3	191
	October	136.6	148.4	184
	November	137.6	150.0	181
	December	138.5	151.3	185
1974	January	139.7	153.7	198
	February	141.5	157.6	202
	March	143.1	159.1	194
	April	144.0	158.6	183
	May	145.6	159.7	175
	June	147.1	160.3	165
	July	148.3	160.5	176
	August	150.2	162.8	185
	September	151.8	165.0	181
	October	153.2	166.1	186
	November	154.3	169.2	182
	December	155.4	170.4	178

U.S. Bureau of Labor Statistics, *Monthly Labor Review* (July 1974), pp. 103–5; (December 1974).
USDA, ERS, *Farm Income Situation, July 1974*, pp. 8–9.
USDA, Statistical Reporting Service, U.S. Crop Reporting Board, *Agricultural Prices* (28 June 1974); (15 December 1974).
New York Times, 23 October 1974; 22 November 1974; 22 January 1975.

for cattle raisers, the price per hundred pounds dropped from $53.24 to $44.84, just between August and September. Prices slipped even further when the expanded herds and flocks began to reach market in early 1974. Meanwhile the costs for the farmer of feed grains, already the most rapidly increasing item in his budget, rose even higher. With supplies up, prices down, and costs up, some cattlemen were losing $50 to $100 for every steer they sold in 1974. Once the preceding year's corn crop had been exhausted, more and more animals were kept in pasture; numbers at the costly feedlots declined. In the fall of 1974, 28 percent fewer cattle were on feed than in the preceding year; in a few isolated but widely publicized incidents, farmers shot calves they could not afford to feed and donated the meat to famine relief. The sacrifices may not have been as great as the stories seemed to indicate; the great majority of all male dairy calves become veal during the first weeks of their lives anyway.[68]

Before attributing inflation in food prices to increased prosperity on the farm, it should be recalled that the farmer-producer typically receives between one-half and one-third of the dollar spent at the supermarket. The estimated annual retail cost of a "market basket," which averaged $1,537 in 1973, rose to $1,751 in the third quarter of 1974.[69] In 1973 the farmer's portion had been about 46¢, up from 40¢ in 1972. The U.S. Department of Agriculture attributed most of the gains in consumer prices in 1973 to these higher returns for the farmer. Then, when prices for farmers turned downward from their 1973 peak, a radical change took place. The higher prices at the grocery store in 1974, USDA charged, were mostly because of a marketing margin increase of 21 percent which left the farmer's share of the market basket dollar at about 43¢.[70] Don Paarlberg, chief economist of the USDA, charged that farm retail spreads had gone up 15 percent for beef, 68 percent for white flour, and 300 percent for sugar. Prices received by farmers in September 1974, as table 2 shows, were 7 percent below September of the preceding year—the retail price of food was 11 percent higher.[71]

Food processors and retailers were quick to respond, the retailers the most vehemently.[72] New York City bakers, trying to explain a price increase from 33¢ a loaf in 1973 to 61¢ in October 1974, reported that the wheat in a retail loaf cost them about 8¢. Milling costs at Pillsbury and General Mills had doubled since 1972; the price of shortening was up 80 percent, sugar costs had tripled, and wages were rising. Wonder Bread in the New York area was sold wholesale for 48½¢ a loaf, so the 61¢ price represented a 21.5 percent retailer markup.

In the wake of the USDA charges, A & P opened its books just far enough to divulge its "meat margin." The chain's vice president for merchandising denied that the marketing margin was going up because of profiteering by supermarket chains. At the same time, he revealed that A & P's markup on meats, 21.89 percent, was the highest since 1968, but hastened to add that marketing expenses of the chain consumed 19.09 percent of the retail price markup.[73] A representative of Colonial Stores supplied no figures, but admitted that his firm had not passed on reduced meat prices to consumers; at the same time when meat costs hit an all-time high in 1973, the chain had refrained from charging its customers higher prices.[74] Given that the usual profit of supermarkets is about 1¢ for every dollar of sales, the president of the National Association of Retailer Grocers admitted to a general increase to about 1½¢ in the summer of 1974. W. S. Mitchell, president of Safeway Stores, Inc., conceded a profit of 1½¢, but this was the result, he argued, of his company's more efficient operation. A & P, still nursing a hangover from "WEO," reported that its margin in the first nine months of 1974 was only 0.4 percent.[75]

Despite rising costs, most food processors chalked up record earnings in the inflation year of 1974. In the years preceding, the earnings of processors had grown at an annual rate of about 7 percent. In the first months of 1974, Esmark, producer of Swift brand name meats, the largest company in the industry in terms of dollar value of sales, boasted a generous 33 percent earnings increase; Kraftco's earnings went up 22 percent, Ralston-Purina, 14 percent, and Campbell Soups, 15 percent. On the other hand, earnings of the diversified giant, General Foods, were a modest 4 percent, and actually declined in the last quarter of 1974.[76]

The financial record of the supermarket chains wasn't so impressive. The best performer was Safeway, which surged into profit leadership in the industry by doubling its net profit in the third quarter of 1974 ($1.24 per share) from that of the preceding year. In September 1975 the company boasted of a 43 percent rise in profits in the preceding twelve weeks. Meanwhile poor A & P's temporary recovery evaporated; its new management sadly informed shareholders at the June 1975 annual meeting that the annual deficit for the fiscal year was $157 million and no dividends would be paid. More and more closings of stores were announced, and a new advertising blitz, for which the company managed to come up with $4 million in a six-week period in the summer of 1975, attempted to impress upon the public the company's new slogan, "Price and Pride."[77]

Perhaps these were not windfall profits, but rather than being buffeted by price inflation, most food processors and retailers had successfully turned the situation to their own profit advantage.

Even when the portion of the consumer's dollar, siphoned off by processors and retailers, is subtracted and escalating production costs taken into account, the striking per capita income figures for 1973 indicate that farmers' wallets were fatter than ever before, and some of their bank accounts must have been growing. Were these increments in farm income distributed equally among all farmers? Table 10 tells the story. The princely share of increased farm income went to the largest producers. Farms with sales over $100,-000 increased from 2.4 percent of all farms in 1972 to 3.8 percent in 1973.[78] At the same time their percentage of realized net income rose from 21.4 to 34.8. Stated more emphatically, of the total increased farm income in this two-year interval, $14,707,000 (51 percent of it) went to the 3.8 percent of farms in the very largest sales class. On the other hand, the share in realized net income of more than half of American farms, those in the two lowest sales classes, declined, and the actual income in the lowest class fell off a sizeable 21.8 percent. The farm prosperity of 1973 brought the greatest financial gains to those operators already at the top. It actually disadvantaged the small farmer and will likely work to speed his demise. Lest we hasten to pour out sympathy for the producers in the lowest sales class, it should be noted that most are part-time operators, deriving much of their income from work off of the farm. From 1972 to 1973 their actual estimated per capita income rose from $10,000 to a little above $15,000. The major changes had occurred between 1972 and 1973. A comparison of income distribution for 1974 with that of 1973 shows almost no percentage change according to class of farms. (See Epilogue, table 13.)

TABLE X

Classes of Farms by Sales and Net Income, 1972–1973[79]

Class of Farms	Percent in Class		Realized Net Income (Millions of Dollars)		Growth Rate	Percent of Realized Net Income	
	1972	1973	1972	1973		1972	1973
$100,000 +	2.4	3.8	3,697	11,206	67.0	21.4	34.8
$ 40,000 – 99,999	7.7	11.9	4,124	8,209	49.7	23.5	25.5
$ 20,000 – 39,999	14.1	19.8	4,440	7,519	40.9	25.4	23.3
$ 10,000 – 19,999	12.8	11.7	2,265	2,411	6.	12.9	7.5
$ 5,000 – 9,999	12.2	9.2	1,203	1,046	–15.	6.9	3.2
$ 2,500 – 4,999	15.4	17.2	799	1,022	21.8	4.6	3.2
$ 2,500 –	35.4	26.2	993	815	–21.8	5.6	2.5
ALL FARMS	100.0	100.0	17,521	32,228	45.6	100.0	100.0

To explain how the shrunken consumer food dollar is divided up among big farmers, processors, and retailers still doesn't answer why the shrinkage occurred in the first place. The demand for and the supply of food products is determined by the aggregated preference choices of millions of consumers; but it is also influenced by deliberate policy decisions of powerful political and business leaders.

Because of the patterns of choice ingrained by two decades of experience, consumers themselves were partly responsible for the high food prices they were paying in 1973 and 1974. Traditionally, Americans have enjoyed cheap food, as the historic lower income for the farm sector testifies. In addition, since 1933, government price support policies insulated the price of key commodities from the untrammeled operation of a free market economy. Sustained by such indirect subsidies, per capita food consumption shot upward in the affluent postwar years, and people developed tastes for costly products such as handy prepared and convenience foods, attractively and expensively packaged. Urged along by seductive television advertising, pampered taste buds demanded juicy steaks and greasy hamburgers so often that meat consumption soared from 60 pounds a person in 1950 to 116 in 1972. Surprisingly, compared to other necessary cost items in middle-class budgets, it wasn't costing that much. In 1960, 20 percent of total disposable income of Americans went for food; this had declined to 16.4 percent in 1973, even with price inflation. For whatever consolation it offers, food price inflation in the United States has been less than in most other industrialized countries.[80] Statistics such as these, frequently cited by spokesmen for the Department of Agriculture, while valid in the aggregate, ignore the bitterest consequences of food price inflation. Higher prices mean emptier market baskets for the poor, the retired, and those on fixed incomes. The Bureau of Labor Statistics records that in 1972 a family with a $12,700 income spent 24.5 percent of it for food; a family earning $9,000 spent 27.2 percent, and a family with income of less than $6,300 spent 30.5 percent.[81]

The most important influence that has made food prices the domestic leaders in a worldwide inflationary cycle has been a series of policy decisions that have had important implications, both domestically and internationally. Devaluation of the dollar in 1971 and 1973, designed to rectify adverse balances of payments, was followed by a series of events that quickened demand for American farm products abroad. Grain harvests in 1972 were poor in China, India, Australia, Indonesia, and the Soviet Union, the world's leading wheat producing nation. Disappearance of anchovies from Peruvian waters increased demands for American feed grains abroad. Enhanced demand, due to the rising standards of living in middle-level developing nations such as Taiwan, Korea, Mexico, and Spain, prompted the record high exports of 1973 and 1974 already noted. Confronted with soaring foreign demands, the Nixon administration chose to implement its program to "get the government out of agriculture." The historic grain reserves were released into the commercial market. Every encouragement was given to bolstering exports, for dollars earned by farm commodities were desperately needed to balance off the inflated price of imported oil.

Increased demand and deliberately decreased supply forced farm prices so high that the price supports in effect since the New Deal became a redundancy. Rising world market prices made sales abroad highly profitable; and in a free enterprise system the great grain exporting corporations sell to the highest bidder, whether an American baker, a German importer, or a representative of the Soviet Union. Accordingly, the great American grain surplus drained away to foreign markets. Whether they realized it or not, American consumers were competing for products in finite supply with shoppers in Yokohama or Munich.[82]

In the summer of 1974, fields that were fallow since the 1930s were being cropped again. Government payments to agriculture, which had reached an all-time high of $3.9 billion in 1972, fell to $2.6 billion in 1973. Payments in 1974, a meager $534 million, were the lowest since 1955.[83] If the aim of government policy was to remove the old surplus-preventing restrictions in order to allow American farm production to expand freely, it was no spectacular success.

Production for 1974 fell behind that for 1973.[84] Neither was the American farmer so noticeably smiling in the winter of 1974, for his income was not keeping pace with the steady march of inflation. Computed in preinflation 1967 dollars, net income per farm was $5,169 in 1972; it shot up to peak at $9,235 in 1973, but in the third quarter of 1974 it fell to $5,970. For the year 1974 disposable personal income of the farm population, $4,258, again sank below that of the nonfarm population (farm=91.8 percent of nonfarm).[85]

At a time when greater efficiency and increased production seem the most hopeful ways to correct an imbalance of supply and demand, "progress" has thrown some substantial obstacles in the way of the classic expectation that capital and manpower should flow to areas where demand is great and supply is short. Inflated interest rates (if there is money to borrow at all), high equipment costs, and delays in deliveries of eight to twelve months hardly facilitate easy entry into farming. Land values are at unprecedented highs. Ironically, labor is not available in the countryside. Nothing can lure back the sharecroppers. The dispossessed family farmers have retired to the village or sleep in the country churchyard. Part-time farming has become a way of life: truck drivers and factory workers who reside in the countryside have neither capital nor the impulse to abandon it.[86]

The food price increases of 1973–1974 caught economists by surprise. Perchance what is happening is a temporary phenomenon, and the dislocations may be adjusted by increased technological advances, greater efficiency, and new government policies. On the other hand, the inflationary spiral of the mid-seventies may be symptomatic of the unpredictable consequences rapid technological change can produce. Ruthless centralization and consolidation have made agriculture into a big, integrated business and driven small producers out; it has reaped profits for the large farmers, processors, and retailers; it has stimulated luxury demands at home. Long conditioning to surpluses and relatively low prices have blunted any serious consideration of whether American food producing capacity, as it has been structured in the last twenty years, is adequate to meet the severe demands now being placed upon it. If Americans are to continue to enjoy a standard of living that consumes 40 percent of the energy used in the world each year, exports of farm commodities are vital to maintain a favorable trade balance. Moreover, America, the "bread basket of the world," was already confronting in 1974 what may be the most portentous problem of all: in the poorest nations of the world, rampant population growth was already exceeding global food production capacities. For at least 700 million people the bitter Malthusian equation was becoming grim reality.

Notes

1. Earle E. Gavett and Robert E. Frye, "Food and Fiber Employment Opportunities," *USDA Yearbook, 1970,* pp. 338–45; Denis F. Dunham, "Marketing Costs are Double the Farm Value of Food Products," *USDA Yearbook, 1970,* pp. 107–12; Everett Rogers, *Social Change in Rural Society,* (New York: Appleton-Century-Crofts, 1960) p. 345.
2. A "market basket" consists of 65 retail items, theoretically the food supply for a family of 3.2 persons for an entire year. It is a statistical measure and is not intended to reflect "actual" costs, since only domestically produced farm produce is included.
3. *New York Times,* 15 September 1974.
4. Allen B. Paul and William T. Manley, "The Marketing System for Food, Fabulous and Dynamic," *USDA Yearbook, 1970,* pp. 99–100; U.S., Federal Trade Commission, *Economic Report on the Structure and Competitive Behavior of Food Retailing* (Washington: U.S. Government Printing Office, 1966), pp. 76–77.
5. USDA, *Handbook of Agricultural Charts, 1973,* p. 33.
6. Ingrid Jones, *Some Corporations and Conglomerates That Are Marketing Brand-Name Food Products* (Washington: Agribusiness Accountability Project, n.d.).
7. North Central Regional Extension Service, "Who Will Control U.S. Agriculture?" Special Publication 27 (Urbana: University of Illinois, August 1972), p. 8, as quoted in Susan Sechler and Susan DeMarco, *Some Facts and Figures Supporting Action Against Concentration in the Food Industry* (Washington, D.C.: Agribusiness Accountability Project, December 1973), p. 5. The Agribusiness Accountability Project, source for some of

the data in this discussion, is a nonprofit, nonpartisan public interest group financed in part by grants from The Field Foundation, Stern Fund, Norman Foundation, Ottinger Foundation, Cummins Engine Foundation, and Janss Foundation. In all instances where I have been able to verify statistical data I have found their research to be impeccable.

8. Dunham, "Marketing Costs," p. 108; Kermit Bird and Charles O'Dell, "How They Saved the Soup: The Technology of Marketing," *USDA Yearbook, 1970,* p. 78.

9. Bird and O'Dell, "How They Saved the Soup," p. 78.

10. Sechler and DeMarco, *Some Facts and Figures, p. 10.*

11. Jennifer Cross, *The Supermarket Trap* (New York: Berkley Medallion edition, 1971 [Bloomington: Indiana University Press]), pp. 39–40.

12. Jennifer Cross, "The Politics of Food," *Nation* 219 (17 August 1974): 115.

13. William G. Shepherd, *Market Power and Economic Welfare* (New York: Random House, 1970), table 13, pp. 274–81.

14. Linda Kravitz, "Who's Minding the Co-op?" (Washington, D.C.: Agribusiness Accountability Project, March 1974), p. 41n.

15. Standard and Poor's Corporation, "Standard NYSE Stock Reports," vol. 41, no. 27 (7 February 1974); see also A. V. Krebs, *Ralston-Purina Company:* A Report of the Agribusiness Accountability Project (Washington, D.C.), January 1973. Ralston-Purina's profits for the period September to December 1974 were up 16.4 percent from the same period the preceding year. This was an impressive advance, but paltry compared with that of the sugar giant Amstar which reported the same day a gain of 278.3 percent. *New York Times,* 17 January 1975.

16. Smith, Barney & Co., "DeKalb Agresearch," Research Report 24–75 (22 May 1974).

17. Standard and Poor's Corporation, "Tenneco, Inc.," *Standard NYSE Stock Reports,* vol. 41, no. 107 (5 June 1974); George L. Baker and Ronald B. Taylor, "The Conglomerate Green Giant," *Nation* 214 (13 March 1972): 332–35; Peter Barnes and Larry Casalino, *Who Owns the Land?* (Berkeley, Calif.: The Center for Rural Studies, 1972), pp. 4–5, 15; Robert D. Hershey, "Tenneco's Profit Pipeline," *New York Times,* 17 November 1974, p. F1.

18. Parenthetically, James T. Halverson, director of F.T.C.'s Bureau of Competition, noted that throughout the nation forty-three wholesale bakers with eighty plants went out of business during 1972 and 1973, *New York Times,* 11 December 1974; A. V. Krebs, *International Telephone and Telegraph Corporation* (Washington, D.C.: Agribusiness Accountability Project, December 1973).

19. Cooperatives could still, however, be prosecuted for monopolistic practices in violation of the Sherman and Clayton acts.
20. Kravitz, "Who's Minding the Co-op?," pp. 9, 137–41.
21. Ibid., pp. 127–29. Agway is a taxpaying corporation founded, in 1964, by merger of two long-established regional cooperatives: Cooperative Grange League and the Eastern States' Farmers' Exchange.
22. Linda Kravitz's study is a thorough analysis of a topic deserving greater discussion than the brief treatment here.
23. Rogers, *Social Change in Rural Society,* p. 363.
24. Kent Pollock, "How That Co-op Scandal Came to Be: Who Milked the Lehigh Valley Co-op," *Philadelphia Inquirer,* 25 August 1974, p. 1A; *Philadelphia Inquirer,* 28 November 1974.
25. *New York Times,* 18 November, 23 November 1974.
26. These supports, in effect since the New Deal, are designed to smooth out milk prices, particularly in the spring when pastures are green and cows are calving, hence supplies abundant.
27. Kravitz, "Who's Minding the Co-op," pp. 27–28.
28. *New York Times,* 4 August 1974.
29. *Philadelphia Bulletin,* 14 August 1974.
30. *New York Times,* 14 October 1974.
31. Standard and Poor's Industry Survey, *Food Processing* (22 August 1974), pp. F–25.
32. *New York Times,* 26 November 1974, 29 January 1975; *San Francisco Chronicle,* 1 August 1975.
33. Eighty-eight percent of cases involving preferential discounts of processors to retailers, 1959 to 1965, that came before the Federal Trade Commission involved food firms. All of the nine top grocery chains were implicated. Cross, *Supermarket Trap,* pp. 28, 54.
34. *New York Times,* 18 December 1974.
35. *New York Times,* 12 January 1975; Cross, *Supermarket Trap,* p. 83.
36. U.S., FTC., *Economic Report on the Structure and Competitive Behavior of Food Retailing,* p. 276.
37. Cross, *Supermarket Trap,* p. 126.
38. *New York Times,* 5 November 1974.
39. Ibid., 28 October 1974, 12 January 1975.
40. Jim Hightower, *Corporate Giantism in the Food Economy* (Washington, D.C.: Food Action Committee [Agribusiness Accountability Project] December 1973), p. 11.
41. Paul and Manley, "The Marketing Systems," pp. 94–98.
42. "The American West and Foreign Markets, 1850–1900," in David M. Ellis, ed., *The Frontier in American Development* (Ithaca: Cornell University Press, 1969), pp. 381–406.
43. USDA, ERS., *U.S. Foreign Agricultural Trade, Statistical Report, Fiscal Year, 1974,* p. 2; USDA, ERS., *Foreign Agricultural*

Trade of the United States (November 1974), p. 4; (December 1974), p. 4; USDA, ERS, Outlook and Situation Board, *Outlook for U.S. Agricultural Exports* (10 December 1974). USDA, ERS, *Agricultural Outlook,* AO–5 (October 1975), p. 16.

44. USDA, ERS, *U.S. Foreign Agricultural Trade, Statistical Report, 1974,* pp. 1, 3–19, 23–25. The Netherlands and Canada are among the major importers but substantial portions of deliveries to them are transshipped elsewhere. Purchases by the Soviet Union declined from 900 million in 1973 to 509 million in 1974, less than P.R.C. USDA, ERS, *Agricultural Outlook,* AO–5 (October 1975), p. 16.

45. In the first quarter of the 1975 fiscal year slower export volume and a reduced U.S. grain crop caused a substantial drop in net income.

46. Seth S. King, "Five Grain Dealers Dominate in a Hungry World," *New York Times,* 10 November 1974, p. F3; *New York Times,* 25 June, 9 October 1975.

47. Cook shipped 570,000 metric tons of corn and 900,000 of wheat in mid-November in compliance with the president's guidelines. The original Soviet order was for 1.3 million tons of corn and 900,000 tons of wheat. Part of the balance of this and other outstanding grain contracts were cancelled by the Soviet Union in late January 1975, *New York Times,* 16 January 1975.

48. Dewain H. Rahe, "U.S. Foreign Trade is Vital to Our Farmers and to Our Economy," *USDA Yearbook, 1970,* pp. 255–63; William A. Faught and Edward H. Glade, Jr., "Younger, Bigger, Richer—The Farm Market of Today," *USDA Yearbook, 1970,* p. 64; D. Gale Johnson, "Interrelations in Our Policies for Agriculture, Trade and Aid," *USDA Yearbook, 1970,* pp. 244–46.

49. M. Louise Perkins, "Fiscal 1974 Exports Under Government Financed Programs Moved Below Billion Dollar Mark," USDA, ERS, *Foreign Agricultural Trade of the United States* (November 1974), p. 29; O. H. Goolsby, G. R. Kreur, and C. Santmyer, *P. L. 480 Concessional Sales,* USDA, ERS, Foreign Agricultural Economics Report No. 65 (Washington, D.C.: U.S. Government Printing Office, September 1970), pp. 20–21.

50. "World Hunger: Enemy of U.S. Prosperity," *Forbes,* 1 March 1966, quoted in William and Paul Paddock, *Famine, 1975!* (New York: Little, Brown & Co., 1967), p. 180.

51. In December 1974, an amendment to P. L. 480, sponsored by Sen. Hubert Humphrey, stipulated that no more than 30 percent of food aid could be given to countries not classified by the United Nations as "most seriously affected" by food and capital shortages, *New York Times,* 21 January 1975.

52. USDA, ERS, *Foreign Agricultural Trade of the United States* (December 1974), pp. 27–40, 45–46.

53. USDA, Foreign Agricultural Service, Trade Operations Division, Import Branch, *Import Controls Under Section 22 of the Agricultural Adjustment Act, As Amended* (July 1972). Import quota fees on wheat were suspended subseqent to the date of this publication.
54. *New York Times,* 12 December 1974, 3 February 1975.
55. Paul A. Samuelson, *Economics,* 9th ed. (New York: McGraw-Hill Book Co., 1973), p. 420.
56. Legislation of October 1974, which became effective in April 1975, established a new five member Commodities Futures Trading Commission outside of the Department of Agriculture. The new commission regulates all commodities, including some previously free of controls; it has power to issue injunctions to arrest trading abuses and can levy fines for violation of trading rules. *New York Times,* 11 October 1974, 24 September 1974.
57. *New York Times,* 18 January 1975.
58. For information on the operation of the commodities market I have relied upon a helpful booklet, Merrill, Lynch, Pierce, Fenner and Smith, *How to Buy and Sell Commodities* (May 1974); Thomas A. Hieronymous, *Economics of Futures Trading* (New York: Commodities Research Bureau, 1971); Gerald Gold, *Modern Commodity Futures Trading,* 6th ed. rev. (New York: Commodities Research Bureau, 1971).
59. Isadore Barmash, "Soaring Sugar Costs Arouse Consumers and U.S. Inquiries," *New York Times,* 15 November 1974, p. 1; *New York Times,* 29 November 1974. Seth S. King, "The Money Plant," *New York Times Magazine,* 9 September 1973, pp. 36–37.
60. Some leeway is permitted on the grade of the commodity delivered and a premium or discount from the stated price will accordingly be allowed.
61. This is not an irrational result. Feeding grain to cattle on feedlots, given the low food efficiency ratio of cattle, is not the most efficient use of grain.
62. *New York Times,* 5 December 1971.
63. Publicity materials sent to writer by Jerry Arrego, vice president, marketing, Cal-Ag Farms.
64. *New York Times,* 5 December 1971.
65. For a technical discussion of these tax reforms, see Hoy F. Carman, "Tax Loss Agricultural Investments After Tax Reform," *American Journal of Agricultural Economics* 54 (November 1972): 627–34.
66. Because of different base years, annual estimates are not precisely comparable. For long range data, see U.S., Bureau of the Census, *Historical Statistics of the United States, Colonial*

Times to 1957 (Washington, D.C.: U.S. Government Printing Office, 1960), p. 125.

67. USDA, ERS, *Farm Income Situation* (July 1974); p. 50. Compare with the historical statistics in chap. 1.

68. *New York Times,* 29 November 1974, 5 November 1974.

69. *New York Times,* 14 November 1974.

70. Ibid., USDA, ERS, *Agricultural Outlook,* AO–5 (October 1975), p. 12.

71. *Philadelphia Bulletin,* 1 November 1974.

72. This is understandable. USDA's charges seemed to place more of the responsibility for widening marketing margins on the retailers, not the processors. *New York Times,* 20 October 1974.

73. *New York Times,* 20 November 1974.

74. *Philadelphia Inquirer,* 22 September 1974.

75. *New York Times,* 16 June 1974, 18 December 1974, 20 January 1975.

76. *New York Times,* 2 December 1974, 21 January 1975.

77. *New York Times,* 28 September, 1 October 1974, 14 March, 18 June, 29 September, 30 September 1975.

78. This is partly the result of farms below the $99,999 margin in 1972 pushing over the magic breaking point in 1973.

79. USDA, ERS, *Farm Income Situation* (July 1974), pp. 68, 72. Growth rate as used in the chart = (1973–1972) / 1973.

80. USDA, *Handbook of Agricultural Charts, 1973,* pp. 39, 41, 42.

81. Citied in Martha M. Hamilton, *The Great American Grain Robbery and Other Stories* (Washington, D.C., Agribusiness Accountability Project, 1972), p. 5n.

82. Wright Investor's Service estimated that the export-dominated increase in U.S. food prices resulted in a 17.2 percent increment in 1973 and 1974; the total increase was about 21 percent. *New York Times,* 26 January 1975.

83. USDA, ERS, *Farm Income Situation* (July 1974), pp. 6, 9, 64; USDA, ERS, *Farm Income Situation* (February 1975), p. 7.

84. With 1967 = 100, 1972 = 110, 1973 = 112; 1974 = 106. Production increased in 1975.

85. Daniel J. Balz, "Farm Problems Remain to Be Met," *National Journal Reports* (21 December 1974), p. 1922. USDA, ERS, *Farm Income Statistics,* Statistical Bulletin 547 (July 1975), p. 32.

86. James T. Bonnen, "Discussion of the 1973 Economic Report of the President: Implications for Agricultural Policy," *American Journal of Agricultural Economics* 55 (August 1973): 391–97.

CHAPTER SEVEN

The Role of the Federal Government

Agricultural opinion is not made by some undifferentiated group of hard-working farm operators. It is made by the articulate, the prosperous, and the influential both within and without the primary community of agricultural producers.

—Charles Rosenberg

The role of the federal government in American agriculture has been relegated to a separate chapter and its discussion postponed not because it is unimportant but because it is *vitally* important. In no small measure the modernization and transformation of farming has been aided, abetted, and subsidized by the United States government. Although little more than 4 percent of the population remain farmers, agricultural policy in the mid-seventies is one of the critical issues that confronts the American political system.

Neither the press nor the media devote much attention to the often dreary details of agricultural policy. In discussions of the world food crisis there has been little analyses of policy alternatives, and historical perspective has been lacking. How many informed citizens have contemplated the implications of the fact that since the thirties the so-called individualistic farming enterprise has been the most politically controlled segment of the American economy, the only one where, without stretching the concept, national planning might be said to exist? How many know that the United States Department of Agriculture administers more regulatory laws and programs than any other government agency?[1] How many are aware that legislation of August 1973 altered policy precedents a quarter century old, and that by 1974 the Department of Agriculture's expenditures for food relief were greater than the cost of its services to farmers?

Research, education, and regulation are the major functions of the sprawling Department of Agriculture, which employs eighty-three thousand persons, placing it third behind the Department of Defense and the Post Office. The regulatory functions of the department have multiplied since the thirties and, understandably, are in the spotlight of most policy discussions; still it is debatable whether historically they represent the most significant government activity in the agricultural sector.

Since its inception in 1862, and its elevation to cabinet status in 1889, the department has functioned as an immense and efficient scientific arm of American agriculture, conducting extensive and far-reaching research to improve farm output, find new uses for farm products, protect American agriculture, statistically monitor the production and marketing process, and disseminate its findings to the farm population. Although sparsely publicized, such innovations as frozen orange juice, wash and wear cotton fabrics, instant mashed potatoes, penicillin, aerosol cans, and a variety of pesticides, including 2,4–D, have come from USDA laboratories. The Economic Research Service makes agriculture the best served by statistical intelligence of any segment of the American economy.

Structurally, in the "old" department, scientific research was carried on in a number of independent bureaus, often headed by dedicated scientists such as Harvey W. Wiley, father of pure food and drug legislation and the first chief of the Bureau of Chemistry.

In 1953 the various scientific agencies, among them the Bureau of Animal Husbandry, the Bureau of Soils, the Bureau of Entomology, and the Bureau of Home Economics, were consolidated into the Agricultural Research Service. Much of the scientific activity takes place in the Agricultural Research Center at Beltsville, Maryland, probably the largest such establishment in the world. In addition, the department, in 1967, operated more than one hundred field stations, located in nearly every state, and in 1965 more than fifteen thousand persons were employed in the research and disease-pest control programs.[2]

A network that encompasses two other vast institutions complements and occasionally conflicts with the research programs of USDA. The Morrill Act of 1862 underwrote, through the sale of public lands, the establishment of a series of state land grant colleges designed primarily for agricultural education. Their pioneer attempts to carry on agricultural research and disseminate the results were supplemented in 1887 by the Hatch Act, which provided for federal subventions to each state that established an agricultural experiment station. The Adams Act of 1906 doubled appropriations and, at the same time, increased the authority of the department to coordinate and supervise the vagrant and sometimes trivial researches of the experiment stations. The Smith-Lever Act of 1914 relieved overworked scientists and professors from time-consuming lecture and field work by providing for the appointment, in each agricultural county of the nation, of a county agent, nominally attached to the faculty of the land grant college, who would work with farmers to encourage new technology and introduce scientific farming. In the following years, the Smith-Hughes Act subsidized the teaching of vocational agriculture in secondary schools across the country.

On few investments by the federal government has the social rate of return been so high. Contemporary econometricians who have devised statistical measures of government contribution to economic growth estimate an overall social return on agricultural research of 30 percent. In the case of the development of hybrid seed corn, if the hypothetical value of corn production without the innovation is compared with the actual value of output that resulted from the innovation, a research expenditure of about $3 million produced a net social return of $248 million, even with the costs of research and development subtracted.[3]

Who is the constituency for agricultural research? Who ought to be the constituency? From the days of the Hatch Act to the present, conflicting claims of scientists, administrators, consumers, producers, rival farm organizations, and strategically placed congressmen have made the issue of research priorities a bitterly contested political battleground. At one level, the goals of scientists concerned with basic research conflicted with the objectives of college and experiment station administrators who, beholden to niggardly state legislatures for funds, insisted upon practical experiments like testing soil for farmers and servicing the needs of powerful business and agricultural interests in the states. At another level, USDA sparred each budget year with the state bodies over how federal appropriations should be divided. (Nevertheless, budget conscious rural congressmen were usually not sparing in their support for agricultural research.) In broader perspective, while the social benefits of disease eradication, nutrition research, and discoveries such as penicillin cannot be denied, the research activities of USDA, the extension stations, and the land grant colleges have showered benefits disproportionately upon those groups best organized, more prosperous, and more influential. Professor Charles Rosenberg summarized the problem:

Agricultural opinion is not made by some undifferentiated group of hard-working farm operators. It is made by the articulate, the prosperous, and the influential both within and without the primary community of agricultural producers. Educated and more highly capitalized farmers, editors of farm and rural papers, country bankers, insurance agents, merchants and implement dealers make up the visible agricultural concensus. They were the men active in most farmers' organizations and specialized producers' associations and who had come to accept scientific knowledge as necessary for successful economic competition.[4]

Despite its apparent timeliness to the circumstances of 1937 or 1973, the quotation's point of reference is the problems of the agricultural experiment stations in the early years of the twentieth century.

The most determined attempt to realign the priorities of the Department of Agriculture came in the heady reform atmosphere of the early New Deal years when dedicated social scientists like M. L. Wilson, Howard Tolley, L. C. Gray, and Rexford Tugwell, coordinating their activities with the various New Deal relief agencies, embarked upon a series of land-use projects and assistance programs for the rural poor. They even attempted to create a viable political constituency among small farmers. One result of their efforts was the model farm communities created under the Resettlement Administration. The later Farm Security Administration underwrote small low-interest loans to farmers and to tenants for the purchase of property; it operated camps for dispossessed migrants, like the Joads in *The Grapes of Wrath,* in California. Attempts were made to establish grass roots committees to provide democratic participation in long-range planning, the ultimate objective of the social scientists.

The ambitions of the planners clashed with the objectives of some of the most powerful interest groups in American agriculture. The American Farm Bureau Federation, a private association linked closely with the extension service and land grant colleges, perceived USDA primarily as a service agency for commercial farmers and feared the political consequences of a counter-organization of the small and less affluent operators. Influential congressional allies in the House and Senate agricultural committees abhorred public planning and feared centralization of authority. Once Secretary of Agriculture Henry A. Wallace, who was sympathetic to reform, was replaced by successors less competent, and wartime needs caused a shift from production control to production expansion, Congress and department administrators chipped away at the innovative programs, and by 1948 most had been dismantled and their sponsors removed from positions of responsibility.[5]

In the decades since World War II, while technology and migration were transforming American farming, the technical and scientific infrastructure of the Department of Agriculture has functioned as a service agency for processors, organized commodity associations, big farmers, and powerful organized interest groups.[6] Chiefly lip service has been directed to the rural poor and the small, marginal farmers; the benefits to consumers of the research activities of the Agriculture Research Service have often been by-products of projects whose principal beneficiaries were those who produce, manufacture, and sell food.

Hard Tomatoes, Hard Times, a report of the Agribusiness Accountability Project, attacks the priorities of the land grant colleges and the associated experiment stations and boldly charges that the millions of displaced rural dwellers who have poured into cities are "the waste products of an agricultural revolution designed within the land grant complex." It goes on to say: "Today's urban crisis is a consequence of failure in rural America. The land grant complex cannot shoulder all the blame for that failure, but no single institution—public or private—has played a more crucial role." The report charges that the $750 million annual subventions were being devoted to projects that aided agribusiness and the largest of producers. One illustration, which gave the report its title, was the research that developed "hard" tomatoes, designed to expedite mechanical harvesting. The author estimated that only 5 percent of the 6,000 man-years of research annually were devoted to "people-oriented" projects, such as plans to improve the quality of rural life.[7]

Closer to home, a group within USDA, the "Young Executives," warned, in October 1974, that in an era of spiraling food prices, increased ecological awareness, shortages, and consumer advocacy, the department was ignoring the needs of the largest of all inchoate constituencies: people who eat. Public confidence in the agency was eroding, the report stated, and it was commonly regarded as catering to the needs of big business and farming interests. Unless the department's information program was liberalized and its image changed, the overwhelming majority of congressmen who represent urban constituencies could seize control of farm policy and the USDA would "fade as an instrument of public policy."[8]

The agricultural policy that guided the United States from 1933 to 1973 was forged in response to the severest crisis American farmers ever confronted, the depression of the 1930s. In seminal legislation of 1933, 1936, and 1938, fundamental concepts were defined which still set the boundaries of farm policy. As important as these decisions were, there is no need to join company with the able historians who have made the New Deal the pivot for most analyses of the farm issue over the last thirty years.[9] The seminal New Deal programs were conceived in an era of over-production; the objective since has been to limit supply, increase demand, and buttress a volatile price structure. That era of plenitude abruptly ended in the mid-seventies. In a context where demand is escalating and pushing commodity prices prohibitively high both for domestic and foreign consumers, New Deal agricultural precedents are an anachronism. Further, viewed in historical perspective, the technological innovations of the postwar period that were revolutionizing farming and driving the traditional yeoman into oblivion had more significant social consequences than all the legislative enactments, no matter how appropriate they may have been at the time. It is in this context that we will examine some of the milestones in the process that carried farm policy through an era of abundance into one of scarcity.

Given their complexity and the tortuous interest group politics that produced them, agricultural programs, once adopted, assumed a life of their own and tended to persist and place boundaries upon future decision making. The result has been a confusing disparity between the pious legislative debates, authoritative policy pronouncements, and the rhetoric of politicians, and the realities of social change in the agricultural sector. Policy precedents set during the New Deal period served as guidelines through the 1970s, despite the fact that during that long interval at least 22 million people had moved away from farms, a technological revolution greater than any in the history of American agriculture had taken place, and economic power in the food production industry was being concentrated in the hands of oligopolistic processors and retailers. In part it has been one vast masquerade, because the powerful interest groups that are the movers and shapers of agricultural policy find it convenient to hide behind the myth of the family farmer and to cloak their campaigns for commercial advantage in the nostalgic rhetoric of agrarian fundamentalism. As with the fruits of the research carried on by the USDA, the principal advantages of its regulatory policies since the 1940s have been bestowed upon the big, heavily-capitalized commercial food producers. As for the rural poor, remaining behind in the depleted countryside, their problems could be conveniently relegated to such government agencies as the Office of Economic Opportunity. The policing of abusive practices of food processors and retailers (or big dairy cooperatives) was the responsibility of the Justice Department or of one of Washington's notorious "powderpuff agencies," the Federal Trade Commission. By 1974, as a new agricultural crisis developed, the changing circumstances began to force alteration of entrenched policies. By 1975, the Food Stamp program, for example, was serving purposes far different from those originally intended.

Accordingly, why discuss agricultural policy at all? It is in the political arena that interest group objectives are balanced, weighed, and compromised. The kind of decisions that result, although serving purposes different from those openly declared, affect such mundane things as the prices consumers pay at the supermarket and such critical matters as the international economic and political security of the United States.

In another sense, I have asserted that agriculture is the only economic sector in the United States where in any sense national planning may be said to have existed. Tangentially, then, tracing the complexities of four decades of farm policymaking may be the best case study possible of what kinds of national plans ensue from a polity where private interest, not public interest, reigns supreme.

Concretely, what are the interest groups that, since the forties, have been the movers and shakers in the forging of agricultural policy? Powerful, entrenched congressional committees and their leaders have often exercised determining influences. Cotton-state congressmen, disproportionately represented in the House Committee on Agriculture, were able to beat back for years ceilings on total payments made to any single farm enterprise, for the biggest checks always went to some of their constituents. Lack of concern for small farmers, tenants, and the food needs of the urban poor was in no small measure attributable to the influence of House committee chairmen like Harold Cooley and W. R. Poage or Jamie L. Whitten of Mississippi, long-time chairman of the House Appropriations Subcommittee on Agriculture.[10] During World War II crucially placed farm-state congressmen successfully insulated their commercialized rural constituents from any adverse effects on their incomes that wartime price controls might have imposed. The Senate and House agricultural committees, with a generous assist from the Farm Bureau Federation, presided with obvious relish over the dismantling of the "people-oriented" planning programs of the Farm Security Administration and the Bureau of Agricultural Economics.

Within the infrastructure of the Department of Agriculture, many of the political appointees have been spokesmen for and in some cases officials of agribusiness corporations. Chester Davis, in the New Deal period itself, Secretary Ezra Taft Benson, during the Eisenhower administration, and

Clifford Hardin and Earl Butz, the two secretaries of agriculture in the Nixon-Ford administrations, are examples. Butz was a member of the board of directors of Ralston-Purina before becoming secretary; Hardin, upon his resignation, assumed a position with the firm. Butz and his economic alter ego, Don Paarlberg, moved to the department from key positions in the college of agriculture of a major land-grant college, Purdue University. Such academic establishments are in as close liaison with major commercial farm and food processing industries and the American Farm Bureau Federation as schools of business are with the corporate industrial community and its adjunct trade associations.

Buttressing implanted agricultural interests in the Congress and inside the Department of Agriculture is the agricultural lobby, one of the largest and most diverse in Washington. The American Farm Bureau Federation, the largest and most important voluntary association of farmers, claimed to represent, in 1974, 2.3 million member families, organized into county organizations in forty-nine states—more than the total combined membership of all other general farm groups. Although farm population dwindles, the number of member families increases each year. The term, it should be noted, is "member families," not "farm families." The reason is that lawyers, doctors, teachers, banks, and business corporations can also be members of the Farm Bureau, and so can town dwellers who buy the organization's insurance or patronize its cooperative stores.

Allegedly nonpartisan in its political persuasion, the Farm Bureau, for the last thirty years, has lined up on the Republican side of most major issues. This has not always been the case. In the dark days of the depression in the thirties, Farm Bureau officials helped draft and administer the Agricultural Adjustment Act, and only started to move in a free market direction as conditions improved, technology wiped out more small farmers, and a few intrepid planners within the USDA seemed bent upon creating rival organizations of smaller, poorer farmers than the Farm Bureau was able to attract. By the seventies, the oft-stated objective of AFBF was "to create a climate which will enable agriculture to operate under the market price system," which has been translated into a determined campaign to demolish government price supports, acreage allotments, and restrictions on exports. Spokesmen for the largest and most prosperous of farm proprietors, the Farm Bureau lionized Ezra Taft Benson, and smiled with favor on the policies of Earl Butz. In 1974, the AFBF was enthusiastically pushing for expanded exports and, somewhat anomalously for an organization whose ritual anti-Communism predates Senator Joseph McCarthy, endorsed most favored nation status for the Soviet Union. (A bit of ideology here and there ought not to stand in the way of higher incomes for farmers.)

On other agricultural issues, the Farm Bureau (especially in California) has orchestrated a counter-campaign against attempts of the United Farm Workers to organize agricultural laborers. The 1974 resolutions called for action (apparently by the federal government) to suppress secondary boycotts such as the consumer boycott of nonunion grapes; in 1972 the AFBF joined with grower and processor interests in California to sponsor an unsuccessful initiative petition which, if it had been approved by the state's voters, would have seriously hampered farm worker unionization. In a stance that was surprising for an association long at loggerheads with organized labor, the AFBF, in 1974, favored legislation to require handlers of agricultural products to bargain in good faith with qualified producer associations; and they busily engaged in organizing such bargaining associations.

Farm Bureau membership is strongest in the corn-producing Midwest; the Illinois organization is the most influential of the state units. The AFBF, however, is more than a political interest group. Because of its large insurance business (sold to farmers and nonfarmers under the trade name "Nationwide") and a series of cooperative business enterprises, its assets and financial position equal those of major corporations.[11]

The 250,000 members of the National Farmers' Union come largely from wheat-producing regions; the NFU is the major farm organization in North and South Dakota, Minnesota, and Montana. For the last twenty-five years, the NFU has been nearly as close an ally of Democratic farm policy as the Farm Bureau has been of Republican. This, too, has not always been the case. In the thirties, when the Farmers' Union was under the leadership of neo-Populist firebrands like John Simpson and Milo Reno, currency inflation and guaranteed cost of production prices, not reduced acreages and benefit payments, were its preferred solutions. As leadership changed and the Roosevelt administration considered Farm Bureau demands in the war years too extreme, Union policies reversed, and by the end of the war an alliance, almost as close as that of organized labor with the Democratic party, had been forged. Secretary of Agriculture Charles F. Brannan, proponent of the controversial and radical program spurned by Congress in 1948, moved from his Washington post to a major position with the Farmers' Union. In its current policy stances, the Union calls for high government price supports linked with rigid production controls. In 1974, Tony Dechant, NFU president, vigorously attacked the Nixon administration for dumping abroad the reserves of the Commodity Credit Corporation.[12]

The National Grange, the oldest of voluntary farmer associations, is the least active politically, although its membership is greater than that of the Farmers' Union. It is the principal general farm organization in most northeastern states, including Pennsylvania and New York. The cooperatives that the Grange pioneered a century ago are represented now only by a group of insurance companies: the fact that only members can hold policies explains an upswing in membership in the 1970s. The Grange has not always been crystal clear in its political stances; in the past it was usually allied with the Farm Bureau. Its positions have been even less predictable the last few years, although

John Scott, Grange president, states the organization generally favors less federal involvement in farm programs.[13]

Newest and most aggressive of the farm associations, the National Farmers' Organization, founded in 1955, staged a series of "holding actions" in the sixties in an attempt to force processors to negotiate collective bargaining contracts that would, among other things, establish the price farmers would be paid. A spokesman declared in 1974: "... our organization is trying to get the farmers organized so we can get as big and powerful as the corporations we deal with."[14] Dues, like those of a labor union, are high and precise membership figures vague. The NFO's areas of organizational strength overlap those of the Farm Bureau; the fact that the conservative AFBF has endorsed bargaining contracts indicates that the NFO's program must have some farmer appeal and may have been drawing off Farm Bureau members. On national policy issues the NFO spokesmen are consistently Democratic party allies of the National Farmers' Union.

Specific commodity organizations are of increasing importance in this era of agricultural specialization. Most of them maintain lobbyists in Washington, and representatives appear as witnesses on major farm bills. When committee hearings were being held on the Omnibus Farm Bill of 1973, in addition to the NFU, NFO, and AFBF, testimony was heard from the National Corn Growers' Association, National Association of Wheat Growers, National Cotton Council, Southern Cotton Growers, Inc., and the National Wool Growers' Association. Associations of processors and retailers keep surveillance over agricultural legislation as well. Among the lobbying organizations registered in 1972 were the National Broiler Council, Milk Industry Federation, American Feed Manufacturer's Association, American Frozen Food Institute, and National Council of Farmers' Cooperatives.[15]

The pioneer New Deal farm legislation embodied in the Agricultural Act signed by President Roosevelt in May 1933 sought to reduce the output of American farms. At a time when the market was choked with burdensome surpluses and farm prices were at historic lows, the Agricultural Adjustment Administration rented land from producers of seventeen commodities, reimbursing the owners with "benefit payments," paid before the crop was planted in order to get cash into farmers' pockets immediately. The rented land was held out of production. Participation was voluntary, except severe tax penalties were imposed on tobacco and cotton producers who chose not to cooperate. The ultimate objective was to balance domestic supply with domestic demand in such a way that farm prices would be restored to parity—the price that would bring the farmer the same purchasing power his dollar had enjoyed in the base period, 1910–1914, a hypothetical "golden age" before the disruptions of World War I, when supply and demand for farm products were in equilibrium.

Invalidated by the Supreme Court in 1936[16] because of provisions that financed the program through a processing tax on the first purchaser of any commodity, the Agricultural Act of 1933 left behind important legacies. First, a tradition-shattering precedent had been established by the federal government's direct intervention in the alleged free market operations of the farm sector. Second, the Commodity Credit Corporation was created. Originally established as an ancillary to the crop reduction program, it was destined to become the principal mechanism for the price supports that were, after 1938, the mainstays of agricultural policy. As first conceived, a producer of corn or cotton could obtain a government loan by putting up as collateral commodities sealed in bins on his own property. If at the end of a set period, usually eight to ten months, the market price was above the loan value, the farmer paid off the loan with interest, sold his corn or cotton, and pocketed the profit. On the other hand, if at the end of the time period the market price was lower, he kept the full amount of the loan, forfeited his crop, and the government hauled the commodity away to its own storage bins. It should be obvious that the loan rate became a floor under farm prices—commodities would not be commercially marketed for any amount less than the prevailing loan value. Coverage was extended to other commodities, and the political question of where the loan rates—that is, price supports—should be pegged became the nucleus of most battles over farm legislation during the succeeding thirty-five years.

The Supreme Court decision hastened a reevaluation, already underway in the Department of Agriculture, that sought to supercede the emergency measures of 1933 with longer-range recovery and reform programs. The Soil Conservation and Domestic Allotment Act of 1936 was a stopgap measure but it introduced some significant modifications, and the years it was in effect marked the high point of influence on farm policy by the social and economic planners who perceived of agricultural policy as something more than a service to commercial agriculture.

The emphasis was soil conservation, not simply acreage reduction. Individual farmers were paid benefits with money appropriated directly from the treasury for acreage they refrained from planting with soil-depleting crops and given bonuses for those they planted with soil-conserving crops. The distinction was actually an expedient, because the soil depleting crops were cash grains—that is, wheat and corn—where reduction was desired, and the soil conserving crops were forage legumes and grasses, usually marketed only sparingly. Parity was redefined: in 1933 the objective was price parity, in 1936, income parity. Since the new aim was to restore net income per farm to a purchasing power equivalent to that of 1910–1914, the actual support prices could fluctuate above or below parity, as they subsequently have. High price supports, it was feared, would stimulate greater production and more surpluses; flexible supports would provide the financial stimulus for farmers to reduce production when carry-over was great. By 1936 this was no trivial problem. Already the Commodity Credit Corporation had accumulated cotton surpluses of 6.2 billion bales—greater than that in the Hoover administration.

Provisions for assistance to low income farmers, authorized by the Bankhead-Jones Farm Tenant Act of 1937 and implemented by the Farm Security Administration, represented an innovation, albeit a small one. Funds were made available for tenants to buy their own farms, but they reached only 12,234 families in the peak year of 1939–1940. Rehabilitation loans, usually in amounts of less than four digits, were made available to farmers who could not qualify for credit from usual sources. The final recovery rate from these high risk loans was greater than 80 percent.[17]

The Agricultural Adjustment Act of 1938, much amended, remained the basis of federal farm policy until the 1970s. The conservation features of 1936 remained. There were, however, some significant changes. Allotments were determined not by base acreage but by a quota approximating an individual farm's contribution to total national output. If for any given year the estimated supply of some commodity was greater than normal, the secretary of agriculture specified a mandatory quota that could be marketed. Farmers who exceeded it were subject to tax penalities similar to those imposed upon noncooperating cotton and tobacco producers in 1933. Once a quota was announced, it was submitted within thirty days to a referendum of producers; it went into effect if two-thirds approved. If a referendum failed, price supports were to be suspended for two years or levels of support substantially reduced. Cooperating farmers received payments for not planting soil-depleting crops. If the market price of a commodity fell below the stipulated parity level, it was possible to make direct subsidy payments to farmers equal to the difference between the market and the parity price.[18]

The Commodity Credit Corporation, which was the stimulus for Henry Wallace's "Ever-Normal Granary," became central to agricultural policy. The 1938 act raised parity levels and prescribed a complex formula: corn would be supported at 70 percent of parity if the supply did not exceed the normal by more than 10 percent. Rather than a device to calibrate farm supply with domestic and foreign demand (the original purpose of AAA), CCC became a means, thanks to the pressure of commodity-conscious congressmen, to maintain support levels in excess of what the price would have been on the open market.

The 1938 act more or less completed the repertoire of regulatory devices available to the USDA to deal with the most pressing agricultural problem of the depression years: a productive capacity greater than demand. Emphasis, to the dismay of planners like Tolley and Wilson, was upon supply regulation rather than demand expansion. Legislation included, however, authorization for a Surplus Commodities Corporation, which distributed some perishable commodities to the poor. Section 32 of the original act assigned to the secretary of agriculture 30 percent of the agricultural customs revenue to use for price support and surplus removal programs, including school lunches, some direct food distribution, and special free or low-cost milk programs. The 1938 act included a provision for distribution of surplus to the poor through a free food-stamp program.

Only a series of Acts of God and acts of men not related to farm policy spared this misplaced emphasis upon supply constriction from becoming a national disaster. The crop reduction program was a failure, for it overlooked a critical variable—farm technology was already growing more sophisticated. When acreage was reduced or quotas assigned, farmers simply cultivated more intensively, poured on more fertilizer, and coaxed an ever increasing output from their cropland. A crushing surplus of cotton, corn, and wheat was building by 1934; two successive years of drouth fortuituously intervened. The surplus was absorbed, farm income rose, and the CCC earned a small profit. Again in 1938 and 1939 government storage bins swelled to capacity —the outbreak of war in Europe suddenly opened the markets of the world to American farm products and the reserves became not a liability but a godsend.

The years 1942–1945 were halcyon days on the farm. To stimulate more production, price support levels were set at

90 percent of parity on most commodities.[19] Once price controls were established, legislation required that no ceiling price on farm products be less than 110 percent of parity. A spectacular 33 percent increase in farm production took place with only a minimal increase in acreage; the war years, as we have noted, marked the takeoff of the mechanical revolution in American farming. Technologically efficient farms met all the needs of the military, satisfied foreign demands, and provided for an expanding domestic market; despite rationing, higher wartime incomes raised domestic food consumption to the highest levels in U.S. history. Unlike in the years 1917–1918, farmers refrained from land speculation, debts were reduced, and, by 1945, American agriculture was stronger financially than ever before.[20]

The emergency of the years 1946–1948 assumes new significance in the perspective of the world food shortages of the seventies.[21] Government policy in 1945, sometimes described as a "bare-shelves policy," reflected the apprehensions of men like Secretary of Agriculture Clinton Anderson, who recalled all too vividly the disasters that had followed in the wake of expanded production in the years 1917–1919 in American farmlands. Fearful of overproduction and a collapse of the market for farm products, American policymakers failed to detect the severe food shortages that were developing across a war ravaged world. Suddenly the problem wasn't abundance, it was scarcity. The United Nations Relief and Rehabilitation Administration channeled American grain to Europe. When humanitarian pleas failed to unlock sufficient amounts from farmers' bins and warehouses, price controls were reluctantly removed. Inflation in America was less costly, it was argued, than starvation in Europe. Americans found themselves short of meat, prices shot upward when ceilings were removed, farm prices held near their wartime highs, and, at the same time, starvation stalked much of the European continent. Again, disaster, not foresight, had saved American farm policy.

The congressional debates of 1948 and 1949, culminating in the agricultural act of the latter year, avoided long-range planning objectives and failed to consider such alternatives as a permanent food reserve or emphasis on increased consumption rather than decreased production. Republicans, who controlled the Eightieth Congress, sought to substitute flexible and declining supports for the high support levels of the war years. They sought further to restrict the quantity of commodities that could be stored in government facilities. These proposals, while even perhaps realistic in terms of the surpluses that would accumulate after 1953, had allegedly disastrous political consequences for Republicans in 1948. Nevertheless, it is doubtful that the farm vote alone gave Harry Truman his unexpected presidential reelection. Democrats indeed were able to capitalize upon historic fears of dwindling markets and falling prices. Already by 1948 revived European production was reducing foreign demand for American farm exports. However, in the heated political discussions little note was made of the fact that Truman had supported some type of flexible price supports rather than the high wartime levels insisted upon by powerful leaders in the House Agriculture Committee. Neither was it noted that only one Democrat had voiced any objective to the minor provision in the temporary 1948 bill that limited and partially curtailed government storage facilities.

Debates over agricultural policy in the Eighty-first Congress centered around the Brannan Plan, authored by the secretary of agriculture and sponsored without notable enthusiasm by the Truman administration. The most change-oriented legislative proposal since the New Deal years, the Brannan Plan would have updated agricultural policy through: (1) computing price-support levels not by parity standards, but by a ten-year moving average beginning in 1938–1947; (2) supporting major farm products at full income standard levels; (3) supporting the incomes of growers of perishables by direct government payment of the difference between market prices and established support prices; (4) restricting support for large-scale farmers; (5) requiring compliance with conservation practices and with production and marketing controls in order to receive benefits.[22]

Democrats from the cotton South skillfully sidetracked the Brannan Plan and, at the same time, beat back Republican advocates of lower supports. As a result, flexible price supports originally authorized in 1948 were continued but at a higher level. The net effect of all this intricate legislative maneuvering was to project the high price guarantees of wartime into the indefinite future and, accordingly, stimulate production.[23]

The day of reckoning for the high support policies in effect since 1938 came only with the winding down of the Korean War. The continuation of a quasi-wartime economy kept men at work and incomes up.

The rapid increase in agricultural output guaranteed cheap food for a citizenry who, in their new found affluence, were deserting the cities for the suburbs and finding that two automobiles were a necessity not a luxury. The agricultural dam broke in 1953; for the first time since the late thirties surplus farm products glutted the warehouses and storage bins. The CCC, burgeoning with excesses of wheat, cotton, and corn, stored commodities in circular aluminum bins scattered about the countryside, poured wheat into the holds of the navy's mothball fleet, and paid out an estimated $1 million daily in storage costs.[24] Against this backdrop, the Republican-controlled Eighty-third Congress responded to President Eisenhower's requests, and in the Agricultural Act of 1954 reverted to flexible price supports, ranging from 70 to 90 percent of parity, which was redefined in such a way as to further reduce supports; acreage allotments were reimposed on wheat, corn, and cotton. The effect was that when price supports went down farmers predictably poured on more fertilizer in a losing attempt to maintain their income level by producing more. Per capita personal income from farm sources declined each year, from 1951 to 1956, and didn't achieve the 1951 level until a decade later. In an experiment reminiscent of the original program in 1933, farmers were awarded generous rental payments for retiring land into a soil bank; by 1960, 28 million acres were held in such a reserve. Only the least productive of land was withdrawn and, having had minimal effect, the soil bank was allowed to expire in 1960. Surpluses continued to mount; by the end of the Eisenhower administration government holdings of wheat and feed grains alone approached $7 billion in value. In 1952, price stabilization programs had cost $288.6 million; by 1959 the costs topped $2 billion.

For the first time agricultural policymakers had to give serious consideration to the demand side of the equation. Public Law 480, passed in 1954 (discussed earlier), was in part a humanitarian measure, but it was more important as a way of disposing in foreign lands a precious bounty that had become a liability. The Farm Bureau, fearful of price-depressing surpluses, supported the measure. Despite shipments abroad of more than $6 billion in excess commodities (largely grains) between 1955 and 1961, in the latter year the ratio of carryover stocks of wheat to domestic use stood at 2.3 years; in 1954, before Public Law 480 exports began, the ratio had been 1.5 years.

Like their predecessors in the thirties, Democratic party policymakers in the sixties were concerned with supply management. The objective was to remove surpluses and force market prices above support levels, hence allowing the government to withdraw from the costly business of acquiring and storing farm commodities. Farmers in general, and the Farm Bureau in particular, were emphatic, in May 1963, that they would not tolerate mandatory farm programs. Although referenda in the past had typically been near unanimous, 52 percent of the wheat growers rejected an administration plan that included strict production controls but raised the income guarantees.[25] In voting "no" they were choosing to entrust their fortunes to a free market—a "free" market, that is, without government controls or guarantees, but in no sense a "free" market independent of the powerful consolidating mechanisms of agribusiness and financial institutions. In 1964 Congress passed a Cotton-Wheat Act which incorporated most of the provisions of the program that were rejected the preceding year, but made participation voluntary. Farmers who chose to cooperate received one level of support for that portion of their crop destined for domestic production and a lesser amount for exports. In a program suggestive of the processing tax of thirty years earlier, direct subsidies were paid to wheat producers with funds provided by wheat certificates purchased by millers and redeemable at seventy cents per bushel, extra costs being passed on to the consumer. In addition, under authority granted in the 1933 act, export subsidies were being paid on shipments of cotton and wheat abroad. Price support payments gravitated downward through the sixties, but amounts paid to farmers in direct subsidies rose. By the end of the decade they totalled up to $3 billion annually, about 7 percent of the cash receipts of farmers. It was hoped that this procedure would bring down American prices on the world market and, at the same time, sweeten the incentives for producers of wheat, cotton, and feed grains so that they would participate in the only kind of program they would accept, a voluntary one. Typically, 70 to 80 percent of all producers were sufficiently attracted by the benefit features to participate in the reduction programs.[26]

Two programs dating back to the thirties were rejuvenated during the Kennedy and Johnson administrations. Free food stamps and milk and cheap school lunches began as surplus disposal measures. The New Deal food stamp dispersals ceased during the World War II, but the milk and school lunch programs had been continually funded and supplied with surplus commodities, purchased by the states. Despite problems of administration, appropriations, and allocation of responsibility between the states and the federal government, these two programs expanded during the Nixon administration and, by 1971, 6 million school children received free or reduced-price meals, and millions more received lunches at less than cost. The cost of the program rose from $301 million in 1970 to $581 million in 1971, and to $797 million in 1972.[27]

The Food Stamp Act of 1964 permitted low income families to purchase coupons redeemable at the grocery store for selected foods. The cost to recipients was based upon a sliding scale, geared to the family's income. In 1974 a family of four with an income of $475 a month would pay $126 for stamps that would buy $150 worth of food. If family income was $209 monthly, $53 would purchase the same amount ($150) in stamps. A family earning less than $30 monthly could receive free food stamps. The average cost of food stamps was about 23 percent of a family's income.[28] Through the late sixties and early seventies, the relief activities of the Department of Agriculture expanded. Numbers receiving food stamps tripled from 3.2 billion in May 1969 to 9.5 billion in February 1971. In 1970, federal expenditures for food stamps totaled $1.9 billion; this more than doubled to $3.1 billion in 1972 and to $8.3 billion in 1975, making this the most rapidly increasing item in the department's budget.[29]

With the return of a Republican administration to Washington in 1969, emphasis shifted from income guarantees for farmers toward a flexible policy package that would ease government controls and facilitate movement of American farm products in international markets. A three-year program authorized by the Agricultural Act of 1970 abandoned crop-by-crop acreage allotments and, through a set-aside feature, left farmers qualifying for price supports free to raise all except a few specified crops on land that remained after the owner had withdrawn a specific percentage from production. For the first time in the history of agricultural legislation, a ceiling of $55,000 was placed upon the payment an individual producer could receive.[30]

When net farm income was sagging in 1971, the Nixon administration replaced an ineffective secretary of agriculture with the experienced, aggressive dean of Purdue University's College of Agriculture, Earl Butz. While the new secretary crusaded through the farm country in the spring and summer of 1972, extolling the virtues of Republican agricultural policies in general and Republican candidates in particular, he bought up surplus corn to prop up prices, raised the level of price supports, and increased the acreage set aside. As a result, government payments to farmers in 1972 were the highest in history, nearly $4 billion. More wheat and feed grain acreage were held out of production than ever before.[31] While farm prices crept up, so did the costs of food for consumers. Butz pried loose $200 million from the penurious Office of Production Management to supplement the Food Stamp program, and obtained a bigger appropriation for the already heavily subsidized Rural Electrification Administration. To facilitate the disposal of what was regarded as a price depressing reserve, one-third of the American grain crop was sold to the Soviet Union in 1972. The sale was negotiated by private grain traders, but Butz had visited the Soviet Union in the spring of 1972 to facilitate just such a transaction.[32]

The rain of financial benefices across the countryside in 1972 was politically motivated; Butz took justifiable pride in his abilities as a Republican campaigner. The record high price supports and the huge amounts of acreage set aside were not intended to be permanent. Earl Butz had long been on record, prior to his becoming secretary, as a believer in a free farm market devoid of government controls, particularly controls on exports. The objective of Republican agricultural policy was to move the government out of agriculture, obliterate government-held food stocks, and expand foreign markets for American commodities. Once this was done, farm prices would rise to a permanently high level where the costly government guarantee programs of the past would no longer be necessary. In another of the ironies that have haunted United States farm policy, Earl Butz and the Republican economic planners succeeded in doing just that, but in a way and at a cost that never had been anticipated. While American farmers in 1972 were paid record-breaking amounts to hold the largest acreage ever out of production, commercial export sales drained American reserves, and shipments under Public Law 480 declined; for domestic consumers the price of food was touching record highs, and in India, Bangladesh, and the Sahel, the vaunted Green Revolution was failing. By late 1974, 700 million among the world's population hovered near starvation.[33]

The Agriculture and Consumer Protection Act (P. L. 93–86), signed into law by President Nixon in August 1973, was the most important farm legislation since 1938. For the first time since the New Deal, farm policy was being created against a backdrop of scarcity, not surplus. As Congress debated the bill, the consumer price index was pushing up to 6.4 percent over January, and income for farmers was at an all-time high. Total agricultural exports were increasing 60 percent over the preceding year. Never had there been so few farmers, and even among them, the greatest share of the new profits went to the small portion who were the most efficient and commercialized. "Drafting the new farm legislation," declared Senator Herman Talmadge, chairman of the Senate Agriculture Committee, "comes at what is perhaps the poorest possible psychological and political moment."

Had the Nixon administration had its way, the Omnibus Farm Bill of 1973 would have buried all the legacies inherited from the days of Henry Wallace. Parity would have been eliminated and all direct payments to farmers terminated. A farmer's income would come from the marketplace, not from the government. Two expectations underpinned these objectives: first, it was estimated that migration out of farm areas would have stabilized by 1980; the farms that remained would be viable economic units run by businessmen engaged in commercial production; second, increased domestic and foreign markets would provide enough extra income for farmers to offset any losses caused by the disappearance of government payments.

The final bill, tortured and compromised through Senate and House committees, opposed at some time by all major farm organizations, and upstaged by the more dramatic Ervin Committee hearings that were going on simultaneously, nonetheless came remarkably close to administration objectives.

The old parity formula was replaced by a system of "target prices." Compensatory payments would be made to producers of wheat, cotton, and feed grains—the three commodities covered by the bill—in the event market prices fell below the designated targets. An escalator clause made possible increases in the target prices after 1976 to reflect increases in farmers' costs of production. The target prices were a compromise, opposed by the Farm Bureau and accepted only reluctantly by Secretary Butz, for the whole operation smacked of the long-discarded income payments contained in the old Brannan Plan and certainly represented a direct payment to farmers. The final target prices would have been ever higher had not the threat of a presidential veto reduced their levels. In matter of fact, the entire target price structure was redundant. On the day the bill was signed, wheat, with a target price of $2.05 per bushel, was pushing above $4.50 on the commodities markets; corn, pegged at $1.38, was marketing at $3.28. Given the radically changed demand factors of an inflationary international economy, spot prices, between 1972 and 1976, never dropped even close to the target price minimums.

Historic price supports through nonrecourse loans were again extended. With prices at record highs, however, there was no need for farmers to forfeit, and all grain was sold on the commercial market. Accordingly, the 1973 price supports served two functions. First, as they always had, they provided a means of getting credit to farmers at the beginning of the growing season. Second, and most important, they were a fail-safe mechanism to guard against the unlikely possibility that world demand would fail and the surpluses of the fifties return.

Over protests of the no longer dominant cotton bloc, Congress lowered the subsidy ceiling for a single farm to $20,-000. The less complex target price guarantees eliminated the need for the cumbersome wheat certificates. Public Law 480 was extended, with the stipulation that the president assure that supplies were available to meet commercial export demands.[34]

The food stamp program was extended through fiscal 1977. The most heated debate over the agricultural bill erupted over a strictly tangential issue: Should strikers be eligible for food stamps? Congress refused to approve an amendment specifically excluding them. This obscured an important development: by 1973 the Department of Agriculture was spending more for food stamps, school lunch programs, and related welfare activities than it was paying out in benefits to American farmers.[35]

With unemployment rising throughout 1974, the number of food stamp recipients grew proportionately. In December 1973, 13 million people were purchasing their groceries with the coupons; in June 1974 the figure was 13.5 million, and by December it was 17.1 million. This represented 8 percent of the population of the United States. Costs seemed likely to reach $4 billion a year. The projected budget for fiscal 1976 alloted $7.7 billion to the Department of Agriculture, $5.4 billion of which went to the various relief programs.[36]

Both the total budget and the welfare budget of the Department of Agriculture were to be slashed in fiscal 1976 as a part of the Ford administration's inflation-checking economy drive. Accordingly, the department announced a change in guidelines: beginning 1 March 1975, all food stamp recipients would pay out a flat 30 percent of their income for the coupons. The new policy would save $650 million yearly and would have raised the cost of food stamps for 95 percent of the recipients; 10 percent would have been forced out of the program. The new rate never materialized. The Ninety-fourth Congress, in its first legislative action following organization, approved by veto-proof margins in both houses a one year freeze on the cost of food stamps.

This was only a first round—the food stamp issue had escalated into a major political controversy by the end of 1975. By October, 18.8 million Americans were receiving stamps, and the cost to government was estimated at $6 billion, not the originally projected $4 billion. USDA figures showed that 85 percent of recipients were below the poverty level of $6,000, but at the same time 6 percent earned more than $9,000. Some critics charged that by skillfully manipulating the complex deduction formula (including allowances for rent, home maintenance, or dependents), families earning $16,000 or more annually could qualify for food stamps. Nevertheless, the Senate Select Committee on Nutrition and Human Needs reported that only 38 percent of eligible families were being reached by the Food Stamp program. Responding to conservative critics of the program, and urged on by Secretary of Agriculture Butz and Senator James Buckley of New York, President Gerald Ford had introduced into Congress a reform bill that would reduce the benefits for nearly half of the recipients and limit participation to families whose income fell below $5,050 (for a four-member family). Given alternate proposals by Senators George McGovern and Robert Dole, the food stamp issue remained deadlocked in Congress at the end of 1975.[37]

If the transformation of the Department of Agriculture into a relief agency was not proof enough, other emerging concerns of farm policy in 1974 added to the evidence that a new era for agriculture had already begun. The Soil and Conservation Service of USDA estimated that nine million acres of formerly unfarmed land, much of it in semiarid areas such as the southern High Plains of eastern New Mexico and the Texas and Oklahoma panhandles, came back into cultivation in 1974. Most of the land had lain fallow since the 1930s; as the renters and owners sought quick profits and expected rapid depreciation, erosion control was practiced on less than half of this newly farmed land; an estimated 60 million tons of topsoil were lost to wind and rain. Thus the same geographical regions and the same farm practices that spawned the dust bowl of the thirties seemed to be creating another for the seventies.

The prestigious National Academy of Sciences warned in January 1975 that the long time-pattern of continuing increase in farm output seemed to be faltering just when the demands for foodstuffs were the greatest in history. Those gains of the past, achieved through overly-generous application of fertilizer to croplands, had reached a point of no further return. If land was to be cultivated more extensively, it could be done only through clearing, drainage projects, and improved irrigation. Lamenting that scientific research in food production had been given low priority during the decades of plenty, the report called for new scientific pioneering to better utilize sunlight and carbon dioxide, improve plant and animal breeds, and create better irrigation technologies. The authors concluded:

> ... If we expect great difficulties to arise in increasing agricultural output to meet demands and therefore urge great expenditures of effort on research, and the difficulties do not arise, the worst that can be said is that we over-expended our resources and expended them too soon. If, on the contrary, we assume that agricultural output will always rise to meet demand, but in fact it falters and does not, the lead time for research is so long that severe economic and social dislocations could arise.[38]

"In general, U.S. farm policies were designed against a background of chronic farm commodity surpluses, an excess supply of farm labor and substandard farm incomes. Today all these conditions have changed," a recent report of the Council on Economic Development declared.[39] Some observations about the long decades of trial and error in formulating agricultural policies provide a bridge to carry us to what will be our final consideration: American farming in world perspective.

The technological and organizational revolution in agriculture, one as great as any that has transformed contemporary society, has, by the mid-seventies, only a little bit more to run. Looking to the policies of the future, the "Young

Executives" group within USDA speculate: "Agriculture should be viewed as an industry. . . . National policy should be directed toward maintaining agriculture as a viable industry, not as a way of life."[40] Modern commercial food producers, utilizing the fruits of government-sponsored scientific and technical research, are rapidly acquiring the capacity for production control and adjustment that characterize all other mass industries. Farmers learned long ago to manipulate and adjust their production according to the intricacies of programs designed in Washington. When acreage was reduced, more intense cultivation of the remaining land thwarted the goal of reducing output. Low price supports, as in the fifties, stirred farmers to produce more to offset losses; high prices stimulated more production in order to reap the attendant financial rewards. In 1946 wheat supplies for hungry Europeans remained sealed in bins and warehouses until the government agreed to raise ceiling prices on grain. Livestock producers followed the example and, in the autumn of 1948, created a serious meat famine in American cities, until President Truman was obliged to capitulate and remove all OPA ceiling prices on meat.[41] Given such market powers, traditional distinctions that segregate agriculture from other commercial activities fade into obscurity. If history is any guide, commercial food producers will respond but little to consumer protests, to political exhortations, or even to moral obligations that might be owing to starving people in afflicted foreign lands. They will respond, however, to price incentives.

That farm policies have been shaped against a backdrop of chronic surpluses and assumptions that food was cheap and abundant is axiomatic; it is not so clear in retrospect that the underlying rationale of these policies was correct. The fortuitous circumstances that have periodically necessitated dramatic reversals in these policies are not so fortuitous as has been assumed. Drouth in 1934 and 1935, war demands from 1939 to 1945, the requirements of the Korean War in the early fifties, and the squeeze of the Malthusian ratio upon world food supplies in the seventies all belie the tacit assumption that abundance has been the norm. Indeed, the only extended time periods when commodity surpluses seriously weighted down the supply-demand balance were prior to 1933 and the years between 1953 and 1972. Emergencies have been frequent enough to defy the predictive capacities of the most polished economic research operation in the world. Attempting to analyze the precipitate rise in meat prices in April 1973, Don Paarlberg, chief economist of USDA, said that members of his staff could not find the reasons. "Even looking back," he confessed, "we can't answer why the exuberance [in prices]."[42]

The current uncertain world economic climate, where skyrocketing oil prices bring about redistributions of national wealth, where population increase outruns food supply, and where vagaries of weather may bring famine to millions of people, challenge policy premises that barter away vital reserves, play politics with food production, and make decisions on the basis of the short-term interests of well organized interest groups.

Some years ago a wise scholar of federal farm policy, addressing himself to the problems of another day, cautiously concluded:

One of the lessons to be drawn from the experiences of this period [World War II] is that the world's largest producer of surplus foodstuffs cannot afford, in any period of greatly disturbed international conditions, to operate only on the basis of such stocks of storable foodstuffs as will be maintained privately in the normal channels of trade. Had these stocks not been in existence, the food situation would inevitably have been much tighter, even with the phenomenal increase in agricultural production that occurred during the war years.[43]

Throughout the sixties and early seventies, a food reserve was available to provide sustenance for all the world's people for approximately ninety-five days; in October 1974, reserves were available for twenty-six days.

Notes

1. Wayne D. Rasmussen and Gladys L. Baker, *The Department of Agriculture* (New York: Praeger Publishers, 1972), p. 80.
2. For a detailed, authoritative discussion of the research activities of the Department of Agriculture, see Ernest G. Moore, *The Agricultural Research Service* (New York: Praeger Publishers, 1967).
3. Theodore Schultz, *Economic Organization of Agriculture* (New York: McGraw-Hill, 1953), chap. 7; Douglas C. North, *Growth and Welfare in the American Past,* 2d ed. (Englewood Cliffs, N.J.: Prentice-Hall, 1974), pp. 102–4.
4. Charles E. Rosenberg, "The Adams Act: Politics and the Cause of Scientific Research," *Agricultural History* 38 (January 1964): 4; see by the same author, "Science, Technology and Economic Growth: The Case of the Agricultural Experiment Station Scientist, 1875–1914," *Agricultural History* 45 (January 1971): 1–20.
5. This significant chapter in American agricultural history, treated here in truncated fashion, is authoritatively detailed in Richard S. Kirkendall, *Social Scientists and Farm Politics in the Age of Roosevelt* (Columbia: University of Missouri Press, 1966). See also Graham Taylor, "The New Deal and the Grass Roots," (Ph.D. diss., University of Pennsylvania, 1972).
6. The largest and most important of these, the American Farm Bureau Federation, has, however, since 1950 opposed price support policies.
7. *New York Times,* 1 June 1972; Jim Hightower et al., *Hard Tomatoes, Hard Times* (Washington, D.C.: Agribusiness Accountability Project, 1972).

8. *Philadelphia Inquirer,* 6 October 1974. My attempts to obtain a copy of this report from the usually accomodating Department of Agriculture have been unavailing.

9. See Van L. Perkins, *Crisis in Agriculture: The Agricultural Adjustment Administration and the New Deal, 1933* (Berkeley: University of California Press, 1969); Chester C. Davis, "The Development of Agricultural Policy Since the End of the World War," USDA, *Yearbook of Agriculture, 1940,* pp. 297–326; Prof. Theodore Saloutos is at work on what promises to be the most comprehensive study of the Agricultural Adjustment Administration; some of the early results of his researches are reported in Theodore Saloutos, "New Deal Agricultural Policy: An Evaluation," *Journal of American History* 61 (September 1974): 394–416. For more specific studies, see William D. Rowley, *M. L. Wilson and the Campaign for Domestic Allotment* (Lincoln: University of Nebraska Press, 1970; Christiana McFadyen Campbell, *The Farm Bureau and the New Deal* (Urbana: University of Illinois Press, 1962); Sidney Baldwin, *Poverty and Politics: The Rise and Decline of the Farm Security Administration* (Chapel Hill: University of North Carolina Press, 1968); Donald H. Grubbs, *Cry From the Cotton: The Southern Tenant Farmers' Union and the New Deal* (Chapel Hill: University of North Carolina Press, 1971); David Eugene Conrad, *The Forgotten Farmers: The Story of Sharecroppers in the New Deal* (Urbana: University of Illinois Press, 1965).

10. That representatives Poage and Whitten were prime targets of the reform-minded Democrats in the Ninety-fourth Congress, as the seniority system was dismantled, is ample evidence of the power these congressmen were believed to control. Their removal from their critical positions marks the end of a legislative era.

11. American Farm Bureau Federation, *This is Farm Bureau* (n.p., n.d.); American Farm Bureau Federation, *Farm Bureau Policies for 1974* (January 1974); Samuel R. Berger, *Dollar Harvest: The Story of the Farm Bureau* (Lexington, Mass.: Heath Lexington Books, 1971).

12. *New York Times* 21 January 1974.

13. Daniel J. Balz, "Agricultural Report: Angry Cotton Interests Join Fight with Administration to weaken House Farm Bill," *National Journal* (24 February 1973), p. 261.

14. *New York Times,* 31 January 1975.

15. Ross B. Talbot and Don F. Hadwiger, *The Policy Process in American Agriculture* (San Francisco: Chandler Publishing Co., 1968), pp. 90–121.

16. U.S. v. Butler, 296 U.S. 1 (1936).
17. Murray R. Benedict, *Farm Policies of the United States, 1790–1950: A Study of Their Origins and Development* (New York: Twentieth Century Fund, 1953), pp. 350–64. This is the most detailed, comprehensive account of the subject.
18. Only about half of commodity types have been covered by price supports; the principal ones have been grains, tobacco, cotton, soybeans, wool, sugar, and dairy products. Benedict, *Farm Policies of the United States,* pp. 377–90.
19. Not only was this high support level guaranteed through the war years, but legislation of 1941 extended the 90 percent support prices for two years following the formal declaration of the end of the war.
20. Benedict, *Farm Policies of the United States,* pp. 302–453.
21. Allen J. Matusow, *Farm Policies and Politics in the Truman Years* (New York: Atheneum Publishers, 1970 [Cambridge: Harvard University Press, 1967]).
22. Rasmussen and Baker, *The Department of Agriculture,* p. 105.
23. Benedict, *Farm Policies of the United States,* pp. 453–520.
24. A few speculators such as Billie Sol Estes reaped some dishonest financial rewards through speculative dealings involving storage facilities.
25. Results are not strictly comparable to earlier ballots, since growers of less than fifteen acres were entitled to vote in 1963. Most opposed the program and they made up two-thirds of all wheat producers.
26. Don F. Hadwiger and Ross B. Talbot, *Pressures and Protests: The Kennedy Farm Program and the Wheat Referendum of 1963* (San Francisco: Chandler Publishing Co., 1965).
27. U.S., Department of Commerce, *Statistical Abstract of the United States* (1972), table 619, p. 390; (1973), table 628, p. 393.
28. *Philadelphia Bulletin,* 6 October 1974.
29. *Statistical Abstract of the United States* (1973), p. 393. USDA, ERA, *Agricultural Outlook,* AO–9 (April 1976), p. 12.
30. *Congressional Quarterly Almanac* 29 (1973): 290; Rasmussen and Baker, *The Department of Agriculture,* p. 111.
31. U.S.D.A., *Handbook of Agricultural Charts, 1973,* p. 25.
32. See Appendix.
33. Julius Duscha, "Up, Up, Up—Butz Makes Hay Down on the Farm," *New York Times Magazine,* 17 April 1972, pp. 34–35; Lauren Soth, "The Operations of Dr. Butz," *Nation* 219 (26 October 1974): 396–98.
34. Daniel J. Balz, "Economic Report: Target prices, escalator clause leave cost, effect of new farm program uncertain," *National Journal Reports* 5 (11 August 1973): 1179–83; *Congres-*

sional Quarterly Almanac 29 (1973): 285–321. Proposed amendments to the 1973 act in 1975 called for increasing the target prices to $3.35 for wheat, $2.25 for corn in order to assure farmers that if their drive for all-out production results in surpluses, they would still be guaranteed a reasonable price. Approved by Congress, the increases were vetoed by the president; the veto was not overridden. *New York Times,* 13 January 1975.

35. In 1973, total government payments to farmers under various programs = $2,607,000; food stamps alone (appropriated) = $2,-500,000. USDA, ERS, *Farm Income Series* (July 1974), p. 64; *New York Times* 14 October 1974.

36. None of the programs involve direct relief. Standards for distribution of food stamps are determined by the several states within guidelines specified by the federal government.

37. *New York Times,* 29 January, 5 February, 6 February, 17 March, 7 October, 21 October, 20 November 1975.

38. Boyce Rensberger, "Danger of Soil Erosion Arises in Food Shortage," *New York Times,* 11 January 1975, p. 1; William Robbins, "Rise in Food Output Said to Falter as Need Grows," *New York Times,* 13 January 1975, p. 1; National Research Council, Committee on Agricultural Production Efficiency, *Agricultural Production Efficiency* (Washington, D.C.: National Academy of Sciences, 1975), p. 185.

39. Quoted, *New York Times,* 29 October 1974.

40. Daniel J. Balz, "Economic Report: Exports, high food prices boost Administration efforts to reverse farm policy," *National Journal* 5 (24 February 1973): 258–59.

41. Matusow, *Truman Years,* pp. 32, 59.

42. Quoted, Daniel J. Balz, "Economic Report: Unexpected increases in meat prices cited as major factor in decision to impose controls," *National Journal* 5 (7 April 1973): 509.

43. Benedict, *Farm Policies of the United States,* p. 407.

CHAPTER EIGHT

The World Food Crisis

We have, in effect, a revolution of rising expectation,
superimposed on a population explosion, in a world of
fixed dimensions and limited productive capacity.

—Emile Benoit

The scourges of pestilence, famine, wars, and earth-
quakes have come to be regarded as a blessing to over-
crowded nations, since they serve to prune away the
luxuriant growth of the human race.

—Tertullian, a third-century theologian

During the last months of 1974, the macabre threat of death
by starvation haunted the lives of more than 700 million
people in 32 nations. A hunger belt, stretching from Hon-
duras and El Salvador in Central America, across sub-
Saharan Africa, through Pakistan, India, and Bangladesh,
to Laos and Cambodia, encircled the globe. Energy, food,
population, and finance are the modern analogues of the
four horsemen of the Apocalypse, according to President
Valery Giscard d'Estaing of France. The nations of the hunger belt made up a vast "fourth world," distinguished from
other nondeveloped countries because they have too much
of population, too little energy, food, and capital. In Novem-

ber, when delegates from 130 nations met at Rome in the First World Food Conference, Addeke Boerma, head of the United Nations Food and Agricultural Organization, pleaded in vain for a minimum of 11 million tons of relief grain. The grim estimates were, that before the winter passed, one million might perish in stricken Bangladesh, and the total in India might reach 10 million.[1]

The food crisis of 1973–1974 caught the experts by surprise. An observer as knowledgeable as Henry Kissinger admitted that "Until 1972 we thought we had inexhaustible food surpluses and the fact that we have to shape our policy deliberately to relate ourselves to the rest of the world did not really arise until 1973."[2] Some argued that the shortages were transient—the result of adverse weather conditions, a lack of fertilizer, monetary inflation, or an energy crisis of uncertain duration. Others, with credentials equally prestigious, contended that with world population likely to double in 35 years, the crisis of the seventies was the harbinger of the fatal squeeze of too many people upon too few of resources that Thomas Malthus prophesied 175 years ago.

Discussion of this most fundamental of human issues has been blurred by ideology, obscured by faulty statistical data, and confused by projections into the future that ignore critical variables and take little account of a historical past more than a decade removed.

Opposition to population control measures made ideological bedfellows, if not allies, of the Vatican, the People's Republic of China, and that group of scientists on the "Dr. Pangloss fringe" who insist that the abundant earth, its resources unlocked by the magic of science, can feed the present population many times over. Thus, Pope Paul VI told the delegates to the Rome conference: ". . . is it not a new form of warfare to impose a restrictive demographic policy on nations to insure they will not claim their just share of the earth's goods?"[3] The Chinese delegation at the First World Conference on Population led an "anti-Malthusian" bloc, insisting that existing resources could sustain comfortably ten times those living on the earth today. Malcolm Muggeridge, although not a scientist, regards it as strange that demands for population limitation should be made "precisely when the possibilities in the way of food production are seen to be virtually illimitable, and when the whole universe is about to be opened up, providing space to accommodate a million, million times our present squalid little human family."[4]

The data that underpins long-range statistical projections of population growth and food supply, including that of the U.N. Food and Agricultural Organization, is notoriously flawed. In 1960, United Nations projections of world demographic trends postulated three alternate models: optimistic, reasonable, and pessimistic—the latter predicted six billion people by the year 2000 unless demographic brakes were immediately applied. By 1964 the rate of world population increase already had exceeded that envisioned in the most extreme, pessimistic, model. The predictions were subsequently revised—upward.[5] Raw population data from many Fourth World nations is simply guesswork; the only general rule is that the direction of bias runs consistently toward underestimation. Dramatic statistics that rank nations by the extent they fall below some minimal nutritional standard overlook both the questionable nature of the national estimates and the fact there is no concensus as to what the minimum nutritional standard ought to be. For example, a 1964 study demonstrated that if the then-current Food and Agricultural Organization standards were rigorously applied, then a substantial portion of the population of Japan would have to be considered as starving.[6]

Statistically elegant predictive models often pay scant heed to historical trends and omit crucial variables. Scientists and economists alike failed to anticipate the dramatic increases in output brought about by the Green Revolution of the late sixties, an oversight nearly as serious as their failure to prepare for its collapse in the mid-seventies. A USDA analysis of May 1974 projected the supply of and demand for world food supplies in 1985 from a ten-year time base, 1963–1972, the usual interval employed. The study discounted the existence of a serious world food shortage and envisaged American farms as capable of meeting their share of global food needs in the target year. The authors deliberately excluded as too vacuous for measurement the increased costs and diminishing supplies of petroleum and other energy resources.[7]

Confidence in the state of knowledge in this most critical area is little enhanced by the fact that the Department of Agriculture, with perhaps the most sophisticated economic research facilities and staff in the world, predicted a 3 percent annual rate of inflation for domestic food prices in 1973; the actual figure turned out to be close to 20 percent. The massive Soviet grain purchase of 1972 was unanticipated, just as the possibility of mammoth future imports of food by the People's Republic of China is but little reckoned with in policy discussions. The doubling of world prices for wheat, rice, feed grains, soybeans, and sugar between 1972 and 1974 was unexpected, and few foresaw that by 1974 all the vast reservoir of once idled cropland in the United States would be back in production.[8]

There has been famine before; there will be famine again. Grim prophets of doom, from Thomas Malthus in 1798 to the gloomy advocates of "triage" in the present, have periodically forecast an imminent apocalypse when burgeoning numbers of people would outpace the limited capacity of the environment to supply them with food. In most discussions where the consequences weigh as heavily as in this one the maligned discipline of history is invoked only judgmentally or pejoratively to hone off the rough edges of incomplete analyses or lend credence to thinly disguised value judgments. Yet history alone of the social sciences rests by definition upon a time perspective; it is the one discipline that should be most sensitive to the crucial issue of whether the trends and patterns observable in the present break sharply with those of the past. It is from this perspective, and with considerable humility, that we hypothesize that although the worst ravages of the current

crisis may flow from transient causes, factors quantita-
tively and qualitatively different from any that have gone
before point to the decade of the seventies as the beginning
of a time of chronic global scarcities that portend social,
political, and moral catastrophe, unless there is very soon
a radical change in the ways peoples and governments interact and cooperate.

Famines of the past were geographically confined—to
Ireland in 1848, to Bengal in 1943, to India in 1966, and to
Europe in the aftermath of World War II. The present crisis
discriminates neither by region nor by man-induced social
upheaval; it affects three continents and afflicts diverse nations, bound together only by their common lack of energy
and capital and their inability to check rampant population
growth. It follows in the wake of the Green Revolution, the
most significant technological take-off in world food production that history records; it occurs at a time when most
of the world's arable land is in production. In 1972 the
world's food output dropped for the first time in twenty
years, falling 33 million tons from a level of 1,200 million
in 1971. Another ominous drop occurred in 1974. In 1975,
despite a bumper grain crop in the United States, world
production declined because of short-falls in Europe and in
the Soviet Union.[9]

At the root of the problem is the exponential expansion
of the world's population. One-quarter of all of the human
species who have ever lived on the earth are living now.[10]
In 1900, world population was estimated at 1.55 billion; in
1950, 2.5 billion; at the end of 1974, 4 billion. At this rate of
increase, the number of people doubled in the fifty years
from 1925 to 1975 and will double again in the next thirty-
five years. Should this rate be sustained for a century, the
equivalent of the present world's population would be
added every forty-six months. The present estimated rate of
increase, 2.3 percent in 1973, is a deceptively small figure
which translates into two added persons (births over
deaths) every second, 200,000 every day, 6 million each
month.[11] In 1973 the earth's population grew by 76 million

—the greatest annual increment in history. Thirty-seven percent of this increase took place in just two nations: India and China. Minimal subsistence, just for the new people who joined the world's dinner table in 1974, would have required 40 percent of the total grain exports of the United States in that year.[12]

Can runaway demographic growth be halted? In 1968 the government of India set as its objective the reduction of its birthrate of 41 per 1,000 to 25 per 1,000, by 1980. In 1973, only a decrease to 37 per 1,000 had been achieved, and population grew at a rate of 2.1 percent yearly. Confronted by famine, escalating costs of imports, oppressive debts, and depleting currency reserves, appropriations for the nation's birth control programs were slashed from $106 million in 1972–1973 to $72 million in 1974–1975. It was estimated (although all such estimates must be questioned) that of the nation's 100 million fertile couples, only 15 percent practice any form of birth control. In Bangladesh, the most overcrowded nation in the world, no birth control program at all had taken shape.[13]

Confronted by such discouraging potentials, one group of influential biologists and demographers have borrowed a text from Aristotle: "From time to time it is necessary that pestilence, famine, and war prune the luxuriant growth of the human race," and a term, "triage," from wartime medical practices. Triage was a policy of restricting care only to those who had a reasonable chance of survival, hence not wasting precious time and medication on those among the wounded whose chance of survival was hopeless. Since the United States is the world's principal grain exporting nation, they argue that in the future American food aid and technological assistance should be confined to those nations which, in our best assessment, have made substantial efforts to reduce their population, have an efficient and stable political system, possess raw materials necessary for American industry, or are strategically important for American foreign policy. Even benevolent grants of food for emergency relief to others, they contend, would only keep fitfully alive those who are doomed anyway, and would encourage bringing into the world children whose fate would be a pitifully brief life of misery and hunger. Wasting resources on nations in hopeless condition could create worldwide shortages which would make it impossible to provide for nations which could be saved, thus reducing them to the hopeless category. The policy might, at the same time, encourage recalcitrant governments to make the hard decisions and emphasize those priorities that might bring their population into stability with their resources. Writing in 1967, William and Paul Paddock, the most forceful advocates of triage, classified India, Haiti, and Egypt as "hopeless," Libya and Gambia as "walking wounded" (that is, nations that could with minimum outside assistance provide for themselves), and determined that, on the basis of their performance at that time, Pakistan and Tunisia were worthy of receiving American food and technological assistance.[14]

While there are certainly no grounds for euphoric optimism, perhaps the pessimists complain too much. Apparently the aggregate world birthrate is declining, albeit at snail-like pace. Three nations, East Germany, West Germany, and Luxembourg, achieved zero growth rates in 1973, and eight others (including the United States, the United Kingdom, and Belgium) had increments of less than 1 percent. These examples, of course, may be dismissed, for these are all industrialized and urbanized nations. Not so easily disregarded is the experience of the several underdeveloped and less developed nations that have reduced their crude birthrates over the last decade by more than 1 percent annually. Thus, Barbados, Taiwan, Hong Kong, and Singapore had crude birthrates of less than 25 in 1972, and Tunisia, Mauritius, Costa Rica, South Korea, Chile, and Egypt had substantial declines.[15]

This listing includes a variety of nations: some are Catholic, some are Moslem, but in none is the level of deprivation so grueling as in Bangladesh, India, Mali, or Chad. This is the significant point. Limiting population growth is more complex than distributing contraceptive devices and information or establishing birth control clinics. Checking demographic expansion is a social issue. As living standards rise ever so slightly, as literacy increases, as alternatives are posited to traditions that tie women to the confines of hearth and home, birthrates decline. Privation, civil upheaval, and the threat of starvation may actually have the adverse effect of increasing crude birthrates; parents throughout the developing world seem to have the understandable desire to produce enough offspring (preferably male) to have reasonable assurance that some will survive to care for them in their old age.

To transform population control from a technological to a social issue is not to disregard the importance of making contraceptive devices available and disseminating birth control information. Throughout much of the world, family planning services are the exception, not the rule. Even in advanced and liberated America, such services have been available to everyone, irrespective of economic class or place of residence, only since 1970. Lester Brown has estimated that an expenditure of about $2 billion could make family planning services universally available to all people.[16]

Yet in all this, there is a rub, and a serious one, too, that underscores the extent to which the issue of population limitation is linked intricately to a galaxy of complex problems. Even a minimal improvement of living standards to the point where some effect might be manifest in the birthrate would require capital resources that nations already financially hard-pressed, with little to export—the very nations where the problem is most critical—do not possess and are unlikely to attain even in the distant future. The potential for grants or loans from the more affluent industrial nations is not only limited, but is diminishing in a time when world prices are skyrocketing and domestic economic crises press even the most stable of governments. The substantial American food and technological aid in the fifties and sixties did little more than allow the nations that were assisted to keep just a little bit ahead of rising population pressures. It must be noted, however, that ravenous military budgets still expand in the face of inflationary pressures: the United States has been able to find $105.2 billion for new weapons systems currently in the stage of development or procurement. The newly rich Arab world has the raw material and the investment capital (currently being funneled into speculative ventures in Western countries) to finance needed fertilizer production, support food research, and underwrite famine relief programs.

The formidable obstacles that stand in the way of curtailing the demographic explosion are epitomized in the results of the international conference on population that met at Budapest in August of the World Population Year, 1974. The conference became trapped in a debate between Western nations who demanded deliberate population reduction, Communist nations who opposed it, and Third and Fourth world nations whose greatest interest was in funds for development. The final declaration eliminated all references to any urgent label on collaborative efforts to curb growth, and in its final form it turned out to be a series of compromises, tortuously worded to avoid the implication that any nation's sovereignty was being infringed. Laudably enough, the resolutions avowed: "This plan recognizes that social and economic growth is a central factor in the solution of the population problem. National efforts of developing countries to accelerate economic growth should be assisted by the entire international community." The delegates, however, went home with no plan for implementation, and none has been forthcoming since.[17] Oil prices, world inflation, tensions in the Middle East: these are the concerns of statecraft and diplomacy in the mid-seventies. Triage may not be a conscious, deliberate choice at all, but one implemented and effectuated by inaction.

Another dynamic of increasing importance taxes the finite food-producing capacities of the world. As Professor Emile Benoit expresses it, "We have, in effect, a revolution of rising expectation, superimposed on a population explosion, in a world of fixed dimensions and limited productive capacity."[18] As wealth accumulates and standards of living rise, the people benefited become more demanding and selective in their dietary habits. A prime example is the increased demand for meat, particularly beef, the consumption of which is one of the most inefficient means conceivable of converting grain into foodstuff. Cattle require six to nine pounds of food for each pound they gain in live weight. In the United States, growing ever more prosperous in the years after World War II, beef consumption soared from 60 pounds annually per person in 1950 to a peak of 116 in 1972. Georg Borgstrom has estimated that the livestock population of the United States eats enough each year to feed 1.3 billion human beings.[19] As nations join the ranks of the prosperous or nearly prosperous, meat consumption seems automatically to rise. Per capita consumption in Japan leaped from 14 pounds in 1960 to 51 in 1972; in Italy it rose from 70 to 136; in the Soviet Union, 80 to 104. One of the stimuli for the 1972 grain purchase from the United States was the decision of the Kremlin leaders to import grain to feed cattle, thus maintaining the higher levels of meat consumption to which Soviet citizens were slowly becoming accustomed.[20]

The world's favored nations draw disproportionately not only upon foodstuffs but upon other resources necessary for agricultural production. The United States, with 6 percent of the world's inhabitants, consumes 40 percent of the energy used up every year. More fertilizer is poured upon suburban lawns, gardens, cemeteries, and golf courses than is used by all of the farmers in India.[21] Add together the energy needed for tractor fuel, for packaging, for transportation, for driving to the supermarket, and it is estimated that for every single food calorie an American consumed in 1970, nine calories of energy were needed to produce it.[22]

"In a world of scarcity, if some of us consume more, others of necessity consume less," writes Lester Brown of the Overseas Development Council. "The moral issue is raised by the fact that those who are consuming less are not so much the overweight affluent but the already undernourished poor."[23] Accordingly, both Brown and Dr. Jean Mayer, a nutritionist from Harvard, urge that if Americans would cut back their meat consumption just 10 percent—that is, to the levels of a decade ago—12 million tons of grain, an amount greater than India's food deficit in 1974, would be saved. Mayer has coined a sardonic slogan, "Have a drink and starve a child!" pointing out that the 4.1 million tons of grain (1.6 percent of total U.S. production) used to manufacture alcoholic beverages is sufficient to feed at a subsistence level twenty million people for one year.[24]

As morally assuaging and laudatory as such voluntary reductions might be, they would be only short-range responses. Recall that, at the present rate of increase, to feed just those who are added to the world's population in a period of a little more than two years would absorb the entire annual grain exports of the United States, both commercial and charitable. Moreover, the idea that food Americans refrain from eating would reach empty dinner bowls in India or Bangladesh is elusively simple. In the first place, the group that would be most immediately affected would be the already beleaguered American livestock producers. Second, grain diverted from meat or liquor production, under present circumstances, would flow into the commercial market, there to be sold to the highest bidder. The highest bidder would not likely be the capital-deficient, famine-stricken nations. Diverted grain could reach them only if it were purchased and transported by the government or charitable organizations. In that case it would be more efficient for the government to enter the grain market and purchase the grain directly.[25] Less generous applications of fertilizer to lawns and cemeteries would be a token gesture. Only about 4 percent of fertilizer produced in United States is for nonfarm use; most of this is a low-nitrogen mix specially formulated for grass and not comparable to the high nitrogen bulk fertilizer needed for the hybrid grain and rice crops that spurred the Green Revolution.[26]

To argue that benevolent abstinence is little more than symbolic is no counsel for complacency. Already the gregarious consumption habits of the United States and other privileged nations are being challenged by global scarcities of food and other resources, and in ways that are both involuntary and more direct. As competition for food intensifies through the developed and underdeveloped world, American shoppers are competing with every other food buyer in the world, rich and poor, and are paying the now current higher prices as a result. This competition will not slacken. The reason is the international trade position of the United States. Obviously, certain raw materials not available on the North American continent, such as manganese, must be imported. Less widely acknowledged is the fact that vaunted American production techniques have been outpaced and accordingly underpriced by more efficient technologies of foreign nations. Thus, in 1971, imports to United States from abroad accounted for 90 percent of home radios purchased, 96 percent of motorcycles, 51 percent of black and white television sets, 68 percent of sweaters, 42 percent of shoes, and 16 percent of new automobiles. The United States trade deficit with Japan mounted up to $4 billion in 1972.[27] The products of its farms are the principal exchange the United States has to offer on the international market to surmount a negative trade balance and to keep in reasonable bounds ever growing deficits in the international balance of payments. Mounting shortages and escalating prices of oil (which will be exacerbated if Canada, source of 40 percent of American oil imports, follows through in its determination to cease all sales to the United States by 1985) are alone the reason why the United States cannot hoard its foodstuffs for its own use. The days of idled acreage and low food prices seem unlikely to recur again.

To turn from the demand to the supply side of the equation, if world food output is to be increased, in macro-view, two principal means are available: first, extensification— more land can be brought into production and new sources of subsistence utilized; second, intensification—the yields of lands already being cultivated can be increased through improved technology and new plant and animal breeds. Crops are now cultivated on about 11 percent of the earth's land surface. Acreage that is double that amount is in savannahs, high mountain meadows, low rainfall areas, or sloping foothills, usable only for livestock grazing. Fully 70 percent of the world's surface is unsuited to agriculture because of dryness, inclement temperatures, or altitude. The most prolific lands are located in a broad temperate zone north of the equator that reaches around the world from the Ukraine across northern Europe and North America into China. Most of the usable land is being cropped or grazed today.[28]

The potential for extending farming into the area of the earth least cultivated, the vast tropic belts of Africa and South America, is severely limited. Tropic soils are infertile and organic materials decay quickly when the protective forest cover is removed. The primitive cultivators of the tropics were rational men who learned long ago to slash, burn, plant, harvest, and move on to new fields every three to four years.

As for the scientific optimists who assume that miraculous new technologies will emerge so that some day the Sahara may be yellow with ripening wheat and fertile green pasturelands may reach all the way to the Arctic Circle, we can point to several defects that blunt their euphoria. First, the lands where they envisage extensification taking place are more forbidding than any ever cultivated. Energy and capital needs would be gargantuan—even the slopes of Mt. Everest can be considered amenable to cultivation with the proper technology and the immense investments needed to build and operate it. Second, their argument is predicated upon an assumption of continued, undifferentiated growth and takes no account of the impact of such growth upon the fragile world ecosystem. Third, it is by no means logically demonstrable that wherever great needs exist, scientific magic will automatically rise to the challenge to meet them. Finally, if carried to extremes (as it has been by the skilled propagandists of the People's Republic of China), and faith in scientism becomes a deterrent to population control, the argument is positively dangerous.

On the negative side, there is evidence, still controversial, that acreage available for agriculture may be shrinking, not expanding. At the conclusion of an international meeting of climatologists in 1974, Dr. Walter Orr Roberts, a leading expert, declared: "The study of many scholars of climatic change attest that a new climatic pattern is now emerging. There is a growing concensus that the change will persist for several decades and that the current food-production systems of men cannot easily adjust." The mean temperature in the northern hemisphere rose steadily from about 1900 to 1940, when a downward, colder cycle commenced. The net change, although only about half a degree, is sufficient, some scientists insist, to trigger serious adverse effects upon world agriculture. Perhaps this is one reason the monsoon belt in South Asia is shifting and the Sahara advances southward nearly thirty miles each year. Other scientists argue that weather patterns oscillate in cycles of about twenty years duration and that a period of drouth is beginning now. Not all climatologists accept these pessimistic hypotheses,[29] but there is general agreement that weather patterns of the past two decades are not normal— if normality is defined in terms of the experience of the last several centuries.[30]

Whatever the consequences of inanimate change may be, the very fact of man's increased numbers depletes the quality of land available for agriculture, particularly for grazing. In the poorer countries, more people means more livestock for food and draft power. Overgrazing by sheep, goats, and cattle has already denuded millions of marginal dry acres on the desert fringes in Africa, Asia, the Middle East, and in the Andean highlands of South America.[31]

Not the land, not the climate, but water utilization may be the principal constraint upon extensification of cultivatable and productive land. Since the dawn of history seasonal and uneven rainfall patterns have compelled men to turn to some form of irrigation. The greatest expansion ever in the amount of irrigated land has taken place just since 1950, an extension from 100 million to 460 million acres. Nearly half of the world's irrigated land is in India and China. Rice is the principal cereal grown there, and more of it is grown on irrigated land than the combined total of all other crops. Barring catastrophic climatic changes, water for extending irrigation is available in those parts of the world where it is most needed; in fact, much is lost in floods. In India and Pakistan, when the Green Revolution was at its peak, small private tube wells proved more efficient sources of water than huge, costly dams and combined hydroelectric projects. The major restraint on the irrigation facilities required for the dwarf wheat and rice varieties that initiated the Green Revolution is not the supply of water. The problem is the source of the capital that will finance new tube wells and pay for the energy needed to fuel them. Stricken India and Bangladesh, for example, would need to develop a massive export economy to even approach meeting the capital requirements for building and fueling the irrigation systems that would make it possible for the Green Revolution to revive.[32]

There appears to be no immediate possibility that some miraculous scientific breakthrough is about to unlock new sources of food supply. There is little hope in looking to the oceans. The world fish catch has been declining precipitately since 1970; several nations, concerned with diminishing supply, are theatening to extend their territorial waters as far as 200 miles offshore.[33] French scientists are seeking to develop synthetic foods by such processes as fermentation, using micro-organisms growing on petroleum extracts. Mass production of food substitutes are a long way off in the future, and they entail high costs; and scientists have yet to overcome a formidable problem: the stuff tastes awful.[34]

It has been argued that significant increases in world food supply can be achieved only by the means which prompted the great American production achievements since 1945 and accounted for 80 percent of world production increments during the early seventies: more intense cultivation of existing acreage through greater application of technology and increased scientific farming. Let us examine the potentials.

"Today many experts are concerned about the specter of feast rather than famine and a single phrase—'The Green Revolution'—signals the new attitude and the growing vogue."[35] These words, written in 1970, typify an optimism that was widely prevalent—and justifiable—just a few years ago. Planting of new high-yield dwarf varieties of wheat, rice, and other cereals, developed by scientific projects such as that headed by Dr. Norman E. Borlaug in Mexico and the International Rice Research Institute in the Philippines, raised Pakistan's wheat production 60 percent, from 1967 to 1969; India's food output in 1970 was 100 million tons, compared to 89 million in 1964. Eighty percent of India's fertile Punjab was planted with miracle wheat, and in the Philippines triple-cropping of new rice varieties yielded 8 tons to the acre rather than the traditional 2. The amount of acreage planted in the new breeds in Asia and North Africa alone is dramatic evidence of the rapid pace of innovation:

TABLE XI[36]

Year	Acres
1965	200
1966	41,000
1967	4,047,000
1968	16,660,000
1969	31,319,000
1970	43,914,000
1971	50,549,000
1972	68,000,000
1973 (est.)	80,200,000

Despite the fears of political and social observers, the technological revolution did not provoke serious maladjustments. Jobs lost to technology were more than offset by the need for more hands to deal with increased output and new forms of cultivation.[37] The promise of the Green Revolution deteriorated as precipitately as it had arisen. In December 1974, Norman Borlaug, the father of the Green Revolution and winner of the Nobel Peace Prize, grimly predicted that millions of people were going to die of starvation in the months that lay ahead.[38] Like one of Lewis Carroll's legendary characters, a scientist attached to the Mexican wheat project observed: "We've been running hard for thirty years and we're still at the starting line."[39] Lester Brown concludes that the Green Revolution was just a means of buying time (fifteen years, at the most) to discover some means of checking runaway population growth.[40]

India's 1974 wheat crop fell seven million tons below original projections; each million tons would have fed five million people for a year. The short-fall in India epitomized the problems that beset the technological transformations required to offset the hungry future. The production impetus of the Green Revolution was exaggerated; the lands of the Punjab where the miracle seeds were first planted were already the most productive on the subcontinent. More important, the key to the successful cultivation of the productive new varieties was generous applications of fertilizer. In 1973–1974, world fertilizer prices multiplied three to four times over. Fertilizer with high nitrogen content, the most valuable and most frequently used, has a petroleum base. The same shortages and contrived price increases that caused Americans the inconvenience of waiting in lines to fill their automobile gas tanks meant for many small Indian farmers a return to old grain varieties and old methods of cultivation—the inflated price of nitrogen fertilizer was greater than the increased return from high yield varieties.

Exacerbating the price increases, world fertilizer output fell short of demand. Only a few years ago, production had been over-expanded; prices declined and producers throughout the world were threatened with bankruptcy. Cheap fertilizer encouraged generous use, and often over-use. With no new plants being built, shortages, by 1974, were so severe that major producing nations (Japan, U.S.S.R., and the United States) were forced to restrict exports. With the already inflated American price still 50 percent less than that on the world market, farm interests in the United States, in 1973, successfully pressured the government to place a quasi embargo on exports.[41]

Nevertheless, of all the variables that enter into the complex food supply system, the possibility of meeting expanded fertilizer needs is one of the more auspicious. The required natural resources are relatively abundant— Morocco, U.S.S.R., United States, and Canada have major phosphate, sulphur, and potash deposits. Natural gases, insufficient to power motor vehicles, but usable in nitrogen fertilizer production, are flared off and lost in most major oil fields. Important natural gas reserves have been found in Bangladesh and India. Moreover, the greatest potential for substantial production increments are in those underdeveloped areas where fertilizer has thus far been sparingly applied and food needs are greatest. Professor Raymond Ewell, a major authority, has estimated that an increase in food production of 100 million tons would require 24 million tons of fertilizer if it were applied to the already impregnated fields of the United States, but only 10 million tons if spread on the rice fields of Bangladesh. New mines and fertilizer plants are being opened in several parts of the world; China reputedly is building eight nitrogen fertilizer complexes. Unfortunately, availability of raw materials and need for the finished product are not enough. Production of large quantities of nitrogen fertilizer involves an enormously complex technology and consumes huge supplies of energy. To satisfy their fertilizer needs, the hard-pressed nations of the Fourth World would need the capital, the expertise, and the electric power systems to leap quickly into a demanding technological enterprise.

Once again the independent variable is not resources or motivation; it is capital.

Insects, rodents, leaf molds, and birds may seem trivial matters to interject into a serious discussion of agricultural technology. But this illusion quickly dissipates in the face of estimates that reveal that half the world's food supply is lost to such pests in any given year. Even in a technologically advanced America, with all its elaborate control devices, a third of the harvest is destroyed. One reason India failed to meet its productive goals in 1974 was the vulnerability of the high yield varieties to disease and insect infestation. In addition, some have estimated that 70 percent of food in storage in India is often destroyed; about 90 percent of the nation's food grains are stored in inadequate facilities. Four and a half million square miles of grazing land in central Africa are deserted because of the presence of the tsetse fly, carrier of the dread sleeping sickness. The knowledge and the means to build better storage bins—even such simple precautions as traditional American farmers used eighty years ago—are available. Chemical fumigants, insecticides, and resistant breeds of rice and wheat are used in developed nations, and new ones are being created in research laboratories. But, like expending irrigation facilities and building fertilizer complexes, they are costly and require an advanced technology.[42]

Weaknesses in political and administrative leadership, elusive to measure and defiant of any easy remedy, seriously impair the potential both for immediate relief and long-range technological advancement. In oppressed Bangladesh, charges of corruption, smuggling, and profiteering have been rampant, and grain reportedly has rotted in the warehouses of Chittagong.[43] The government of Chad peremptorily halted American food aid when the *New York Times* reported that it was the concensus of donor officials that the government was mismanaging the distribution of relief supplies.[44] The food distribution system in India is notoriously inefficient. Planners there must struggle with hard decisions whether to invest scarce capital in heavy industries to make exports possible or in agricultural developments that will enhance the food supply. A member of the planning commission, who resigned in anger in 1973, charged that, confronted with mass starvation, the government had reduced its outlay for agricultural development from $1.03 billion in 1972 to $850 million in 1973—and that in the wake of an inflation rate of 30 percent. Accusations of myopic, interest-centered decision-making need not be confined to nations of the Third and Fourth worlds. One need but observe the policy of the United States government that held the delegates and the hungry world in suspense through the course of the Rome Food Conference, before summarily rejecting a plea of its own delegation to increase American commitments to a short-range world grain reserve.[45]

Neither can any analysis overlook the innovation-depressing consequences of archaic methods of land tenure in many of the underdeveloped lands. *Latifundiaries* in many South American countries and *zemindars* in India and Pakistan (often friends, allies, or relatives of the politically powerful) are nonresident landlords who extract profits from the hard labor of peasants and accumulate profits for lucrative investment elsewhere. Shortages may actually accrue to their financial benefit, increasing their earnings as supplies run short. Sadly enough, technological aid often yields greater benefits for privileged, parasitic land holders than for productive indigent farmers. Equally sad is the fact that peaceful methods of social change and evolution have been less successful than revolutionary violence in divesting this parasitic class of its power.[46]

Finally, the key problem that lies athwart all attempts to revive the Green Revolution through induced technology must be confronted. How will the costs be met? Can they be met at all? The most elaborate efforts to project long-range world needs and to control for such variables as population growth and shortages of food and energy are the computer studies carried out by a German-American team under the auspices of the Club of Rome. The original study of this group several years ago, reported in *The Limits of Growth,* was criticized as being simplistic and prone to doomsday predictions; its policy recommendations were scarcely distinguishable from triage.[47] A recent study, *Mankind at the Turning Point,*[48] revises the earlier analysis in calling not for a halt to growth but for "organic growth," where the development of the world economy would be controlled like that of the human body. It would permit of differentiation of growth into many lines of development. Most critically, the study postulates that only an *annual* investment of an astronomical $250 billion in the developing countries for the remaining quarter of the twentieth century would permit them to achieve self-sufficiency and avoid apocalyptic upheavals. If, however, action were to be deferred for twenty-five years, the cost by that time would be five times greater.

Two hundred and fifty billion dollars! The Rome Food Conference proposed a World Food Authority that would spend $5 billion yearly to stimulate agricultural development in poorer countries. The total food aid of the United States since World War II totals $40 billion. The newly enriched nations of the Organization of Petroleum Exporting Countries had a net income in 1974 slightly above $50 billion, of which they committed $8.4 billion to foreign assistance, a quarter going to those nations most severely hurt by inflated oil prices. The World Bank, the major international lending agency, made loans in 1974 of about $4.5 billion, approximately $800 million of which involved agricultural projects. The budget request of the President of the United States for fiscal 1976 added up to $330 billion.[49]

Even if the Club of Rome projection is grossly exaggerated, and even if only half $250 billion were required, an international cooperative effort of sacrifice and resource reallocation, unprecedented in history, would be required. Ironically, the favored among the world's nations have in the recent past mobilized their technology, manpower, and resources for efforts of an even larger scale—but they have been for the purpose of destroying lands and peoples, not for stimulating their development. Neither the concern nor the intent to make the sacrifices that a full-scale war on poverty and underdevelopment would require appear on the agenda of any nation or group of nations. Despite the unwillingness of those who have it to invest capital anywhere proximate to the amounts needed for large-scale efforts, not all scientists are pessimistic. Dr. Robert F. Chandler, Jr., founder of the Rice Institute in the Philippines, sees production and yields of Asia's principal cereal crop increasing as breeds are improved through better armoring against pests, making them responsive to smaller applications of fertilizer, and better adapting them to seasonal variations. Similar developments in wheat research lead scientists at Dr. Borlaug's center in Mexico to hope that food production can keep in step with population explosions for perhaps another thirty years.[50] Scientific developments such as these—the most promising on the food front—stress less mechanization and more manpower, for this is the most abundant resource the Fourth World possesses. Techniques are being sought that can be used by small farmers at reasonable costs within bounds that modify traditional practices as little as possible. Double, and even triple, cropping are among the prospects. There are several promising examples. In Taiwan, where the average farm consists of 2½ acres, the mean yield is 3,320 pounds per acre yearly; the yield from the huge agribusiness food factories of the United States is 3,050 pounds of grain yearly.[51]

Ten leading American food scientists, including Dr. Borlaug, who visited the People's Republic of China in the summer of 1974, came away impressed that the world's most populous nation seemed not to be suffering serious food deficiencies. Eight hundred simple backyard factories turned out nearly half of China's needed inorganic fertilizer in 1973. Special cropping systems that grew several grains simultaneously or in close succession on the same plot of land were widely used. New varieties of rice similar to those developed in the Philippines were almost universally being planted. A highly structured organizational scheme that begins with a production team of thirty to forty households provided an efficient medium for transmitting information and formed the basis for an incentive system where individual income was geared to the success of the team in achieving its production target.[52]

Not all the world is or can be a showcase such as Taiwan or a disciplined society like China. Nevertheless, these examples point the most auspicious direction development strategies in the immediate future ought to take.

The analysis we have attempted here, drawn from a variety of sources and disciplines, suggests the following. A permanent crisis brought about by the pressure of population upon resources in finite supply has already begun. The potential for remedying this crisis through the extension of production—cultivating fallow land or finding in laboratories miraculous new ways of providing foodstuffs—is small. On the other hand, intensification of production through existing technological methods appears less discouraging. The fertilizer shortage is remediable. Enough water is available; the problem is its efficient usage. The lands where the most momentous gains in output, through application of nitrogen fertilizers and cultivating of new crop breeds are possible, are those very underdeveloped countries where the needs are the greatest. All of the factors that enter into the complex problem of development are interrelated. Once the worst ravages of potential pestilence and famine have been somewhat mitigated, it becomes possible to create the social stability that affords the security for more willing acceptance of family planning.

Yet formidable obstacles bar the way to the kind of technological development strategy these conclusions suggest. Thus far we have stressed but one recurring one, the maldistribution of capital. Simply stated, as the world's capital resources are now distributed, only a social reorganization of revolutionary proportions could meet the kind of goals such projections as that of the Club of Rome's second report calls for. A continuing crisis exacerbates the complex finance problem: the precious resources India expends to meet immediate food demands is subtracted directly from those development funds that that nation so desperately needs to develop the industries that will earn the exchange to pay for high-priced oil and provide other export revenues. Finding, as we have, little evidence of programs to provide the kind of capital assistance needed, perhaps we are then trapped in a problem made insolvable by our own logic.

To this must be added another paradox of cosmic proportions—one that has had as yet but a shadowy presence in this analysis. The nitrogen fertilizers poured generously on the fertile fields of Illinois, the poisonous wastes emanating from the feedlots of the Southwest, and the pesticides sprayed across fields and gardens in America are but the tips of the iceberg of an ecological problem, the complete significance of which is nearly impossible to fathom. The environmental problem is so vast that it cannot be equated with other issues—the environment is the very arena, the context, wherein all the problems and developments occur. If the technological development that an age of scarcity requires reverses the cycle of the Asian monsoons or turns to barren desert the grassy savannahs of North Africa, then all the logical analysis or all the goodwill in the world have created not betterment for mankind but catastrophe. If this be the case, should we not begin immediately to implement the callous policy of triage?

Indeed, then, we have reached through this tortured analysis to a paradox. The most elemental rule of logic tells us, however, that a paradox results when the frame of reference is wrong. Therefore, to escape a paradox, the frame of reference must be changed. New techniques, new objectives, new priorities in the ways people and nations interrelate and interact are called for.

Through the long decades of unrecorded and recorded history, when population grew at a snail-like pace, when vast areas of land for exploitation remained untilled in the vast prairies of the North American continent or in the virgin lands of Siberia, the luxury of growth and wealth accumulation was possible. When technology and mechanization advanced slowly (witness the constancy in American traditional farming techniques over more than a century), reckless gobbling up of resources in the name of progress was equally possible. However one might criticize the land policies of the United States government in the last decade of the nineteenth century, they had scant impact upon the daily lives of Indian or Chinese peasants. That atomistic era is indeed the "world we have lost." Statecraft and diplomacy oriented in terms of individual nation states as the actors, and national power as the objective, are the essence of the old frame of reference that can only end in paradox. The new frame of reference required is not the quaintly naive world federalism in vogue thirty years ago. Rather it is a pattern of relationships between peoples, mediated through governments, that plans and coordinates growth rather than stimulates it in undifferentiated fashion. Thus, addressing the difficult ecological question, the kind of all-out production currently heralded by technological zealots from the United States Department of Agriculture is positively dangerous, because, to the best knowledge of this writer, it takes into no account the environmental consequences of continued fumigating, disinfecting, and artificially stimulating the fragile soils and air of the North American continent. The all-out production effort must be in India, Bangladesh, and those other nations where manpower is abundant, needs are greatest, and the potential returns infinitely larger. For whatever scant benevolence it affords, the ecological problems there, while dangerous, must (and can) be overlooked until some better balance between population and resources is achieved. Ecology is a luxury in the Fourth World; it is not a luxury in the United States and Western Europe.

To the argument that such a program is an impossible dream or a naive utopianism, several responses can be made. First, there is ample precedent for international cooperation and coordination to meet crises, albeit the crises were military and political. Yet, the longer action is postponed, the more the crisis of scarcity becomes no less pressing than the most serious international political crises of our epoch. Second, the capital, perhaps even in the unprecedented amounts the Club of Rome study calls for, is available; in matter of fact, much of it is currently funneled into waste expenditures for the hardwares of military destruction. Finally, the question of whether a reorientation of priorities can take place is ultimately a political question; the very essence of political questions is that they are by some means—be it compromise, payoffs, reappraisal of self-interest, or strategic advances and retreats—solvable. Likewise, it is the very essence of political questions that they are not solved easily.

In sum, in a world of increasing scarcity and resource depletion, national self-interest is a matter of stability, not power. Security is not gained in terms of military advantage; it is obtained by the availability of vital food and energy resources. To achieve this modicum of stability and security requires more cooperation, less competition. In short, national advantage is no longer a matter of what goes on within confined territorial boundaries, but is rapidly assuming a worldwide frame of reference.[53]

We will conclude by asking what steps can be taken and what steps have been taken to initiate the vast transformation from a local to a planetary arena for interaction.

The first priority is population control. The progress that has been achieved in some of the nations of the developed and nondeveloped world is optimistic. Nevertheless, forestalled by dogmatic ideological and nationalistic arguments, and viewed with indifference by those who mastermind world diplomacy, birthrates are still decreasing at an inadequate pace. To abandon nations as hopeless, as the champions of triage propose, would only lead to social and political upheavals on top of catastrophic problems of scarcity. It would indeed deplete population—by the means of war, pestilence, famine, and death. It would not reduce birthrates, because a world where life is tendentious will only seek to create more life in a desperate attempt to perpetuate itself. Moreover, the effects of the metaphorical "midnight rides of the Four Horsemen of the Apocalypse" are not insulated within political or even continental boundaries. Even the United States seems willing to entertain the possibility that at some time military force might be necessary to assure petroleum supplies for itself. Parallel with policies to curb demographic growth, capital and technical assistance are indispensable if Third and Fourth World nations are to utilize existing scientific developments to slowly revive a Green Revolution. Since 90 percent of the world's food is consumed where it is grown, the most auspicious interventions are those that supply short-term relief in the case of crop failures and then offer knowledge, capital, and basic technical tools to push nations along toward the ultimate goal of self-sufficiency.

Whatever capital is made available to spur and feed agricultural developments on the small farms of India, Bangladesh, or central Africa can come only from those nations made recently rich by their oil reserves or from those who have long been the leaders and movers of world politics and international trade. While the United States cannot be expected to bear the burden alone, the oft-heard generalization that America has done and is now doing more than its share is belied by noting that in 1973 the United States dropped to fourteenth place among the sixteen Development Assistance Committee countries in terms of official development assistance as a percentage of gross national product.[54] The only alternative is whether developed nations such as the United States, Japan, U.S.S.R., West Germany, and the Organization of Petroleum Exporting Countries choose now to cooperate in programs that will underwrite better agricultural development and plan the worldwide distribution of food and energy resources, or wait until the inexorable laws of supply and demand, forcing critical domestic cutbacks, high prices, and potentially bitter rivalries, compel a reallocation of priorities.

At the present time there is no escape from the cruel reality that millions face starvation now and millions more to be born confront a life Thomas Hobbes described as "nasty, short, and brutish!" These sad years require that in the interest of elemental morality, in maintaining some modicum of political stability, and in preventing crude birthrates from further escalation, the nations that *have* will need to share some of their increasingly precious food reserves with those that *have-not.* The contribution of American agriculture, which supplies 85 percent of the grain that flows in international commerce, is central. The problems that the revolution on the American farm have wrought, the vicissitudes of United States agricultural policy, and the economics of modern domestic marketing and retailing processes have a significance that stretches far beyond our borders and may pose the most pressing political and economic question of our time.

All these problems and the formidable difficulties that stand in the way of comfortable solutions came into better focus as a result of the First World Food Conference which met in Rome in the early weeks of November 1974. Convened by the United Nations at the behest of the United States, the purpose of the meeting of 130 nations was to address problems of long-range development and initiate cooperation in efforts to bolster world food production. The acuteness of the emergencies in the autumn of 1974 compelled a shift in emphasis. Pressing problems of immediate relief prompted the major controversies of the conference and monopolized almost the exclusive attention of press reports on the proceedings.

As such conclaves are wont to be, the Rome conference was strong on proposals, effusive in rhetoric, but short on plans for implementation and financing. Admirably enough, among the resolutions approved was one that called for a ten million ton annual food aid program, and which envisioned an international grain reserve to which participating nations would contribute supplies in years of plenty to guard against times of scarcity. The reserve, apparently, would be nationally held, but internationally coordinated. The already developed nations were urged to implement agricultural policies that would encourage the early expansion of food production. The delegates called for raising the annual rate of output growth in developing nations to 40 percent a year, and urged governments there to give high priority to pricing and tax policies that would give farmers greater incentive to produce more. It was agreed that too easy access to foreign food aid might handicap efforts to achieve local production increments.[55] Another resolution approved an international early warning system to provide information on crop prospects, supplies, and changes in demand. In longer term, the delegates called for an agricultural development fund that would help finance irrigation, fertilizer, pesticide, and nutritional assistance. To administer these, the conference asked the United Nations General Assembly to create a World Food Council that would replace the generally ineffective Food and Agricultural Organization.[56]

The omnipresent problem of financing remained unresolved at the end of the conference. The United States cautiously refused to place any price tag upon its contribution.[57] In terms more blunt than the usual guarded language of diplomacy, Secretary of State Kissinger, in the conference's keynote address, threw the challenge for financial initiative to the oil exporting countries with "incomes far in excess of that needed to balance their international payments or to finance their economic development."[58] Two follow-up meetings subsequent to the conference failed to come up with specific proposals on finance, although some of the OPEC nations made aid commitments, largely to other Moslem countries.

Shortly after the Rome meeting, Ambassador Edwin M. Martin, the U.S. coordinator for the First World Food Conference, was guardedly optimistic. "Five years seems the very earliest point at which it would be fair to conclude that the Conference succeeded or failed." He went on to add:

This assumes ... that a prompt effort is made to implement the conclusions of the Conference. We may not have to wait more than six months to be able to judge it a failure. For if steps have not been taken in this period to put into operation the World Food Council, the Agricultural Development Fund, the Consultative Group on Food Production and Investment in Developing Countries and if negotiations are not well underway on a firm agreement among major grain exporters and importers to establish an international system of national grain reserves and among food exporters and sources of concessional finance to guarantee a minimum of 10 million tons of food aid a year, we haven't much hope of success.[59]

On the other hand, Norman Borlaug, disappointed at the failure of the meeting to deal with immediate problems, was categorical: "It was nonsense and you can quote me. Nothing tangible was done. It was just talk."[60]

By March 1975, some of the long-range administrative and procedural suggestions of the conference had been implemented. The World Food Council, disengaged from the cumbersome and inefficient operation of FAO, had been speedily approved by the United Nations General Assembly. The consultative group, headed by Ambassador Martin, was functioning in its designated role of investigating the most propituous areas for investment and assistance. Establishing committees is simpler than soliciting funds and building up food stocks. The consultative committee significantly was a recommending body, not a funding body. The early warning system designed to forecast potential famine, still was nonfunctional; the Soviet Union and China, as usual, balked at revealing crop and agricultural production data. More important, a full year after the conference, no effective world food reserve existed and no progress was being made toward creating one. Among the many stumbling blocks was the reluctance of the United States Department of Agriculture to buy and hold grain; USDA continued to insist—as it had since 1972—that American grain reserves should remain in private hands.[61]

The immediate, acute food scarcities in the autumn of 1974 were not a part of the original agenda of the Rome conference, but given the severity of the crisis, these, rather than the long-range plans discussed above, were the principal issues debated and discussed. These deliberations accentuated not only the worldwide problems of 1974 but the dilemmas that confronted American agricultural policy in a new epoch. While the delegates argued and debated, the harvest was being gathered in the United States from virtually all of the farmland that for decades had been held out of production. And the harvest was hauled away not to a government grain reserve but to the warehouses of Cargill and Continental. The United States' monopoly over world food production is no less extensive than that of the Arab world over scarce oil reserves. As the nations at Rome looked to the OPEC for the initiative on finance, they looked to the United States for the initiative on the crucial issue of emergency food assistance.[62]

In contrast to Secretary-General Boerma's original estimates of 11 million tons of grain needed to meet immediate emergencies in such nations as Bangladesh, Pakistan, India, and the central African states, conferees at Rome finally agreed upon 7.5 million tons, costing $1.8 billion. Two million of these were already provided by the present aid programs of the U.S., Canada, the European Common Market, Australia, and Japan.[63]

Goaded by members of the congressional delegation who observed the conference (Senators Hubert Humphrey, Dick Clark, and George McGovern), the American representatives, including Secretary of Agriculture Butz, who consistently held that the world food situation was "critical" but not a "crisis," cabled President Ford requesting that United States food aid under Public Law 480 be increased from the currently budgeted level of $175 million to $350 million. This would have provided an additional million ton grain contribution from United States. After a week's delay the president rejected the request, arguing that more information was needed on reserves available and that such a commitment would have an inflationary effect upon the commodities market.[64] The refusal was not so callous as it might seem. Secretary Butz hastened to assure that the United States was already committed to export 3.3 million tons, the equivalent of 1973, and an additional million would probably materialize in the natural course of events.

The White House echoed the same sentiments, promising that added relief allocations would be made on a quarterly basis and would depend upon the most timely available crop information.[65]

The president and Butz were true to their promises. On 3 February 1975 the Department of Agriculture announced that the United States' commitment for food aid in the fiscal year ending 30 June 1975 would be raised enough to provide 5.5 million tons compared to the 3.3 originally projected. This would more than satisfy the requests of the delegation at Rome in November.[66] Compared to the tonnage allocated for relief aid, commercial commitments on the grain stocks of the United States in November 1974 included 5.6 million tons for Japan, 6 million for Western Europe, 4.1 million for Eastern Europe, 7 million for China, and 3.5 million for the Soviet Union.[67]

Despite the administration's positive response to international food shortages, it still remained unclear whether American food aid would be distributed according to humanitarian objectives or for political advantages. During the course of the Rome conference, Secretary Butz flew to Cairo to negotiate a concessional sale of 200,000 tons of grain to Egypt under Public Law 480, to be paid for with Egyptian currency. Shortly thereafter, the Department of Agriculture announced a similar concessional sale of 100,-000 tons to Syria and 734,000 bushels of wheat to Jordan.[68] In 1973 a disproportionate 45 percent of American food aid had been allotted to Laos, Cambodia, and South Vietnam. In addition to United States aid, Canada, at the time of the Rome conference, pledged 1 million bushels, Australia, 650,000.

Meanwhile in Bangladesh, India, and Pakistan the gathering of the fall harvest—an inadequate one—had brought some temporary respite from the severities of November. Beneficent rainfall had fallen on drouth-stricken central Africa. By early 1975 some of the most severe shortages envisioned at Rome were partially mitigated. The food gap in February was estimated at 3 million tons rather than the

7.5 million projected in November. India, the most severely afflicted nation, had commitments to import about 7 billion tons of grain. These commercial transactions had cost, however, two-thirds of the nation's currency reserves, and accordingly reduced amounts that could be utilized to improve fertilizer production and initiate other long-term projects to increase domestic production.

In many parts of the world the severe famine conditions of the autumn of 1974 did not recur in 1975. The United States harvested a bumper grain crop—greater even than the record breaking one of 1973. In developing nations, given more favorable weather conditions than the preceding year, output crept upward about 8 percent. Nevertheless, world grain output remained at about the same level as 1974 because of short-falls in Europe and the Soviet Union. American food exports to developing nations increased in the fiscal year ending June 1975 to 37.2 percent of total U.S. agricultural exports, compared to 32.4 percent the preceding fiscal year. Sales to India went up nearly fourfold from 1974 to 1975, but most of the grain that India received from the United States was purchased on the commercial market, thus drawing upon the precious foreign exchange of Mrs. Gandhi's beleaguered government.[69]

Such temporary respites do not ease the problem. Each day the inexorable addition of more members to the human species continues. Each passing week and month drains the supplies gathered at harvest or the exports stored in the warehouses of food-deficient nations. The imprudent policies that drained the American grain reserves in the reckless export binge of 1972–1973, decisions that bargain away the precious remaining reserves for political advantage, render the United States increasingly impotent to provide the emergency assistance the next recurrence of famine will require.

American agriculture at the last quarter of the twentieth century is at the threshold of a crisis as severe as that which prompted the dramatic policy changes of the New Deal years. The products that emanate from the farms of America and the policies that sustain and regulate their production affect intimately the welfare not only of Americans but of millions of people throughout the world. To adapt to a world of scarcity requires of American farm policy, at the very minimum, the restoring of ample grain reserves as quickly as possible. To do so will require the reversal of those decisions that allowed these vital assets to pass entirely into commercial hands. As a further minimum, short-sighted decisions that in past years have cut funds for agricultural research need to be undone. Dr. Jean Mayer crystallizes the issue when he points out that American food policy should have four aims:

1. To stimulate food production on American farms and ensure farmers a fair return.

2. Keep food prices reasonable for American consumers.

3. Help the starving overseas.

4. Contribute to an evening of the American balance of payments.

Unfortunately the four aims are contradictory. To build up grain reserves, ship large amounts of food to the starving, and increase the return to U.S. farmers would necessitate higher prices for American consumers. Shipping grain abroad as gifts, or even long-term loans, does not materially improve the balance of payments position of the United States.[70]

Circumventing such contradictions demands programs that will allow production to expand judiciously within safe ecological boundaries.[71] To maintain sufficient levels of production American farmers seem to require some fail-safe mechanism to provide against the unlikely event that surpluses will recur again, with their concomitant price-depressing effects. The target price mechanism in the Agricultural Act of 1973 seems as well adapted as any to achieve this objective. One might, however, question the motivations of those who, in response to the current USDA drive for all-out production (ignoring environmental consequences), demand that the present target prices be increased to closer proximate the market price. This, they contend, is the only way American farmers will meet the increased demands placed upon them.

No matter how much nostalgia one might have for traditional craft-oriented farming or the agrarian way of life, there is no turning back in the United States from the mechanized and technologically complex agriculture that now exists; it is doubtful if domestic, let alone foreign demands, could be satisfied in any other fashion. Nevertheless, as unemployment rolls grow in the mid-seventies, it now appears that the manpower depletion in agriculture has gone too far. Studies, such as those noted earlier, that point to the efficiency of one- or two-man operations, suggest the advisability of a possible underwriting of a return of manpower to the agricultural sector.

As for the kind of traditional farming that existed in America before the point of disjuncture in World War II and immediately thereafter, it is gone forever. There is a future for a kind of traditional farming, and certainly for some of the shrewd genius and acumen many of those tough old farmers, black and white, possessed. One can only hope there are shrewd, innovating husbandmen as wise as Tarpley Taylor who speak Bengali, Chinese, Hindi, or Urdu.

The gregarious consumption standards of Americans that extract a disproportionate share of food and resources come under increasing challenge in a world of scarcity. It becomes more and more difficult to justify the waste inherent in reckless meat consumption or the frivolous use of precious commodities in high-profit packaged convenience and luxury foods aimed to benefit competitive food processors and retailers. Such vain luxuries of the affluent appear inevitably destined for reduction, not voluntarily but by the relentless pressure of limited supply upon demand and the high prices that therefore result. In an economy out of equilibrium, the most serious domestic consequence of rationing by price alone is the inequity of limiting the availability of material satisfactions to which Americans have grown accustomed to those among its citizens who already are over-fed and prosperous.

In world perspective, if rampant population growth is not soon arrested; if sizeable outpourings of capital for agricultural development are not forthcoming; if the nations of the world delay in implementing programs for food and technological aid, then competition for resources will intensify and prices will rise even more; the vagaries of climate or a series of poor crop years can cause mass starvation; and the slightest political ripples, let alone those as portentous as war in the Middle East, could throw an already unstable equilibrium further out of balance.

In a world where Russian grain purchases precipitate increases in the cost of living in the United States and reduce food reserves, rendering it difficult for the United States to extend aid to those starving in Bangladesh; where food shipments to Japan are necessary to make reasonable priced television sets and electronic parts available to American consumers; where severe crop failures in any part of the world can initiate desperate and costly scrambling for food resources; where the eating habits of the affluent can cause privation among the poverty stricken half a world away, the word "interdependent" becomes a cliché and the aphorism, "In a world of scarcity there are few choices," a self-evident truism.

Notes

1. Boyce Rensberger, "Experts Ask Action to Avoid Millions of Deaths in Food Crisis," *New York Times,* 26 July 1974, p. 31; *New York Times,* 20 October, 13 December 1974. In citations that follow, feature-length signed articles will be designated by author name and headline, news items by newspaper and date alone. In a topic so contemporary as the world food crisis, inordinate reliance upon newspaper reports is unavoidable. I have profited immensely, however, from the perspective and mode of analysis of a work I do not specifically cite, Mitchell Harris Kellman, "World Population Growth and Food Production—A Malthusian Inquiry" (Ph.D. dissertation, Department of Economics, University of Pennsylvania, 1972). Two particularly valuable but now dated works are Rene Dumont and Bernard Rosier, *The Hungry Future* (New York: Frederick A. Praeger, Publishers, 1969) and Georg Borgstrom, *The Hungry Planet: The Modern World at the Edge of Famine,* 1st ed. rev. (New York: Macmillan Co., 1967).
2. Quoted, *New York Times,* 31 October 1974.
3. Quoted, *Philadelphia Inquirer,* 10 November 1974.
4. Quoted, Colin Clark, *Starvation or Plenty?* (New York: Taplinger Publishing Co., 1970), p. 171.
5. J. M. Thoday, "The Problem," in Sir Joseph Hutchinson, ed., *Population and World Food Supply* (Cambridge: At the University Press, 1969), pp. 8–9.
6. Clark, *Starvation or Plenty?* pp. 14–15.
7. Don Paarlberg, "The World Food Situation in Perspective," *American Journal of Agricultural Economics* 56 (May 1974): 351–52. For a critique, see D. E. Hathaway, "Discussion," *American Journal of Agricultural Economics* 56 (May 1974):

372. Apparently these projections were still being used by the USDA in August, when planning for the Rome Food Conference was well underway. *New York Times,* 21 August 1974.
8. Lester R. Brown with Eric P. Eckholm, *By Bread Alone* (New York: Frederick A. Praeger, Publishers, 1974), pp. 241–42.
9. "The World Food Crisis," *Time* 106 (11 November 1974): 68. USDA, *Agricultural Outlook,* AO–5 (October 1975), p. 16.
10. *New York Times,* 27 August 1974.
11. Brown, *By Bread Alone,* p. 179; Lester R. Brown, *In the Human Interest* (New York: W. W. Norton and Co., 1974), pp. 22–23.
12. *New York Times,* 29 October 1974.
13. Ibid., 14 August 1974; 24 November 1974; 2 February 1975. Although India's contribution to total population increase is greater, rates of growth are highest in the world in Columbia, Equador, Venezuela, and Paraguay. China adds more people each year than any other nation, although its reported rate of increase is a modest 1.7 percent. Chinese demographic data must be treated skeptically. The only census in recent times was in 1953 and was almost surely an undercount. See *World Population Estimates, 1974* (Washington, D.C.: The Environmental Fund, 1974).
14. Although the Paddocks, in the title of their book, *Famine, 1975* (Boston: Little, Brown & Co., 1967), predicted with remarkable prescience, their analysis completely discounted the possibility of a "Green Revolution" which was already in progress when the book came into print. They also interpreted Public Law 480 not as a method of disposing America's surplus grain but as a soft-headed humanitarian gesture that would by 1975 have depleted the nation's grain reserves. The grain reserves were indeed depleted by 1975, but for reasons totally different. The precariousness of the tough-minded decisions they advocate is accentuated by their inclusion of Egypt in the "hopeless" category, a choice scarcely conceivable in 1975. Among other supporters of triage are The Environmental Fund of Washington, D.C.; Dr. Philip Handler, president of the National Academy of Sciences; Garrett Hardin, professor of biology at the University of California, Santa Barbara; and Professor Jay W. Forrester, a computer engineer at Massachusetts Institute of Technology and a coauthor of the Club of Rome-sponsored *Limits to Growth* (New York: Universe Books, 1972).
15. Brown, *In The Human Interest,* p. 153.
16. Ibid., 159–66.
17. *New York Times,* 3 September 1974.
18. Quoted, ibid., 19 November 1974.
19. Quoted, Mary Bralove, "World Food Crisis Poses Peril of Star-

vation on International Scale," *Philadelphia Inquirer,* 13 October 1974, p. 9–B.
20. Boyce Rensberger, "Curb on U.S. Waste Urged to Help World's Hungry," *New York Times,* 25 October 1974, p. 1.
21. *New York Times,* 28 August 1974.
22. Brown, *By Bread Alone,* p. 107.
23. Ibid., p. 197.
24. Boyce Rensberger, "How to Help the Starving: Through Eating Less Meat Here," *New York Times,* 28 November 1974, p. 44; Jane E. Brody, "Can Less Drinking Lead to Less Starvation?" *New York Times,* 11 December 1974, p. 50.
25. Rensberger, "How to Help the Starving," *New York Times,* 28 November 1974, p. 44.
26. James J. Kilpatrick, "Food, Famine and Our Image Abroad," *Philadelphia Bulletin,* 11 December 1974, p. 33.
27. Cynical students of colonialism might find something familiar in the pattern by which Japan imports American lumber, foodstuffs, and cotton, and ships back in return high technology and high priced manufactured goods. Paul and Arthur Simon, *The Politics of World Hunger* (New York: Harper's Magazine Press, 1973), pp. 155, 158.
28. Brown, *By Bread Alone,* pp. 77–79.
29. Specialists in the U.S. Department of Agriculture tend to discount all these interpretations.
30. Harold M. Schmeck, Jr., "Climate Changes Imperil World's Food Output," *New York Times,* 8 August 1974, p. 31; *New York Times,* 16 February 1975.
31. Brown, *By Bread Alone,* p. 87.
32. Ibid., pp. 92–99.
33. Harold M. Schmeck, Jr., "World Fish Supply Too Depleted to Fill Needs of the Hungry," *New York Times,* 27 October 1974, p. 1; Brown, *By Bread Alone,* pp. 147–63.
34. Paddock and Paddock, pp. 64–65.
35. *New York Times,* 22 October 1970.
36. Brown, *By Bread Alone,* p. 137.
37. *New York Times,* 23 September, 29 September 1974.
38. *New York Times,* 11 December 1974.
39. *New York Times,* 3 September 1974.
40. Brown, *By Bread Alone,* p. 145.
41. Victor E. McElheney, "Rising World Fertilizer Scarcity Threatens Famine for Millions," *New York Times,* 1 September 1974, p. 1; *New York Times,* 7 October 1974.
42. Jane E. Brody, "Experts for Pest Control to Increase World's Food," *New York Times,* 28 October 1974, p. 1.
43. *Philadelphia Bulletin,* 16 December 1974.

44. *New York Times,* 1 November 1974.
45. Ibid., 16 November 1974.
46. See Rene Dumont and Bernard Rosier, *The Hungry Future* (New York: Frederick A. Praeger, Publishers, 1969), p. 195; Alan Matt Warhaftig, "Famine in Africa—No Act of God," *Nation* 220 (22 February 1975): 197–200.
47. Donella H. Meadows, Dennis Meadows, and Jorgan Randera (New York: Universe Books, 1972). A number of important omissions undercut this "System Dynamics" model. It was quickly pointed out that there was a total absence of adjustment mechanisms in the model, such as price, and that resources are properly measured in economic, not physical, terms. Critics also noted that the advance of technology, like the growth of population and industry, has also been proceeding exponentially, and that the average annual rate of technological growth over the past fifty years had been roughly 2 percent. Thus it would seem possible that the transition from higher to lower growth rates could be achieved without catastrophe. Carl Kaysen, "The Computer That Printed Out WOLF," *Foreign Affairs* 50 (July 1972): 661–66.
48. Mihajlo Mesorovic and Eduard Pestel (New York: E. P. Dutton & Co., 1974), p. 63–142. *New York Times,* 10 October 1974.
49. *New York Times,* 29 October 1974, 17 November, 27 November, 11 December 1974.
50. Boyce Rensberger, "Science Gives New Life to the Green Revolution," *New York Times,* 3 September 1974, p. 1; Victor K. McElheney, "New Miracle in Rice Seen By Some in Asia," *New York Times,* 1 November 1974, p. 1.
51. Boyce Rensberger, "Experts Ask Action to Avoid Millions of Deaths in Food Crisis," *New York Times,* 26 July 1974, p. 31. In India, yield per acre on average farms of less then five acres was more than 40 percent greater than on farms of more than fifty acres. Brown, *By Bread Alone,* p. 214.
52. Boyce Rensberger, "Chinese Farm Gains Impress Visitors," *New York Times,* 7 September 1974, p. 1.
53. Although the analysis in these paragraphs is distinctively my own, I have been influenced by Mesorovic and Pestel, *Mankind at the Turning Point;* David V. Edwards, "Is This a Foreign Policy?" *Nation* 220 (8 March 1975): 263–66, and Dixson Terry, "Report on Central Iowa Food Conference," *U.S. Farm News* (Des Moines) 23 (March 1975): 1.
54. James W. Howe, *The U.S. and the Developing World: Agenda for Action, 1974* (New York: Frederick A. Praeger, Publishers, 1974), p. 108.

55. Edwin M. Martin, U.S. Food Coordinator for the World Food Conference, Address, winter meeting, American Society of Agricultural Engineering, Chicago, 12 December 1974. Copy supplied to writer by U.S. Department of State.
56. *New York Times,* 19 November 1974.
57. Secretary Kissinger, however, stipulated his government's willingness to contribute $65 million to nutritional research and aid programs and to increase the $350 million currently budgeted for international development assistance.
58. *New York Times,* 6 November 1974.
59. Ambassador Martin, Address, p. 11.
60. Quoted, *New York Times,* 11 December 1974.
61. Boyce Rensberger, "Long-Range Plans to Feed World Are Moving Ahead," *New York Times,* 16 March 1975, p. 1.
62. American farms supply 90 percent of world soybean exports, 60 percent of corn and other feed grains, 40 percent of wheat, 25 percent of rice. *New York Times,* 1 December 1974.
63. *New York Times,* 13 November, 30 November, 1 December 1974.
64. Ibid., 9 November, 16 November 1974.
65. Ibid., 16 November 1974.
66. Ibid., 4 February 1975.
67. Ibid., 14 November 1974.
68. Ibid., 8 November, 23 November 1974; *Philadelphia Bulletin,* 28 November 1974.
69. William Robbins, "Food Supplies Up as Hard Hit Lands Find Some Relief," *New York Times,* 2 February 1975. USDA, ERS, *Agricultural Outlook,* AO–5 (October 1975), p. 16; USDA, ERS, *Foreign Agricultural Trade of the United States* (November 1975), p. 40–47. See Epilogue for further discussion.
70. Jean Mayer, "Plenty of Questions and No Answers," *Philadelphia Bulletin,* 25 November 1974, p. A17.
71. Willard W. Cochrane, *Feast or Famine: The Uncertain World of Food and Agriculture and Its Policy Implications for the United States* (Washington, D.C.: National Planning Association, 1974).

Epilogue

Attempts to freeze into a specific time frame a topic so volatile as that of change in modern agriculture incur the risk of being rendered rapidly out of date. Several important developments during the year that has elapsed since the preceding chapters were written demand some further comment.

Anyone who traveled across the farmlands of the West and Middle West in the late summer and autumn of 1975 would have noted how the corn overflowed the barnyard storage bins and that rows of trucks were lined up around the grain elevators. American agriculture, back in full-scale production for the second time since World War II, and spared the drouth that held down output in 1974, produced the largest crop in the nation's history. What have been the implications of this bountiful harvest for two topics that have been central to the analysis in the last three chapters: the price of food in the United States, and the dangers of famine round the world?

The index of prices that consumers paid for food crept upward in 1975, but at a rate of only 9 percent compared to a 14 percent increase in 1974. Table 12 carries the statistics presented in table 9 through September 1975. It will be noted that food prices stabilized and even declined until major spurts upward took place in the summer months, simultaneous with Soviet purchases of American wheat. Prices received by farmers receded through April and then advanced sharply, even as the bountiful new harvest began to flow to market. The small monthly drops in the food price index in August and September reflected declines in the price of fresh fruits and vegetables.[1]

TABLE XII

The Not-So-Steady March of Inflation, 1975 [2]

Month	Consumer Price Index	Food Price Index	Prices Received by Farmers
January	156.1	170.9	172
February	157.2	171.6	168
March	157.8	171.3	165
April	158.6	171.2	170
May	159.3	171.8	178
June	160.6	174.4	182
July	162.3	178.6	187
August	162.8	178.1	187
September	163.6	177.8	193

Despite the greater output in 1975, the products of American agriculture flowed into the same marketing channels as in 1973 and 1974, and in about the same proportions. As indicated earlier, agricultural exports reached record highs in 1974 and 1975. The wheat from the plains and the soybeans from the Middle West remained the critical balancing factors that earned for the United States the international exchange to pay the swollen costs of oil imports. About half the American wheat crop was exported in 1975. If the American standard of living, so dependent upon petroleum products, was to be maintained at any level near its present extravagant one, there could be no turning back from the internationalist policy that bartered the harvests from American croplands for oil and manufactured goods from Europe, Japan, and the Organization of Petroleum Exporting Countries. Given present circumstances, there is no alternative to maximizing American farm output by keeping all available acreage in production. Since American consumers are now competing with buyers all around the world for their bread and breakfast cereal, food prices will remain near their present highs. Poor crop years— anywhere in the world—will push prices proportionately higher.[3]

Likewise, there was very little variation in 1975 in the way the consumer's food dollar was distributed at the various processing and retailing way-stations along the route from the farm to the dinner table. The farmer's share of the market-basket dollar (43¢ in 1974) dropped to 40¢ in the first quarter of 1975 and recovered to 44¢ in the third. Processors and retailers took the rest. The farm retail price spread continued to increase, having risen from 118.9 in 1972 to 163.6 in the third quarter of 1975.[4] Food processors and retailers chalked up only slight profit increases in 1975, but this must be qualified because of the spectacular records of such star performers as Safeway.

Out on the nation's farms, the distribution of real net income according to class of farms showed almost no change between 1973 and 1974 (data for 1975 was not available at the time of this writing). Comparing table 13 with table 10 shows that the most dramatic changes happened in 1973; big, heavily capitalized farms continued to earn a disproportionate share of farm income.

In sum, the short-range effects of a single bumper crop year in no way modify the long emerging economic and commercial patterns that were so sharply accentuated by the developments in 1972 and 1973. Full-scale production, high food prices, mammoth commercial exports, concentration of economic power in the hands of fewer and fewer producing, processing, and retailing units: these are the characteristics of the new American agriculture.

The world food crisis did not go away in 1975. Better weather, short-term relief measures, and the increased pro-

TABLE XIII

Classes of Farms by Sales and Net Income, 1974[5]

Class	Percent in Class	Realized Net Income (Millions)	Percent of Realized Net
100,000 +	4.1	9,572	34.5
40–99,999	12.5	7,168	25.9
20–39,999	20.8	6,606	23.8
10–19,999	11.5	1,955	7.1
5–9,999	8.7	822	3.0
2,500–4,999	17.4	862	3.1
2,500–	25.0	722	2.6
	100.0	27,707	100.0

duction in the United States eased the grimmest manifestations of the emergency, but in stark reality a number of nations faced greater hunger perils in 1975 than in 1974. In one sense, the better conditions were a danger rather than a blessing, because the short-range improvements eroded the sense of urgency that in 1974 had prompted measures to head off potential famine disasters throughout the world.

Unchecked population growth continued. Between 1974 and 1975 about 74 million new people joined the world's dinner table.[6]

Despite better crop yields in undeveloped nations and the bumper harvest in the United States, overall world grain production declined slightly in 1975. More important, a greater percentage of the grain produced was consumed. The world supply of reserve grain, already perilously low in the summer of 1974, was even smaller at the end of 1975. A report of the Overseas Development Council, a private organization concerned with the problems of developing nations, declared in May 1975: "The world in 1975 is more vulnerable to a major new grain shortfall than at any time since World War II."[7]

This vulnerability was heightened by the fact that escalating prices had reduced fertilizer consumption in some of the world's poorest areas by as much as 30 or 40 percent. Although the fertilizer shortage of 1974 had passed, prices for some of the most commonly used soil nutrients had increased as much as 1000 percent. The Food and Agricultural Organization of the United Nations estimated that the resulting reductions in fertilizer use in forty-three of the world's poorest nations was equivalent to the loss of 2.7 million tons of grain. Moreover, higher prices for chemical and petroleum based fertilizers drained increasing proportions of foreign exchange in nations that could least afford it. This forced the postponing of expenditures in other economic sectors and slowed growth rates that were already sluggish.[8]

Forced on to the commercial markets to supply such crucial needs as fertilizer and grain, the trade deficits of nonoil producing developing nations swelled from $9 billion in 1973, to $28 billion in 1974, and to $35 billion in 1975. Their accumulated foreign debt rose to $120 billion. Half of whatever assistance might become available through lending agencies such as the World Bank and the International Monetary Fund would be needed just to meet interest payments. In the wake of spiraling worldwide inflation, the capacity of the poorer nations to develop the export industries that could earn for them the capital to purchase grain and fertilizer from abroad, improve their agricultural technology, and to breathe new life into the Green Revolution, has seriously deteriorated.[9]

After the passage of a year since the Rome Food Conference, a completely pessimistic judgment about its accomplishments would be premature. As noted earlier (page 232), some of the long-range administrative and procedural mandates had been rapidly implemented. In the more concrete areas of food aid, grain reserves, and an international agricultural development fund, progress had been less auspicious.

Food aid of 8.9 million tons had been pledged by July 1975, 1.1 million tons short of the goal set at Rome. The United States' contribution of 6 million tons was an increase of 20 percent over contributions the preceding year, but the nations of the European Economic Community refused to go beyond their 1974 total of 1.3 million tons, and the nations in the Soviet bloc had made no pledges at all.[10]

The world grain reserve remained in the discussion stage. Secretary of State Henry Kissinger reiterated the target set at Rome: a world reserve of 30 million tons of wheat and rice; but the United States, by far the world's leading grain exporter, assumed no leadership initiative, and the government refused any commitment that even approached American holdings in the past. A major stumbling block was the insistence of Secretary of Agriculture Butz and other officials of the Ford administration that American reserves be held by private traders, not by public authority. Thus it would appear that any carry-over from the banner crop year of 1975 will be in the warehouses of the giant grain-trading oligopolies.[11]

During 1975 little progress at all was made toward establishing an international agricultural development fund. Speaking to the United Nations in September, Secretary Kissinger repeated a request for the creation of a "development security fund" of $2.5 billion a year within the International Monetary Fund to meet deficiencies in the export earnings of poorer nations. It was unclear whether the funds would be available as grants or only as debt-increasing loans. Kissinger pledged the United States would contribute $200 million to the suggested agricultural development fund, provided other nations put up $800 million. Saudi Arabia promised, in principle, to contribute but named no specific figure. The dissatisfaction and impatience of many of the developing nations was epitomized by what happened when the World Food Council (established at the Rome Conference) held its initial meeting in Paris in June. Irate that representatives of the more favored nations would not discuss specific pledges of aid, delegates from the African nations and some from Latin America pounded on their desks and clapped disruptively throughout the final session. The conference, remarked one reporter, "seemed to have broken down."[12]

The final chapter of this book, completed a year ago, concluded with a sense of pessimism and of moral urgency. The events that have transpired since that time in no way prompt me to qualify or meliorate those conclusions.

Notes

1. USDA, ERS, *Agricultural Outlook,* AO–5 (October 1975), p. 11.
2. USDA, ERS, *Agricultural Outlook,* AO–3 (August 1975), pp. 19–20; USDA, ERS, *Agricultural Outlook,* AO–5 (October 1975), pp. 20–21. In table 7, 1967 = 100.
3. USDA, ERS, *Foreign Agricultural Trade of the United States* (November 1975), p. 82.
4. USDA, ERS, *Agricultural Outlook,* AO–5 (October 1975), p. 12.
5. USDA, ERS, *Farm Income Statistics* (July 1975), pp. 58–61.
6. Boyce Rensberger, "Food Experts See Several Countries in Greater Peril of Hunger and Possible Starvation Than Last Year," *New York Times,* 3 June 1975, p. 30.
7. Ibid.; *New York Times,* 9 October 1975.
8. Ann Crittenden, "With Fertilizer Shortage Past, Poor Countries Are Still Hungry," *New York Times,* 20 October 1975, p. 1.
9. USDA, ERS, *Agricultural Outlook,* AO–5 (October 1975), pp. 15–16; Ann Crittenden, "Doubt Is Voiced on Impact of U.S. Plan on Foreign Lands," *New York Times,* 19 September 1975, p. 1.
10. Juan deOnis, "Poor Lands Protest Lack of Food Pledges at Parley," *New York Times,* 28 June 1975, p. 3.
11. Crittenden, "Doubt Is Voiced," *New York Times,* 19 September 1975, p. 1; deOnis, "Poor Lands Protest," *New York Times,* 28 June 1975, p. 3.
12. Crittenden, "Doubt Is Voiced," *New York Times,* 19 September 1975, p. 1; deOnis, "Poor Lands Protest," *New York Times,* 28 June 1975, p. 3.

Grain Sales to the Soviet Union

A series of erratic entries of the Soviet Union into the American market to make mammoth purchases of American grain, beginning in 1972, have had a disturbing effect on supplies and, accordingly, on consumer prices in the United States.

The sale of 19 million tons of grain to Russia in the summer of 1972 was a significant turning point for American agricultural policy and a major cause of the rapid food price inflation in 1973. Despite its importance, details of this 1972 transaction remain unclear. The sale, negotiated by the large commercial exporters, particularly Continental and Dreyfus, was arranged secretly, as such sizeable international sales usually are. The Soviet Union, the world's largest wheat grower, makes public no information on actual or estimated production. The purchase consisted of about a quarter of the entire American crop. The price was so low that an export subsidy was paid to the shippers. Due to its secrecy, the huge sale had only a delayed effect on the commodities market, permitting purchases at a low cost, and netting some handsome profits when news of the reserve-depleting sale caused futures prices to skyrocket. Whether the USDA had sufficient information to anticipate the shortfall of the Russian crop or whether the department was fully informed by the negotiators of the amount of wheat involved in the prospective sale remains a mystery —as does the role of Clarence Palmby, the USDA official who traveled with Secretary Earl Butz to the Soviet Union in the spring of 1972, and who subsequently accepted employment with Continental. At any rate, domestic wheat prices rose from $1.68 per bushel in July 1972 to $3.00 in May 1973.

The principal criticism has been that the sale should not have been made in secret. In open trading, free market influences would have prevented a bargain for the shrewd Soviet dealers, avoided a windfall profit for the small trading coterie who purchased the grain at low cost, and saved taxpayers the unwarranted export subsidy.

Negotiated at the peak of the infamous presidential campaign of 1972, the sale was in accord with the Nixon-Butz policy of widening export markets, reducing reserves, and encouraging private commercial transactions; it was consistent with President Nixon's publicized détente with the Soviet Union.

If details concerning the American side of the transaction are hazy, Soviet motives are impenetrable. The 1972 purchase apparently followed upon a disastrous crop failure. The Soviet Union, which produces about twice as much wheat as the United States, is usually itself an exporter. Sovietologists point to several possible motives for the Soviet Union's sudden interest in grain purchases: (1) The Soviet Union has a commitment to supply grain to allies, such as Cuba. Often costs are saved by purchase of American or Canadian wheat rather than transporting grain all the way from the U.S.S.R. (2) Responding to demands of Soviet citizens for a higher standard of living, livestock production is being expanded. Perhaps this explains why the government chose to import wheat in 1972 rather than follow the belt-tightening policies that have been traditional in the past. Since corn and soybeans do not thrive in Russia, about a third of its wheat crop is fed to livestock. Trade data further indicates that the Soviet Union has become a net importer of corn. The Kremlin has embarked upon a policy of bolstering meat production, with its wasteful drain on supplies of feed grains, just at the time when a serious shortage of grains plagues much of the nondeveloped world. (3) Soviet agriculture, never given high priority in the Communist system, is inefficient; incentives for greater efficiency are lacking and production has been unstable. To attempt to reorient this cumbersome sector to produce more livestock may be taxing the best skills of the economic planners. (4) Technological problems impede Soviet production. Shortages of mowers, combines, reapers, and trucks in the critical grain producing areas of Siberia have at times prompted authorities to send as many as 1,000 people into the fields to pick up the grain by hand.[1]

The volume of sales to the Soviet Union declined in 1973 and 1974. Nevertheless, in the wake of a serious drouth in the Ukraine in the spring and summer of 1975, the Soviets contracted to purchase 10.3 million tons of American grain. Negative responses by consumer groups, recalling the inflationary consequences of the 1972 transaction, were instantaneous. Longshoremen at Gulf ports, acting with the support of George Meany, the AFL–CIO president, refused to load grain bound for Russia. Secretary of Agriculture Butz at first denied that the sale would have any consequences for food prices Americans would pay, but conceded in August that the Soviet purchases as of that time would push supermarket prices up about 1.5 percent during the next sixteen months. With the amount of the harvest in the United States still uncertain, a temporary embargo was imposed upon further sales to the Soviet Union.

A five-year agreement, concluded on 20 October 1975, between the United States and the Soviet Union promised to stabilize trade between the two nations and at the same time keep open to the United States the lucrative Russian market. By its terms, the Soviet Union agreed to buy 6 million metric tons of wheat and corn annually during the period 1976–1980. Purchases would be at market prices and would be spaced as evenly as possible over the calendar

year. Additional purchases up to 2 million tons each year
could be made without advance consultation. As a safe-
guard for American consumers, however, if the United
States' supply should fall in any year below 225 million
tons, sales to the Soviets could be reduced below 6 million
tons. American supplies have never dropped below this
minimum for more than a decade.[2]

Notes

1. Lauren Soth, "The Operations of Dr. Butz," *Nation* 219 (26 October 1974): 397; *Congressional Quarterly Almanac* 29 (1973): 320–21; *New York Times,* 19 September 1975.
2. *San Francisco Chronicle,* 22 August 1975; *New York Times,* 21 October 1975; USDA, ERS, *Foreign Agricultural Trade of the United States* (October 1975), p. 89; USDA, ERS, *Agricultural Outlook,* AO–5 (October 1975), p. 5.

A Bibliographical Note

Sources for a study of change in rural life as broad in scope as this one are virtually boundless. Since I have attempted to document rather copiously all of the foregoing chapters, I will dispense with the usual extensive essay on sources and, with a few exceptions, will not note here items already cited in the footnotes.

For the reader who is interested in sampling the broad range of literature there are several excellent bibliographies available. The most comprehensive is John T. Schlebecker, *Bibliography of Books and Pamphlets on the History of Agriculture in the United States, 1607–1967* (Santa Barbara, Calif.: ABC–Clio, 1969). The Agricultural History Center at University of California, Davis, has published several useful lists of references. Especially appropriate for the subject matter of this book are: *A Preliminary List of References for the History of American Agriculture During the New Deal Period, 1932–1940* (Davis, Calif.: Agricultural History Center, University of California, 1968) and *A Preliminary List of References for the History of Agriculture in California* (Davis, Calif.: Agricultural History Center, University of California, 1967).

Some of the features of the general theoretical orientation that I have attempted to bring to the organization and conceptualization of this book are very well articulated in two excellent essays by Samuel P. Hays, "Introduction: The New Organizational Society," in Jerry Israel, ed., *Building the Organizational Society: Essays on Associational Activities in Modern America* (New York: Free Press, 1972), pp. 1–15, and "A Systematic Social History," in George Allan Billias and Gerald N. Grob, *American History: Retrospect and Prospect* (New York: Free Press, 1971), pp. 315–66. A good discussion which applies social theory more directly to the study of agriculture is Robert Swierenga, "Towards the 'New Rural History': A Review Essay," *Historical Methods Newsletter* 6 (June 1973): 111–22.

Any serious student of change in rural America must sooner or later confront the difficult, provocative, and sometimes perverse works of James C. Malin. The best introduction is the often tedious but immensely valuable *The Grasslands of North America* (privately printed, Lawrence, Kans., 1961). Several other good examples of the kind of challenging history Malin has been writing for nearly half a century are: "Man, The State of Nature, and Climax: As Illustrated by Some Problems of the North American Grassland," *Scientific Monthly* 74 (January 1952): 1–8; "The Grassland of North America: Its Occupance and the Challenge of Continuous Reappraisals," in William L. Thomas, ed., *Man's Role in Changing the Face of the Earth* (Chicago: University of Chicago Press, 1956), pp. 350–66; "Mobility and History: Reflections on the Agricultural Policies of the United States in Relation to a Mechanized World," *Agricultural History* 17 (October 1943): 177–91. Malin's pioneer work on rural social mobility, cited in chapter 3, is "The Turnover of Farm Population in Kansas," *Kansas State Historical Quarterly* 4 (November 1935): 339–72.

A cornucopia of statistical data makes the agricultural enterprise one of the most thoroughly documented sectors of the American economy. The decennial censuses of population and of agriculture are indispensable starting points, although data for units smaller than counties is meager. Historians are increasingly making use of the original manuscript schedules for the population censuses of the nineteenth century, as I have done in chapter 3 of this study. The mine of information on individual farms contained in the manuscript schedules of the agricultural censuses has, however, been overlooked. Nevertheless, see Fred Bateman and James D. Foust, "A Sample of Rural Households Selected from the 1860 Manuscript Censuses," *Agricultural History* 68 (January 1974): 75–93.

This book has drawn generously upon the voluminous publications of the Economic Research Service of the United States Department of Agriculture. In fact, without them, this project would have been impossible. Most valuable for synthesis and general interpretation are the annual Yearbooks of the Department of Agriculture. Since they are organized around different themes each year, not all of them are concerned with topics of social and historical interest. Most valuable are the classic *Farmers in a Changing World: The Yearbook of Agriculture, 1940* (Washington, D.C.: U.S. Government Printing Office); *Contours of Change: The Yearbook of Agriculture, 1970* (Washington, D.C.: U.S. Government Printing Office); and *A Good Life For More People: The Yearbook of Agriculture, 1971* (Washington, D.C.: U.S. Government Printing Office). Of the periodic publications of the USDA, a new monthly, *Agricultural Outlook,* inaugurated in June 1975, is the best and most succinct account of contemporary trends. The *Handbook of Agricultural Charts,* published annually, provides comprehensive statistical information that covers the whole gamut of the food production enterprise, from farming, manufacture, and consumption to marketing and price trends. The semiannual *Farm Income Situation* is a detailed balance sheet of the agricultural sector. The monthly *Foreign Agricultural Trade of the United States* is the definitive source on international marketing and price patterns.

Among the various scholarly journals that deal with agriculture and rural life, I found *Rural Sociology* the most valuable, given the objectives of this study. Among its frequent contributors, I found articles of Glenn Fuguitt always stimulating and provocative. See for example his "The Places Left Behind: Population Trends and Policy for Rural America," *Rural Sociology* 36 (December 1971): 449–69, and Harley E. Johansen and Glenn Fuguitt, "Changing Retail Activity in Wisconsin Villages: 1939–1954–1970," *Rural Sociology* 38 (Summer 1973): 207–18. *Agricultural History,* while one of the best edited of historical journals, publishes few articles dealing with recent trends and changes. The *American Journal of Agricultural Economics* (formerly *Journal of Farm Economics*) is more technical and specialized. The *Journal of Economic History* publishes a few articles dealing with agriculture that are consistently good. Two of the best works I encountered were Wayne Rasmussen, "The Impact of Technological Change on American Agriculture, 1862–1962," *Journal of Economic History* (December 1962), pp. 578–91. This article, in fact, provided the model for the organization of chapters 4 and 5. Cited in chapter 5, Philip Raup, "Corporate Farming in the United States," *Journal of Economic History* 33 (March 1973): 274–90, is singularly important for clearing up widely-held misconceptions. The *Annals of the American Association of Geographers* is a source overlooked by historians only at their peril.

While I will not burden the reader with the usual laundry list of books and monographs that have influenced my writing of this book, several are important enough to be singled out for especial attention. I am among that minority of historians who still recognize Frederick Jackson Turner as one of the great masters of historical science, although I reject his much-abused frontier thesis. As any perceptive reader will have detected, I rely a great deal upon his *The United States, 1830–1850* in chapter 2. I believe it is one of the outstanding works in the literature of American history. My frequent references in chapter 4 to Allan Bogue, *From Prairie to Cornbelt* (Chicago: University of Chicago Press, 1963), should make it evident that I regard this book as one of the seminal works in the field. For capturing the texture of traditional middle western farm life, Curtis Stadtfeld, *From the Land and Back,* is unexcelled. Its only rival is the other work that provided much of the data for chapter 4, Charles Henry Taylor, *Tarpleywick: A Century of Iowa Farming* (Ames: Iowa State University Press, 1970).

The data that sustains the chapters of this book dealing with the recent past had to be gleaned mostly from the statistical reports of the USDA, mentioned previously, and from newspaper sources. I relied mostly upon the *New York Times,* but the *Wall Street Journal* and the *Des Moines Register and Tribune* also have comprehensive coverage of current agricultural topics. The *Congressional Quarterly Almanac* and the *National Journal* (especially the timely articles of Daniel Balz) make it possible to keep up to date with the intricacies of agricultural legislation. The Agribusiness Accountability Project (1000 Wisconsin Ave., N.W., Washington, D.C.) is obviously not in the good graces of the Department of Agriculture, but I found their reports and bulletins generally accurate and always informative. A recent book, Jim Hightower, *Eat Your Heart Out: How Food Profiteers Victimize the Consumer* (New York: Crown Publishers, 1975) is somewhat polemical, but it does summarize the project's scattered studies and reports.

The world food crisis has faded from the headlines; one who retains a concern for this serious problem must seek information from the business sections of national newspapers and occasional references in *Agricultural Outlook.* The superb series of articles on the subject in the *New York Times* during 1974 have now been collected into a single volume, Staff of the *New York Times, Give Us This Day* (New York: Arno Press, 1975). The Overseas Development Council (1717 Massachusetts Ave., N.W., Washington, D.C. 20036) continues to issue valuable periodic reports on the world food situation. Lester Brown is a staff member of the organization. Despite their unabashed advocacy of *triage,* the occasional newsletter of the Environmental Fund (1302 Eighteenth Street, N.W., Washington, D.C. 20036), *The Other Side,* often has information unavailable elsewhere. The organization publishes each year a comprehensive chart estimating population in each nation of the world.

Index

249–51; legislation of New
Deal period and, 235–36,
241–45; legislation of 1933
and, 238, 241–43; legislation
of 1936 and, 243–44;
legislation of 1938 and,
244–45; legislation of 1949
and, 247; legislation of 1954
and, 248; legislation of 1970
and, 251; legislation of 1973
and, 253–55; during 1950s,
248–49; under Nixon and
Ford administrations,
251–56; paradoxes of during
world food crisis, 1974,
298–99; priorities of after
1938, 245; rationale for
criticized, 258–59; during
World War II, 245–46
Agricultural Research Service.
See United States
Department of Agriculture
Agway, Inc., 185, 225 n.21
American Farm Bureau
Federation, 231, 237–40, 249
American Indians, 8, 34, 47
Amish, 43–44
Appalachian whites, 10–11, 40
Associated Milk Producers,
Inc. (AMPI), 187–88
Automobile, 94, 99–100, 116

Baltimore and Ohio Railroad,
87–88
Bangladesh, 270
Bankhead-Jones Farm Tenant
Act (1937), 244
Barn lots, 120
Barns, 120
Bayly, Thomas M., 61
Beale, Calvin L., 10
Bedford Academy, 92
Bedford (Pa.) Borough, 81–83,
91–92. *See also* Bedford
County, Pennsylvania

Bedford County, Pennsylvania,
81–107; Beegle farm in,
104–5; Breezewood in, 96–97;
Catholics in, 82; coal and
iron industry in, 83–84,
93–94; crop patterns in,
83–84, 86, 92–93; dairy
production in, 84; decline of
diversified farming in,
102–4; economic activity in
(1963–1964), 100–101;
emigration from farms in,
102–3; Germans in, 82;
immigrants through
Cumberland Borough,
Maryland, in, 82; internal
improvements as important
issue in, 87–88; land use
patterns in, 83–84; Lincoln
Highway passes through, 94;
manufacturing in, 84–86;
motor transport and related
industries in, 100; number of
farms in, 86–87; original
boundaries of, 83; origin of
population in, 82–83;
Pennsylvania Turnpike and,
98; population (1850) in, 83;
population (1860–1890) in,
86–87; population
(1930–1970) in, 101–2;
population changes in, 89;
railroads in, 88–91; real
estate development of, 105;
rural industry in, 84–86;
Scotch-Irish in, 82; tourist
trade of, 98–99;
transportation as issue in,
87–91, 94, 98; "Turnpike
City" in, 97–98; turnpikes in,
87–88; unemployment in,
106–7; voting behavior in,
94–95; water pollution in,
104–96; whiskey distilling in,
83–84